Flesh

The Disappearance of Portia Barrington

KEITH LEE JOHNSON

DARE TO IMAGINE
PUBLISHING

Flesh

The Disappearance of Portia Barrington

Keith Lee Johnson

Dare to Imagine Publishing
PO Box 935
Maumee, OH 43537

ISBN 978-1-935825-02-9

Library of Congress Control Number: 2010942641

First Printing: December 2010

Printed in the United States of America

10 9 8 7 6 5 4 3 2 1

This is a work of fiction. Any references or similarities to actual events, real people, living, or dead, or to real locals are intended to give the novel a sense of reality. Any similarity in other names, characters, places, and incidents is entirely coincidental.

Acknowledgment

I have had numerous editors working on the manuscripts I've written, but none of them were more studious, more indefatigable than Miri Maxon, an amateur. While this book may contain some errors, they will in no way reflect negatively on her, nor will they change my mind about who she is and what she's done for me. I appreciate her attention to detail, the long hours she put in, and the great attitude she had while doing so. I have always been a terrible speller; perhaps that is a result of cheating on spelling tests in the first grade—it all catches up with you people—all of it. Had I known I would grow up to be an author, I wouldn't have cheated on so many tests. Hopefully, Miri caught most of my suffix problems too. Unfortunately, my hands cannot keep pace with my mind when a story is coming to me from only God knows where. I just write what I hear and see in the recesses of my mind. Miri Maxon brought lots of order to my chaos. Thanks so much, dear girl.

Prologue

San Francisco
Russian Hill
175 Taylor Street
10:50 pm

T wo hitters had left Allegro Romano's restaurant ten minutes ago. The 40-seat restaurant closed at 10, but they were still enjoying their Rigatoni alla Amatriciana. The waiter had told them it was former Mayor Willie Brown's favorite. They had been a little start struck when a couple of movie stars walked in just before closing time, which wasn't unusual for the famed eatery. The couple gladly posed for a few photos that would no doubt end up on the celebrity wall along side pictures of Sophia Loren, Warren Beatty, famous politicians and show business royalty. They watched the couple long enough to unintentionally annoy them prior to leaving. They had walked nearly a mile and a half from the restaurant and entered the high rise. They headed over to the uniformed doorman's station to get the key. There was a gold nameplate on the doorman's jacket that read: Clancy.

Clancy didn't ask any questions. He knew better. His boss told him to expect them. Even though he didn't know what was about to go down, he knew to keep his mouth shut. If he didn't someone would be back to shut it permanently even if the hitters were behind bars or dead. He handed the taller man the keys, thinking that he was in charge. He watched them head for the elevator and then picked up his latest edition of *Playboy* magazine and turned to the centerfold.

As the hitters approached the elevator, they saw no less than five bubbled cameras recording their images, but they were unmoved by them. Even though they were about to blow someone away, no one would ever know a murder was committed in the building except the people who ordered the hit. The body would be removed. All bloodstains and gray matter would be cleaned off the walls and repainted. The carpet would be replaced whether it needed to be replaced or not. The entire condo would look like new before the sun rose.

Theodore Twist, a married conservative and the chief justice of the District of Columbia Court of Appeals was in bed with his African-American lover, Gloria Dunes, in a 16th floor condominium. Gloria, in her bid to convince the judge to keep quiet about what he knew, was a complete failure. He was going to the Justice Department the moment he returned to Washington he had told her.

When she realized that no amount of persuasion was going to deter the judge, Gloria put on her robe and went into the bathroom. Reluctantly, she sent the hitters a text message while they were still at Allegro Romano's, letting them know she had failed.

The elevator pinged just before the doors opened on the 16th floor. The hitters exited and turned left. Standing outside the condo, they put on surgical gloves as a precaution prior to entering. They pulled out their weapons, made sure they were fully loaded, and then screwed on their sound suppressors.

As they quietly made their way through the living room, they saw the city lights through the floor-to-ceiling window. They heard Linda Ronstadt and Aaron Neville's, *I Don't Know Much* coming from the bedroom. The smell of olives filled the room as the remnants of wood crackled behind the glass of the fireplace.

Gloria was expecting them at exactly 11:00. She came out of the bathroom when she heard the men enter the bedroom.

The hitters looked at Gloria, waiting for her to say she convinced the judge to play ball. Only she could stop the execution. She closed her eyes and shook her head. They could see the pain she was in.

Gloria turned away. She didn't want to see what was about to happen to the judge. She didn't want to see the shocked look on his face now that he knew she had betrayed him; now that he clearly understood that the romantic weekend in San Francisco she had planned was a charade. She didn't want to be a part of it. She loved him, but the boss was going to kill her if she didn't help him silence the judge. She had tried more than once to persuade the judge not to go to the Justice Department, but he wouldn't listen.

Twist had told Gloria it was his duty as an officer of the court to inform the FBI. He didn't care if their affair came out. He was tired of hiding. He had told his wife he was leaving her before his plane left Dulles. He had offered her a hefty sum to let him go. His wife signed the documents, agreeing to end their twenty two year marriage without a fight.

Twist was planning to spend the rest of his life making Gloria happy. Now his situation was critical. She had trusted him, and he thought he could trust her. Now he knew he couldn't. Even though he realized she had betrayed him, he didn't care. He looked at her and said, "I still love . . ."

Hiss! Hiss! Their sound suppressed weapons discharged. The judge was no longer among the living.

Gloria thought it was over.

It wasn't.

She was next.

"Sorry, Gloria," one of the hitters said. "But the boss says you gotta go too. If it were up to me, I'd let you go. Orders are orders."

"No! Don't! I cooperated! I'm supposed to have my operation in the morning!"

Hiss! A single hole formed in her forehead a split second before her blond wig flew off and landed on the floor before she did. As she fell backward her robe opened. They saw her perfect forty cup silicon breasts, but they were stunned when they saw the long and thick package she was born with.

Her killer pulled out his cell and hit an assigned speed-dial button while looking at his partner. Both of them were shaking their heads. Neither knew Gloria was a man.

"It's done," he said and closed the phone.

Chapter 1

After traveling to Las Vegas, Arizona, Texas, and Memphis, in that order, playing my role as FBI agent, Phoenix Perry, I was finally back in Arlington, where I live with my husband and two children. I was so glad to be home. A couple of weeks ago, I received a troubling call from my deceased father's sister, Ruth, telling me that my cousin, Michelle, had been shot and left for dead. Two murder victims were found at the scene. The Las Vegas Police Department thought Michelle killed the man and his wife in the wee hours of the morning in their own home. The man was bludgeoned before being shot point blank in the face with a double-barrel shotgun. The woman was found upstairs with a knife wound in her eye.

I called Kelly McPherson, my partner, and told her what happened and that I was taking some personal time to fly out to Las Vegas to do some snooping around. Kelly is the liaison officer with Washington, D.C. Metro Police Department. She decided to take some time off too. We were both well aware of law enforcement policy forbidding its agents to investigate crimes of a personal nature, but there was no way I was going to leave my cousin's life in the hands of cops who didn't know her the way I did. That meant Kelly and I would be doing an unauthorized investigation in Sin City. After a week or so of long hours and very little sleep, we solved the crime and now it was time for some much needed shut eye.

When I got home, I looked in on my children. I knew they would be sound asleep, but being a mother and an FBI agent was tough to juggle most of the time. Thank God I had a husband who understood. He and his parents helped out quite a bit, which freed me up to do what I do. First, I looked in on my twelve year old daughter, Savannah. Our relationship was strained because of my commitment to law enforcement. I was planning to remedy that now that the case, which required lots of travel, was over. She was asleep, just as I knew she would be. Then I looked in on my son, who was only four years old. He too, was asleep. I smiled when I saw him. For awhile, I thought he would never get used to sleeping in his own bed.

After that, I headed to the bedroom I shared with the man of my dreams, Keyth Perry, who happened to be awake and waiting for me, it seemed. He wanted my body I could tell, and I wasn't about to turn down the slice of heaven he offered, no matter how tired I was. We decided to shower together before scratching the itch we both had, but we ended up in an argument. I was right and he was wrong. I'll leave it at that. Hell, the husband is always wrong no matter how an argument begins or ends. He had blown his chance of getting some of this. I walked out of our bedroom and went into the kitchen. I was drinking orange juice and looking over the bills when Keyth humbled himself and took full responsibility for the argument.

After that, the mood hit me again. The sex was seriously off the hook because not only was it "I missed you" sex, it was makeup sex and listen . . . there's nothing and I mean nothing like makeup sex. Just when I thought I could call it a night, or better yet, a morning, as it was 6 a.m., my phone rang. Instinctively, I knew it wasn't good news. Who calls at that hour with good news? I looked at the caller ID. The call was coming from FBI Director, Kortney Malone. Getting a call from the Director at that hour meant two things. First, it meant something terrible had happened. And second, it meant I was being called in to handle it.

I knew Kortney Malone long before she became the Director, so I was allowed to get away with calling her by her first name as long as it wasn't in public or when other agents were around. Kelly was excluded, of course. Kortney and I were FBI recruits and trained together at Quantico about fifteen years earlier. Kortney's "rise to power" was a direct result of political nepotism owed to leaders of the Militant Feminist Movement. Kortney fit the bill nicely, being of the female persuasion and African-American to boot—two politically correct birds with one stone.

The former Director and the Assistant Director, both males, one white the other black—excuse me, African-American, had been murdered four years ago, during the summer of 2001, a few months before September 11. That's the official version anyway. It was later found out that both men's hands were dirty. Palmer Davidson was in the Oval Office at the time and he owed the leaders of the movement a huge favor. The move shook up the FBI establishment and they were furious because Kortney didn't owe anybody anything, no favors whatsoever. Immediately after taking the oath of office, she fired several high ranking agents who attended her swearing in ceremony.

Kortney's appointment notwithstanding, I was the first female reparation on a debt long past due. Davidson handpicked me to investigate the murder of Supreme Court nominee, Jennifer Taylor. Taylor was the first African-American woman nominated to the bench. She was murdered three days before her confirmation hearing, which set off a firestorm of racial and gender politics.

The morning after Taylor's murder, Director St. Clair summoned me to the White House for a meeting with President Davidson, where I was told I was going to head up the investigation. I was then told that I would have to answer whatever questions the press asked about the investigation on the White House lawn on national television. I offered negligible protest when I told the president that the FBI had public relations people to handle that sort of thing. Davidson insisted. What's a girl to do when the leader of the free world asks for a favor? All of this happened about fifteen minutes after my Oval Office arrival. I wasn't given any time to think. It was either sink or swim and I swam rather nicely, solving the case to everyone's satisfaction.

I picked up the phone, closed my eyes and flippantly said, "It's a little early to be calling here, Kortney."

"Phoenix, this is *Director* Malone." She sounded so official, like she was in the White House or something. "Find Kelly and get in here immediately."

"Why, what's happened?"

"Defense attorney, Myles Barrington's daughter, Portia, has been kidnapped."

"Kortney . . . surely you can find another agent. I just got home. Sister Girl is seriously whipped, okay?"

"Barrington is a friend of your friend, former President Davidson, Phoenix."

My eyes shot wide open. "I'm on my way," I said.

I sat at the edge of the bed, quietly thinking about the crime, who I would need for the task force, and how many hours of sleep I wasn't going to get because Davidson, while no longer in the Oval office, still wielded lots of power in the Capitol City. Although Davidson and my father never met, they had mutual friends in the intelligence community. Davidson even attended my father's funeral at Arlington Cemetery and handed me my folded flag at the end of the ceremony. I closed my eyes for a moment and was spontaneously transported back to June 2001. I remembered sitting in Arlington Cemetery, seeing an innumerable number of white headstones that marked the graves of our nation's fallen heroes.

I could hear the honor guard fire off several rounds to honor my father's twenty years of service as a Naval Intelligence officer. He also served twenty years with the National Security Agency. I also remembered the ten years my father and I lived in Beijing, where I learned to fluently speak the Mandarin and Cantonese languages. I also studied Shaolin Kung Fu under the tutelage of Master Ying Ming Lo. After ten years of endless study and demanding training, I mastered the art. I was eight years old when we left America and eighteen when we returned.

I took a deep breath, exhaled, and opened my eyes. I turned on my nightstand light and then looked back at Keyth to see if I had awakened him. He was staring at me.

"What's up?"

I said, "I gotta go back into the office, honey."

He cleared his throat. "I figured that much out by myself, Phoenix. What's going on *now*?"

"We got a kidnapping."

Sarcastically he said, "Oh, and they need the great Phoenix Perry to save the day, huh?"

"Something like that, yeah," I offered, playing along with him. Keyth used to be an FBI agent so he knew the drill. He knew that middle of the night calls were a part of being one of the bureau's distinguished agents.

He reached out to me and pulled me back into the bed. "Your daughter needs you now more than ever, Phoenix," he said. "In the blink of an eye, she'll be gone."

"I know," I said. "I'll put in the time right after this case. I promise."

"That's what you said a week ago, remember?"

"I mean it this time, Keyth, okay?"

We kissed passionately and when I was sure he was in a deep
sleep, which didn't take very long, I went into our adjacent bathroom
and called Kelly's cell.

"What, Phoenix!" Kelly screamed in my ear.

"Well good morning to you, too," I said softly,
almost whispering, trying not to wake my husband.
"Did you get a call from our fearless leader?"

"Yeah, but I didn't bother answering. You know I can't stand
her, right?"

"I know. She's by the book . . . blah, blah, blah. She fires agents
for minor infractions. Whatever!"

She yawned loudly. "You only say that because she lets you get
away with everything. Like you know something about her I don't."

"Jealous?"

"Yeah, as a matter of fact, I am."

I laughed a little and quipped, "At least I don't get special favors
for being a hot blond with a body that makes men, young and old,
consider murder just to have one night with me."

"Jealous, Phoenix?"

"A little," I said kidding her. I was hot too, but blonds are supposed to be sex-pots and dumber than bricks. Kelly was far from the
stereotype—at least the dumber than bricks part.

"Well . . . what's up?" She yawned like a sleepy feline. "I'm
worn out."

I laughed. "I just bet you are. So you and Sterling are back together then?"

Silence.

Sterling Wise and Kelly had an on-again, off-again relationship.
He was a high-powered defense attorney turned sports agent. He
makes big bank and lives in Tiburon, California, an affluent town
north of San Francisco. He travels to Washington as often as he can,
supposedly to handle business for Wizards and Redskins clients, but

I suspect that bedding Kelly has much to do with his frequent cosseted bicoastal lifestyle.

"I take your silence to mean that he's awake. And if he's awake, you must've just got finished getting your little swerve on, huh?"

She roared loudly. Still laughing, she said. "Phoenix . . . what do you want? We just wrapped up a case a couple of hours ago. I need to sleep, don't you?"

Completely ignoring her question, I laughed and asked one of my own; one that would put her in an awkward position since her lover was probably in bed with her with his head on her bare breasts. "So was it good to you?"

She laughed again. "Yeah. You know it was."

"And that's why you can't give it up even though he refuses to marry you, right?"

She yawned again. "A girl could do worse, ya know?"

I had already given her my opinion of the relationship several times. She knew full well that I thought he was using her. Apparently, she didn't mind. Perhaps she was using him too. They say all's fair in love and war. The cliché sounds good, but I totally disagree with it. Anyway, I decided to keep my big mouth shut and keep it moving. I changed the subject back to business. "All right. I gotta shower and then I'll be over to pick you up, okay?"

"Yeah, yeah, yeah."

"I take it you're being pampered at the Willard InterContinental, as usual?"

"You know it. We're staying in the Abraham Lincoln Suite."

I laughed and reverted back to girl talk. "You mean you're getting laid in the Abraham Lincoln Suite. Let's see . . . you've been in the Capital Suite, the Oval Suite, the George Washington Suite, the Thomas Jefferson Suite, and now good ol' Abe's Suite? No wonder you can't give it up. You're getting seriously banged and living high on the hog too! Who would want to give that up?"

"Not me." she said. "Give me a call when you leave and I'll meet you downstairs."

"What? You won't offer a sister breakfast at the fancy hotel? No croissants? No wine and cheese? Nothing?"

Laughing, she said, "I work real hard for all of this, okay? Very hard. And by the way, to please me, he does too."

She hung up.

By the time I turned onto Pennsylvania Avenue, it was almost 7:30. I called Kortney at headquarters and told her I was stuck in traffic. She gave me a quick rundown on what happened to Barrington's daughter. Nevertheless, I would have to ask the Barringtons the same questions I had asked Kortney. Who? What? When? Where? Motive? Enemies? Standard police work. Kelly and I would need to get our own visceral reaction to their answers.

After speaking with Kortney, I immediately thought of my own twelve year old daughter, Savannah, and what could possibly be happening to Portia Barrington. It seemed as though perverts were everywhere, snatching kids, raping, and then murdering them. I assumed that's what would happen to Portia if we didn't find her soon. I don't know what I'd do if something like this happened to my family or someone close to me. The Barrington's had to be going crazy like I did when a former nemesis, Coco Nimburu, had kidnapped Keyth and Savannah, all in an effort to get me to come after her. I'd be ready to kill if someone snatched Sydney or Savannah. The Barringtons probably felt the same way. What parent wouldn't?

I pulled up to the entrance of the Willard InterContinental. Kelly was standing on the red carpet, looking like a Hollywood starlet without the glamour of lights, flashing cameras, and throngs of adoring fans standing alongside paparazzi photographers, hoping for a glimpse of their idol while multiple television network interviews were being conducted. She was wearing a pair of Levi's and a crimson and white Dexter Manley throwback jersey, no doubt given to her by Sterling Wise.

I whipped my Mustang Cobra over to the curb and revved the engine several times like an impatient teenager waiting one second too long for his prom date. She got in. I burned a little rubber when I pulled away from the curb. I felt the need for speed.

I filled Kelly in as we drove over to 96000 Ferry Harbour Court. Thirty-five minutes later, I pulled up to the gate and pushed the button on the speaker.

A highly educated and refined female voice answered, "May I help you?"

I said, "Agents Perry and McPherson."

"May I see your credentials, please?"

I looked for the camera. I saw two. One was mounted on a gray brick wall the gates were attached to. The other was right next to the speaker. I held up my badge.

"And the other . . ." the woman said in a commanding tone.

I looked at Kelly and whispered, "I guess she can't be too careful, huh?"

"No, I can't, Agent Perry! Portia's been kidnapped!" the woman snapped.

I assumed she was feeling the stress of losing her daughter, and the daunting idea of never seeing her again.

Kelly shrugged her shoulders and handed me her badge.

I recognized my insensitivity and apologized and then held Kelly's credentials up to the camera. A few seconds later, the gate parted in the middle. As I drove up the path, we saw a purple Bentley, a white Jaguar, and a couple Bureau cars parked in the circular driveway. No press. That meant the Bureau had been able to keep a tight lid on the kidnapping so far. Either that, or perhaps former President Davidson had called in a few favors. That could change at any moment though.

We opened the doors to get out when I remembered something that happened when I got home early this morning. I frowned as the images flooded my mind. I heard Kelly close her door.

I felt her staring at me. She said, "What, Phoenix?"

I closed my door. "When I got home this morning, I decided to take a quick shower before shutting it down for about eight hours of sleep. A few minutes later, Keyth came into the bathroom and got in the shower with me. Things got a little hot and heavy and then I opened my big mouth about the case we just put down. We laughed a little and then we ended up getting into an argument when I told him who had done all the gruesome killings."

"Like I said when we were in Vegas, Phoenix, you can mess up a wet dream."

I looked at her and rolled my eyes before saying, "Thanks, partner. I can always count on your undying support."

Laughing, she said, "Sure thing. You know me, anything I can do to help."

I folded my arms and leaned against the hood of my car. "Anyway, I was so fired up that I lost the urge, ya know?"

Smiling mischievously, she quipped, "Yeah, but I still would've got a piece and been mad later. A good piece helps me sleep more soundly."

"Me too," I said smiling. "Anyway, I knew we weren't going to do it. I was too pissed. So I went into the kitchen to get a glass of orange juice. I sat at the kitchen table and started looking at the bills. Eventually, I see one of those black and white rectangular cards with photos of missing children on it. I hadn't really looked at one for a very long time. Not like I used to when I first saw them, know what I mean?"

"Yeah . . . I don't either. I guess we can be jaded by anything if we see it often enough. I remember seeing my first dead body and couldn't eat for a couple days. Now, I can see the remains of a guy who blew his brains out during masturbation, like we saw during the Sugar & Spice case, and go right over to the food court at Union Station and chow down, like I hadn't seen the horror of what he'd done to himself."

"Yeah, I remember that, too. Anyway, for the first time, I pick up the photo and really looked at the missing girl. I felt bad that I had neglected so many missing children for so many years. Keyth came into the kitchen. We talked. Made up and got our little swerve on and the next thing I know, I'm getting a call from Kortney about another little girl lost."

"Irony? Or a wakeup call?"

"Both. This is one missing little girl that I intend to pay attention to."

"As always . . . I'm with you, partner."

Chapter 2

As we approached the mansion, I saw Jack Ryan, head of the CARD (Child Abduction Rapid Deployment) team, talking to agents Julie Campbell and Steven Boyd between the white granite columns that framed the entrance. Ryan was forty-nine, and had been with the bureau for twenty-two years. I liked Jack, but he could be a little territorial when he was on a child abduction case. He and his wife had a real affection for children, probably because they couldn't have any of their own. They had tried for years but she never conceived. He never told any of us why. They had been foster parents for about fifteen years. I thought what they were doing was quite admirable and a great contribution to society.

Julie Campbell had curly sable hair, was forty-five years old, in excellent physical condition, and had twenty years' experience. She ran a marathon in college and could run a mile in a little under five minutes. Rumor had it that she had a bust reduction, which kind of angered me. Maybe it was jealousy. I don't have enough up top and this woman had so much she could throw some of it away.

Campbell and Steven Boyd, who was thirty-two and had the least experience of the three with only eight years, were quite the item in FBI circles. They were foolish enough to think none of us crackerjack FBI types knew they were sleeping together. Campbell trained Boyd when he graduated from Quantico. Partners tend to get close and when they're the opposite sex, well, things happen that are not supposed to happen. No one would say anything about their relationship unless it started to affect their work, which it would eventually. Then, the boss would act as if he knew nothing of it and make one or both of them put in for a transfer. That's how it normally worked anyway.

Ryan spotted us and said something to Campbell and Boyd. They looked at us and then started making their way over. They didn't look happy. In fact, they looked as if they were about to blow a gasket. Ryan was probably pissed that I was going to be taking over the case when I didn't know a thing about Child Abduction. They were the experts. Combined they had about fifty years experience with kidnappings. All I had was my own nightmare with Coco Nimburu. So, needless to say, former President Davidson's request had stepped on the CARD team's toes.

With much cynicism, Ryan said, "Look, up in the sky . . . it's a *bird*."

He never looked up. None of the CARD team did.

Julie Campbell said, "No, Jack, get your eyes checked. It's a *plane*." When she said, "plane", she kind of sang it, holding the latter part of the word.

Steven Boyd, the youngest of the three, said, "No, its *Super Girl!*"

Kelly, always ready for a fight, said, "Uh, that's Super Woman to you. And don't any of you bozos ever forget it."

Ryan responded first, saying, "Oh and how could we forget the bureau's most *notorious* whore, *Clit* Eastwood."

Kelly took the body blow like a champ. She smiled mischievously and said, "I hear your wife is finally with child. Is it yours? I mean after fifteen years of trying, I figure you must be the problem, right Jack? I think I saw your wife in a Maury Povich Baby Daddy show preview. Maury was saying, 'Jack Ryan . . . you are not the father!'"

"McPherson," Julie said through clenched teeth, "that's way . . . way over the line."

"Talk to your boy, Julie," Kelly said firmly. "If you bring it here . . . I'm bringin' it there." She locked eyes with Jack for a full second and then continued, "I got a lot more if you want it, lover boy. Decide."

Jack didn't return serve. I think he knew better. Kelly's got a mouth on her like you wouldn't believe when she's pushed. Calling her a whore was very unwise.

I didn't bother responding to their derisive chiding. A long pause swirled around us. They were staring at Kelly and me, and us at them. After a few more seconds of loud silence, I got down to business. "Have you set up the command post yet, Jack?"

"Hmmm, let me see," he said, furrowing his brow and tapping his index finger on his cleft chin; his eyes looking toward the sky. "Setting up the command post is one of the most important things I have to do as the leader of the CARD team. Let's see, hmmm . . . did I get that done, Julie?"

"With it being *oh so* important, Jack, and with you having so *little* experience with these kinds of cases, I think it slipped your *neophyte* mind."

"What about you, Steven. Did it slip *your* mind, too?" Jack asked, still furrowing his brow, still tapping his chin with his index finger.

"What mind? None of the CARD team members have high school educations. I don't even know why we're here, do you Julie?"

Julie said, "Steven, you may not know why you're here, but I certainly know why I'm here."

"Do tell," Steven said, playing along.

"I'm here because I was handpicked by a former President *four* years ago to solve the murder of Supreme Court Nominee, Jennifer Taylor," Julie said. "An African-American. What about you, fellas?"

"Yeah, that's why I'm here too," Steven said, staring unflinchingly into my eyes. "Knowing a former President has opened all kinds of doors for me. I mean, after all, I've written a book about the Supreme Court nominee's murderer and everything. I had a desk job over at Homeland Security. Hell, I oughta be running the Bureau by now. After I solve this case, I'm sure I will be."

"That's why we're all here, Steven," Ryan said. "We're here to get favors from the brass." He looked at me. "What are you orders, *Captain?*"

They all snapped to attention and saluted me.

K elly and I looked at each other. We couldn't believe them. A young girl had been kidnapped. Her parents had paid big money to have her returned twice and the CARD team members were crying foul because we were on their turf. Never mind that we were summoned to the Barrington house on orders that came straight from the top. We looked at them and began our own conversational exchange. I said, "Kelly, maybe Portia Barrington's in the house safe and sound and we came out here for nothing."

"You're probably right, Phoenix. Maybe her parents aren't on the cutting edge of an emotional breakdown," Kelly offered, following my lead. "Maybe her parents aren't worried sick about her like we were told by Director Malone."

I said, "Yeah, maybe they think they don't need the FBI to find their daughter. Makes me wonder why they bothered calling us in the first place."

"Maybe the Barringtons think they can handle the situation without us, Phoenix—*any* of us. We should just turn around and go get laid. I know Julie and Steven want to go back to her place and do just that."

Julie's mouth fell wide open, but no words came out. She just stared at Kelly like she couldn't believe she put her business out in the open so callously.

She was about to respond, but I said, "The Barringtons might think we're a bunch of jealous agents who can't work together because our own self-importance has gotten in the way of good police work, Kelly. *Maybe* we gotta show them something different. *Maybe* we gotta show them how much we care and that we're going to do absolutely everything in our power to get their daughter back to them. *Maybe*, just *maybe*, showing them a united front might ease their minds, even if it means taking orders from Super Girl, who has far less experience in these matters."

Kelly looked at me. "Uh, that's Super Woman, Phoenix. *Super Woman.*"

Jack Ryan and his team bowed their heads. They knew I was right.

After a moment or two of silent staring, they looked at us and we at them, Jack said to his team, "All right guys, let's not forget why we're here. Let's find the girl. That's all that matters now."

Julie and Steven nodded.

"All right then," I said. "Resent me if you must, but never let the Barringtons see anything but a team of professionals at all times."

Ryan said, "Here's what we know. The kid was snatched a couple days ago, Wednesday, June 8th. The Barringtons were contacted by the people who snatched Portia. They told them if they contacted the cops, they would never see their daughter again—not alive anyway. They cooperated and paid them two hundred thousand dollars. The kidnappers demanded another three hundred thousand. They paid again. Now they want five. That's when we got the call."

He hesitated.

I sensed he was holding something back. I locked eyes with him and said, "Let's have it, Jack."

"You're not going to like this part, Phoenix," Jack said.

"Go on," I said, having no idea what was coming next.

"The Barringtons hired a bodyguard that doubled as her chauffeur."

"Have you questioned him?" I asked.

"No. He hasn't been seen since he picked the girl up for final exams."

"Well who does he work for? What firm? Or is he an independent?"

"Technically, he works for you, Phoenix," Jack said. "He's employed by your husband's company, Drew Perry Investigative Firm. His name is Joel Williams."

Kelly and I looked at each other, stunned by what we had heard.

Drew Perry Investigative Firm was started by my father, Sydney Drew, when he retired from the National Security Agency. His first client was a billionaire named Adrienne Bellamy, who later helped him establish it by funneling him an endless list of wealthy references. Keyth Perry and I were dating when Former Assistant Director Lawrence Michelson fired him from the Bureau. My father loved Keyth and hired him immediately as an investigator. Before he died, my father made Keyth a partner and put his name on the letterhead. Now, I'm the head of Drew Perry, but in name only. Keyth runs the place and I have complete faith in him. I suppose I should know more about my father's business, but I don't. Law firms, corporations, and politicians are our clients. On occasion, Keyth accepts matrimonial work. The most memorable case of that sort was the Nelson Kennard case. The honeymoon was definitely over. Keyth only took the case as a personal favor for Kelly's boyfriend, Sterling Wise.

When Ryan mentioned Joel Williams' name, he and his team were watching me to see what my reaction was going to be. Ryan was pretending to be disturbed, pretending he was bothered by having to tell me the "bad news" when in fact he and his team were on a fishing expedition. I guess I don't blame him. They had to do it. If I were in his position, I would have done the same thing. They had to know if I knew something I wasn't suppose to know. They had to know if I was withholding information to protect my husband or myself, for that matter. I didn't know Joel Williams and had never heard Keyth mention his name. And if he did, I don't remember.

Seeing their prying, analytical eyes made my skin feel as if a thousand pins were sticking in it. If it were possible, I think my hair would have stood straight up as the pit of my stomach did flip-flops. But I remained cooler than a fan, showing no fear, no stress, no emotion whatsoever. I told myself this was just part of the process of an active investigation. Yet, everything in me wanted to call my husband and have him get Joel Williams on the phone and find out what was going on, but that wasn't going to happen. Unless I missed my guess, Joel was in serious trouble.

I looked at Jack and the rest of the CARD team members. They were staring at me, examining everything I did, no doubt wondering if I had the guts to do what needed to be done; wondering if I would give them the orders they expected. First, they expected me to call the office and find out where Joel Williams lived. Second, they expected me to send them there immediately so they could grill him, *if* he was still alive. I got the feeling they were hoping I wouldn't cooperate so they could have the "amateur" dismissed from the case for cause.

I pulled out my phone and flipped it open. Quickly, I scrolled through my list of contacts until I found the number of the firm. I hit the talk button. After a few rings, I heard Sherry's pleasant voice say, "Drew Perry Private Investigative Firm, how may I help you?"

"Hi Sherry," I said. "Phoenix here . . . Little Sydney's great; growing faster than a stalk of corn . . . Listen. . . I was wondering if you can get me the address of one of our employees. A Joel Williams?" I fought the strong temptation to tell her to tell Keyth to get over to Joel's place before the CARD team got there. It was an incredible battle, but I was victorious. "Yeah, everything is fine, Sherry. Thanks for the info. You have a great day, too. And thanks a bunch." I closed the phone.

I gave Jack and his team the order they had been waiting for. Without a second's hesitation, they hopped in their cars and headed over to Crystal City where Joel lived. I didn't say anything, but deep down, I was hoping they wouldn't find anything that would implicate Drew Perry, knowing all the while they would—at least I believed they would anyway. The idea that someone from my husband's firm could be involved in a high profile kidnapping made me very uneasy.

After they left, Kelly said, "You know that was a test, don't you?"

"Yeah, I know," I said. "They already knew the address. They got it from the Barringtons. But I'm Boo Boo the fool and didn't realize Portia's parents would have his address, phone number, and probably his fingerprints. They've got big money and big connections. No way they don't have Williams' contact information."

"You think they'll find anything?"

I exhaled hard and said, "I'm sure of it."

"Are you thinking what I'm thinking, Phoenix?"

"Yeah. Either Joel's dead, or he and the girl ran off together. And this whole kidnapping thing is a charade."

As we made our way over to the mansion, I said, "Is it me, or is there something strange about kidnappers asking for more than one ransom. In fact three ransom demands. That sounds like blackmail to me. What do you think, Kelly?"

"It does sound strange, but if you think its blackmail, why would Barrington call your buddy, Former President Davidson?"

"I have no idea. If you were a kidnapper, would you ask for more than one ransom? I mean, why not ask for it all at once and minimize the risk?"

"It is puzzling. Maybe the kidnapper knew Barrington couldn't get it all at one time. Who knows?"

I rang the doorbell. The door opened. I was first struck by the emerald and white marbled floors. They reminded me of an elegant and costly chessboard. I could tell the floors had been professionally polished by their high glossy shine. When I looked up, I saw a classy looking, dark-skinned black woman standing in the foyer. She was tall, thin, expensively clad, and strikingly beautiful. Her eyes were greenish blue. I wondered if they were contact lenses. The marquis cut rock on her finger must have cost more than my house. Having learned from the misstep at the gate, we opened our credentials immediately and identified ourselves.

The woman scrutinized our badges and photos before introducing herself as Turquoise Barrington.

Immediately I said, "Mrs. Barrington, I sincerely apologize for my inappropriate comments at the gate. I assure you it won't happen again."

She said, "I apologize as well for responding as I did. I'm not myself these days. This thing with Portia has shaken us both considerably."

"Understandable," Kelly said.

"The rest of the members of the team are in the living room with Myles," Mrs. Barrington said. "I'll take you to them."

As we walked to the living room, I said, "Mrs. Barrington, I know you told agent Ryan and the others what happened to your daughter, but we need to hear it from you and your husband."

"Well," She exhaled, "The day Portia was kidnapped was like any other. When Myles and I woke up, she was gone. There was nothing unusual about that. She's usually gone by the time we get up. We're both attorneys and often keep late hours."

"I'm wondering why you hired a bodyguard," Kelly said. "Have you been getting death threats?"

"No. No threats of any kind in several years, Agent McPherson," she said. "The bodyguard was Myles' idea. It was precautionary. With all the school shootings as of late, he thought there might one day be violence at Portia's school. I thought he was being overprotective, to be honest with you. Men can be like that with their little girls. I never thought something like this would ever happen to us. Nevertheless, to put Myles at ease, that's why we hired your husband's firm, Agent Perry. So that this sort of thing wouldn't happen."

Even though there was no malice in her words that I could tell, my heart sank when she said that. I felt like doubling over. "I'm sorry this happened to your daughter, Mrs. Barrington. We both have daughters of our own. I want you to know that we'll be doing everything we can to get her back safely."

"I'm sure you will," she said. "Palmer still speaks very highly of you in spite of what's happened."

That was another body blow.

We stepped into what most people would call a living room, but it was big enough for a small full-court basketball gym. When Myles Barrington saw us with his wife, he came over and introduced himself. Myles was white, clean-shaven, and athletic looking. He looked to be in his early forties, but given his legal reputation, I assumed he was at least in his fifties. I looked at Kelly. She knew what to do. We had worked together for so long she knew I wanted her to get Myles alone and get his story without Mrs. Barrington being there. Ruthless as it may sound, everybody was a suspect, even the Barringtons, until they were no longer suspects. For all we knew, one or both of them could have killed their daughter accidentally and then trumped up a kidnapping ruse to cover their tracks.

I said, "Mrs. Barrington, could you show me Portia's room while your husband brings Kelly up to speed?"

"Sure. The previous owners had live-in servants." she said. "Portia moved her things to their wing of the house on her fifteenth birthday. Right this way."

As we made our way down the hall, I thought I'd ask some rather personal questions to get a feel for how well she got along with her daughter. Mothers and daughters often have explosive relationships, and that's putting it mildly. The older Savannah gets, the more volatile our relationship becomes, it seems. I find it extremely frustrating sometimes, trying to juggle being an on-call FBI agent and being a wife and mother. My mother died giving birth to me so I never really had a strong bond with any woman other then Kelly. I'm not sure exactly how it's supposed to work, having no schema. Kelly has big trouble with her daughter, Blaze. They go back and forth all the time on the least little thing. It's painful to watch. I hope Savannah and I never get to that point.

I locked eyes with Mrs. Barrington, wanting to both see and feel her reaction before saying, "So, was it her idea to move to the servant's quarters?" I had to see if we were dealing with a rebellious teenager. If Portia was rebellious, she and Williams may have orchestrated this whole affair, which would explain why the ransom demands appeared to be blackmail payments. Since Mrs. Barrington didn't say whose idea it was for the move to the servant's quarters, I decided that something must have prompted the move. Otherwise, why avoid the question. Something made Portia want to separate from her family. What was it?

Mrs. Barrington stopped walking and faced me. "If you're asking me if I get along with Portia, the answer is yes."

Immediately, I found her answer curious. *She got along with Portia?* What did she mean by that? And why didn't she say, she got along with her daughter as any mother would? I didn't want her on the defensive. Not yet anyway, so I exercised patience instead of forging ahead with more penetrating questions. We started walking again. I thought I was being subtle when I said, "Mrs. Barrington . . . how long have you and Mr. Barrington been married?"

We stopped at the house elevator. She pushed the up button and then said, "Portia is Myles's daughter from his previous marriage, Agent Perry."

I tried not to smile. Turquoise Barrington was a perceptive woman. She knew where the conversation was going. Instead of allowing me to meander with seemingly innocent questions, she took charge and got to the point. The elevator doors opened and we got in. Mrs. Barrington pushed the three button.

When the doors closed, I said, "How old is Portia?"

"Fifteen." She said without emotion.

"And you get along?" I asked, watching for any reaction that would reveal how she felt about her stepdaughter.

"As I said, we get along fine. About as well as any mother and daughter, I suppose."

Still watching her, probing for truth, I said, "No problems? No petty arguments? No problems with her girlfriends or boyfriends?"

The elevator doors opened. We stepped out and we faced each other again. She was holding something back. What, I did not know. I was about to ask another question when she fired off one of her own.

"You said you have a daughter, right, Agent Perry?"

"I have two children," I said quickly. "A boy and a girl."

"How old is your daughter?"

She was talking freely now, which was what I wanted. I could tell she was guarded and as long as she was I wouldn't get the truth I was looking for. I said, "Savannah's twelve."

"And has she started her monthly cycle yet?"

I locked eyes with Mrs. Barrington, a little put off by the question. Asking about my daughter's menstrual cycle was beyond the limit of social norms. But I suppose she thought it was fair game since I was getting in her business. Obviously, it didn't matter that it was on a professional level. She probably thought it was okay to get into mine on a personal one. I think she wanted me to be offended. I decided not to be and answered, "Yes she has." My hope was to stun her just a bit. I wanted to let her know that I would hold nothing back even though her question was way out of bounds. I saw her straining to withhold a smile, which told me she knew what I was doing. Now that I had answered her personal question, she would have to answer my professional questions.

Mrs. Barrington turned to the left and escorted me down the hallway. "How well do you two get along, Agent Perry?"

Again, I would be unguarded. "Reasonably well, I'd say."

"Reasonably well?" Mrs. Barrington repeated. "That must mean the relationship is less than perfect."

I let the statement linger for a few seconds before saying, "No relationship, let alone a mother-daughter relationship, is ever perfect. I can only assume that a mother-stepdaughter relationship at best is less than perfect, right?"

We stopped at the entrance of a bedroom. I presumed it was Portia's. Mrs. Barrington inhaled deeply before saying, "Listen, I had a few problems with Portia when her father and I started dating six years ago. And to be honest with you, I initially thought there were some race issues, but I realized my race was just a convenient way for Portia to lash out. Her very best friend in the world, Reilly Vanderpool, is African-American." She paused for a few seconds, looking into my eyes, attempting to ascertain whether or not I was buying what she was selling. "I'm a district attorney, Agent Perry. So, I know you have to suspect the parents, if only a little. And don't think for a moment that I don't know your partner is downstairs giving my husband the business." She paused again, hoping, I guess, for a reaction. I offered her nothing. "Having said that, it's still insulting to be a suspect in your stepdaughter's kidnapping case, you know what I mean?"

"I can imagine," I said. She needed to blow off a little steam, so I let her. I learned long ago, sometimes it's better to keep your mouth shut and listen. People often slip up and give themselves away with their mouths. "So, how did you and Mr. Barrington meet?"

"We met on the Damon DuPont case about seven years or so ago. I was an assistant D. A., at the time, and second chair. Myles was the lead attorney for the defense. After the case was over, he asked me out for a drink. We became acquainted and here we are."

I was thinking, what was so hard about answering my questions. Their story was a romantic one. I suppose, though, being a suspect when you're innocent, the idea of being wrongfully accused automatically puts a person on the defensive, particularly when you're a part of the legal system.

Still standing at the bedroom entrance, I said, "Forgive me for asking, Mrs. Barrington. I know how hard this must be for you. But is there any chance this could all be a hoax?"

She frowned and said, "A hoax, Agent Perry?"

I exhaled softly and said, "Is there any chance that Joel Williams and Portia could have run away together? It doesn't make sense to ask for three ransoms. The risk of being caught increases exponentially each time they attempt to retrieve the ill-gotten booty."

Mrs. Barrington cut her eyes to the left and then to the floor. Before she spoke, she looked over her shoulder and seeing no one, returned her eyes to mine and said, "Between you and me?"

"Between you and me," I repeated, nodding, knowing that she was referring to the racial component she and I had in common.

"It wouldn't surprise me, Agent Perry."

Now that she was finally opening up, I said, "You haven't said this to anyone else? Not even to Jack Ryan?"

"No. I wouldn't dare. If I said one negative word about my husband's flawless daughter, he'd go berserk. He thinks she's still a virgin. I happen to know for a fact, she isn't."

I remained quiet and let her spill whatever secrets she had been keeping. If there's one thing I know, people have incredible difficulty keeping secrets—even their own. They seem to have a burning desire to tell all. It frees them of the burden.

"I can't tell you how many times I've caught her having sex with older boys in this house," Mrs. Barrington continued. "I've literally lost count. And believe me, I'm not exaggerating! I tried talking to her about her conduct and she laughed in my face. When I threatened to tell her father about her extracurricular activities, she told me he would blame me for telling him. And she was right. For a couple of years, our relationship was strained. When I figured out he didn't want to know the truth about his daughter, I stopped telling him. Sadly though, our relationship still hasn't fully recovered. At this point, I don't know that it ever will."

I felt sorry for Mrs. Barrington. She obviously cared about her husband and her stepdaughter. Most people wouldn't care about someone else's child and they certainly wouldn't have the guts to say what needed to be said. They would just look the other way and watch the children go down a path that would one day lead to their own destruction.

"Everything you need to know to confirm who Portia is and to verify the veracity of what I said can be found in her room. If you're half as good as Palmer says you are it won't take you long to find what I found."

I said, "Thanks for being so candid. If it's all the same with you, I need to be in the room alone. It's my process."

"Sure, no problem. Can I get you some refreshments? Coffee or tea? Evian, perhaps?"

"No, thank you. Can you do me two favors?

"If I can, sure."

"I need a list of Portia's friends, their phone numbers, addresses, if you have them, and her class schedule."

"I thought you'd want that, so I typed up a list of Portia's friends and their addresses . . . the ones that we know of anyway. There aren't many on the list, but it should help get you started. Hopefully her friends can tell you something we can't. Now . . . what's the other thing you need me to do?"

"Ask Kelly to come up here when she finishes interviewing your husband?"

"I will. And I'll give her the list."

I thanked her and she turned around and headed back. She stopped, faced me again, and said, "Agent Perry, no matter what you find in there, please, for the sake of my marriage, say you found everything on your own. I had nothing to do with it. I showed you where her room was and then I left you alone, okay? Believe it or not, he hasn't even been up here. He doesn't know, nor does he want to know, what's in there."

I acknowledged my promise a second time with a single nod. But I couldn't help thinking that whatever she found in Portia's room must be off the hook.

I walked through the door opening and eyeballed Portia's room, which was huge. I wasn't looking at or for anything specifically. I was just taking in the décor, basically scanning everything, taking in as much of it as I could from a distance, trying to get a feel for who Portia was. Mrs. Barrington said that everything I needed to answer the unasked questions could be found in the room, which was well-kept. I was immediately drawn to the glass trophy case. I made my way over there to take a look at Portia's awards. She had won a number of swimming trophies, volley ball trophies, softball trophies, and an assortment of equestrian trophies, plaques, and ribbons.

Opposite the canopy bed was a large flat screen television. The walls were covered with brass framed posters of Star Wars: Episode III, Batman Begins, Mr. & Mrs. Smith, along with pop stars, Mariah Carey, Gwen Stefani, Usher, Alicia Keys, and Will Smith. There was a stereo system and an endless supply of DVDs and CDs. Strategically placed beneath the pillows on the bed was a spotted sixteen inch brown and white Jaguar stuffed animal.

I walked around the room, taking it all in, still trying to get a sense of who Portia Barrington was; still trying to learn anything I could about her visually. I stopped at the built-in book shelves and looked at her books. I skimmed the titles to see what she was feeding her mind. Mrs. Barrington had caught her having sex with older boys numerous times. She had to be reading, watching, or listening to something that encouraged that sort of behavior. That's what I believed anyway. I saw the first five books of J. K. Rowling's *Harry Potter* series. I smiled and wondered if every child had her novels. Savannah did. Then, I saw a slew of classic novels like, *National*

Velvet, Treasure Island, The Last of the Mohicans, Robinson Crusoe, A Christmas Carol, The Count of Monte Cristo, The Three Muske-teers, and a host of others.

I browsed her DVD and CD collection next. It looked as if she had every movie and CD released from 1995 to 2005. She even had classic movies like, *A Streetcar Named Desire, Butterfield 8, All About Eve, Giant, Five Gates to Hell, Mackenna's Gold, Footsteps in the Fog,* among other classics. So far I didn't have much of anything that told me who Portia Barrington was. I knew she loved sports, music, and movies, so far. Sports meant she was a competitor. That helped define her too.

I continued scanning the film titles and noticed that a row of them seemed to be set aside, like they were favorites or something. Some of those titles included, *The English Patient, Dangerous Liaisons, The Graduate, Mo' Better Blues, The Age of Innocence, Titanic, Jungle Fever, The Grasshopper, Presumed Innocent,* and about a hundred other such films.

The thing that struck me about all of them is that they were films about love triangles. With the exception of *The Grasshopper,* I had seen all the pictures in the separate stack. I guess that's why it stood out. The other thing that made it stand out was that the film was in a clear plastic container. I picked it up and turned it over. I was looking for the blurb to find out what it was about. There was a piece of masking tape on the back with two names written on it— Jacqueline Bisset and NFL Hall of Fame legend, Jim Brown. I planned to watch the film later. There may be something there. I sat the disc on the desk near the computer keyboard. I was about to take a look in one of the two walk-in closets available. I assumed the previous housekeepers were a husband and wife team. I had taken a couple steps away from the desk before turning around and hitting the power button on the computer tower.

While the computer powered up, I went into the first walk-in closet. I guess I shouldn't have been shocked at all the latest fashions I saw. Portia was obviously into shopping. It seemed as if Portia bought everything she saw, judging by the music and film collection and the endless number of outfits in her closet. I noticed that there were no shoes. I assumed they were in the other closet. I was so impressed with what I saw in the first closet that I forgot all about the kidnapping. I had to see her collection of shoes. It's a woman thing. If they were anything like her designer clothing, I knew her shoes were going to be something else. I went into the other closet and was in heaven. Looking at Portia Barrington's shoes was the equivalent of window shopping on Fifth Avenue and Rodeo Drive.

Among her exquisite collection was a pair of Manolo Blahnik alligator boots with four inch spiked heels that cost $14,000. They hadn't even been worn. The price tag was still on them. They were the most expensive of the collection. She also had everything from Louis Vuitton to Ferragamo to Jimmy Choo to Escada and Givenchy; the latter two being the cheapest, costing $995.00 a pair. Upon further examination, I noticed that several other brand name shoes had never been worn. I just shook my head, envying all of this opulence being lavished on a fifteen-year-old girl who couldn't appreciate it the way I would. And there was more to come.

I hadn't even been in the bathroom yet, let alone down the hall to see what was in the rooms Mrs. Barrington and I had walked past without opening the doors. I was tempted to take the Ferragomos with me. I could say they were evidence or something, I told myself. I took a quick peek toward the bedroom door. Seeing no one, I tried on the alligators. I knew I shouldn't have, but I told myself I wouldn't be hurting anyone if I did. Besides, when was I ever going to try on a pair of $14,000 Manolo Blahnik boots again?

Never! That's when!

I sat on the leather bench and slid into them. They fit like a glove. I stood up and walked around the closet. They felt so good that I lost my mind and started modeling them like I was drop dead gorgeous super model Beverly Johnson or perhaps Gisele Bundchen being showcased on a New York runway. When I turned around to walk back the other way, my mouth fell open. Kelly and Mrs. Barrington were watching me.

Chapter 3

Modeling the shoes of a kidnapped teenager was not the position an FBI agent referred by a former president, should be in. But there I was, with egg on my face a second time in less than thirty minutes. I stood there frozen, looking at Mrs. Barrington, trying to gage what she was thinking of me. The thing about it was that I knew better and I knew someone could come in and I could get caught, but I couldn't resist. It was like the boots were calling me, saying, "Phoenix, try us on for size". We all stood there quietly looking into each other's faces. I noticed that Kelly was doing all she could to keep from laughing. I cut my eyes to Mrs. Barrington again. She didn't look angry, but that didn't mean she wasn't.

"How do they feel, Agent Perry?" Mrs. Barrington asked.

I sat down on the bench again. As I removed the boots, I said, "Wonderful. Forgive me for crossing the line. I just had to know what they felt like. I'm sorry."

"No need to apologize," Mrs. Barrington said. "I tried them on myself. I've never owned a pair of shoes that cost that much in my life. So, I know the feeling and the enticing urge that drove you to try them on."

Immediately I looked at Kelly. We were both wondering why Myles Barrington would spend that kind of money on shoes for his daughter, but would not spend the same amount on his wife. Rather than the direct approach, I said, "All I can say is that your husband is a really big spender."

"Agent Perry, Myles didn't buy Portia those shoes," Mrs. Barrington said. Again she knew what I was asking without asking anything at all. "To my knowledge, Myles didn't pay for much of what's in her closet or what's on the third floor. Again, he's never even been up here."

"Oh, I see." I said, thinking I had figured it out. "Her mother indulges her."

"I thought so, too," Mrs. Barrington said. "But her mother can't afford to spend $14,000 on a single pair of shoes, let alone a vast closet full of shoes and clothes with price tags on them so staggering they boggle the mind. I don't even think Myles could afford to spend this kind of money on Portia. When you add the contents of both closets, and most of the things on this floor, the number runs into the hundreds of thousands of dollars easily, I'm sure."

"So where's she getting the money?" Kelly asked.

"I really don't know," Mrs. Barrington said. "I'll leave you two alone. Keep looking around, you might find a slew of other clues that'll make your hair stand up."

She turned to walk away, and then turned around again. She was about to say something, but I said, "You didn't tell us anything. I got it."

"Thank you, Agent Perry," Mrs. Barrington said, and left the room.

Kelly waited until she was out of earshot and said, "What was that all about?"

I said, "Her relationship with Barrington is strained because of Portia."

"Really? You'd never know it the way he talked downstairs, Phoenix."

"What was he saying?"

"He was just telling me how happy the family was before his daughter was snatched; how they all got along great and how he couldn't believe this was happening to them."

"You believe 'em, Kelly?"

"Not a word of it. If he has to say that, I gotta believe it's just the opposite. I gotta believe the situation is probably critical between them all. But he doesn't want us to think she could have run away or that there was foul play on their part."

"Do you think there was foul play on their part?"

"Honestly, no. I think it's just what it looks like, Phoenix. Sure . . . Barrington is putting on a love show for us, but I don't think he's done anything to his daughter. If nothing else, he definitely loves his daughter. What about Mrs. Barrington?"

I shook my head. "She's been pretty much forthright about everything. She was a little reluctant at first, but then she opened up."

"Well what was that business about not telling anyone she had anything to do with what we find up here?"

"Barrington takes it out on her when he finds out Portia isn't little Miss Perfect. According to Mrs. Barrington, their relationship is strained because she tried to tell him what his daughter was doing up here."

"What was she doing, Phoenix?"

I sighed. I knew what I was about to say was going to force some painful memories to the surface for Kelly. She would just have to deal with it. I said, "Mrs. Barrington says she's caught Portia having sex with several young men that were older than her."

Kelly diverted her eyes away from me. I knew she was thinking about her daughter, Blaze, who she had caught having sex with different boys. Once, she caught Blaze having sex with two boys at the same time. For all I know, Blaze is still off the hook. Kelly doesn't talk about it, but I know it hurts her. I also know she knows much of Blaze's behavior is learned from watching her lifestyle and the rest is probably in her DNA, passed on from Kelly, and probably her father too.

I knew it was time to change the subject when Kelly said, "We probably better continue looking around."

When I got back to the desk, I saw an 8 x 10 photo of a very pretty girl, I assumed was Portia Barrington, that I hadn't noticed when I turned the computer on. I sat in the black leather chair on wheels and studied the photograph. With a face like that, she could easily be a model or a highly paid Hollywood actress. She was wearing what looked like a professional makeup job. If I didn't know she was fifteen, I'd bet the house she was at least twenty-two. No wonder older boys were sneaking over. Long luxurious black mane draped her smallish shoulders and framed her dark tanned face perfectly. Ruby red paint graced her full lips. Silver hoops were in her ears. She had alluring grayish eyes, and a bright attractive smile.

As I looked through Portia's computer, I starting thinking about the money it must have cost to pay for the designer shoes and clothing. Mrs. Barrington had said "hundreds of thousands of dollars in shoes and clothes". I was thinking drugs—a lot of drugs. Was

Portia Barrington a rich kid who got caught up in the drug trade? If so, it certainly wouldn't be the first time rich kids who already had it made, had done so. Is that what this is really all about? Did she owe her suppler serious money and had to suddenly disappear? Did she plan and execute the kidnapping to get money from her father to pay her enormous debt?

According to Jack Ryan, the Barrington's paid a total of five hundred thousand prior to calling Palmer Davidson. The other scenario came to mind. Are Portia and Joel Williams lovebirds? Are they somehow mixed up in the drug underworld—together? If they are lovebirds, if they are involved in the drug underworld, did they somehow get in over their heads? Or was all of this on Williams? Was Williams way over his head in debt and using this young, vibrant girl to pay it off?

Kelly was looking over the closets and the bathroom. In the near distance, I kept hearing her say, "Wow!" over and over again. I knew how she felt. Because of the cases we draw, Kelly and I have been to many different upscale homes. Nevertheless, we are always amazed at how the rich live. Just a couple of weeks ago we were in Las Vegas examining a murder scene. The house was unbelievable. And it had this split staircase I will never forget.

"Phoenix," Kelly called out.

Still searching Portia's computer I said, "Yeah. What did you find?"

"Have you been in this bathroom?" Kelly asked.

"No, I'm afraid I haven't," I said sarcastically. "I'm working my first ever kidnapping case at the moment. That's what I get paid to do. And by the way, my "team" doesn't want me running the show. Apparently you've forgotten that. I don't have that luxury. So I really don't have time for the grand tour you seem to be enjoying."

"You got a lot of nerve," Kelly said laughing.

I could feel her prying eyes staring at me. I looked at her and smiled. She was standing in the door of the bathroom now.

"Who got caught trying on $14,000 boots? Not me."

"That was a part of the case," I said laughing.

"You're lucky she was cool about it, Phoenix. You two must have really hit it off after that shaky start at the gate. I don't think I'd be that cool if it was my daughter and the lead FBI agent was trying on her shoes and modeling them."

"Yeah, well . . . she didn't blow a gasket," I said and double clicked Internet Explorer. "And that's a good thing. What did you find in there?"

"Come and look at this," she urged.

"This better be good," I said, following her.

I gasped when I walked into the bathroom. It was bigger than my bedroom and the connecting bathroom.

"Look at that walk-in shower, Phoenix! I'll bet you can get twelve people in that bad boy!"

"Wow!" I said, without contemplation when I saw how big it was. Then, I made my way over to the sunken tub and looked inside. It was wide and deep with about twelve jets, as I suspected. I looked out the window, which was positioned over the tub. I could see the marina and the stables. Shaking my head, I said, "And Kelly, the girl is only fifteen-years-old and she's living like a pampered Hollywood starlet."

"It just ain't fair, is it, Phoenix?"

"Sounds like class envy to me, Kelly. What does fairness have to do with it?"

"I do envy the rich, don't you?" she said. "I want their lifestyle; a life of ease."

I laughed a little and said, "Well, if I had the money, I would have it like this too. I won't begrudge the rich just because their rich. If anything, I wanna be rich too. The trick is to figure out a *legal* way to live like this. You know what I'm saying?"

"Yeah, I know, but hell, I'm no genius. I'm over forty now. What can I do other than marry someone who's got the bucks to put me in a place like this? I mean this fifteen-year-old girl has a better place to stay than I do. It's better than the Abraham Lincoln Suite at the InterContinental. And you're gonna stand there and tell me you're not the least bit jealous of the rich? Please!"

I smiled and said, "Well, maybe just a little. I'll give you that." Then I looked at the door to my right. "What's in there? Is that the linen closet?"

"No," she said. "The towels and toiletries are in the cabinets next to the sinks. I don't know what's in there. Let's check it out."

I opened the door. It led to a hallway. Opposite the bathroom door was a lavish state of the art Egyptian themed home theater. Above the columned doorway was a sign that read: Elite Entertainment. There were two life size Egyptian statues standing outside the theater on both sides of the double door entrance. Both statues were males covered with rich Mahogany skin, and clothed with golden kilts, black with gold stripped capes. Their biceps, wrists, and ankles were clasped with golden bracelets. Hieroglyphics were on the columns and the entrance doors.

I looked at Kelly, who was looking at me shaking her head. She said, "Are you jealous now, Phoenix?"

"I said, "Yep!"

We both laughed and walked up three stairs and entered what was supposed to be a replica of a Pharaoh's tomb. I looked at Kelly, who was still shaking her head. My jealousy was now full-blown. The place looked like a real ten seat theater, complete with wide tan leather reclining seats and cup holders. The screen had to be at least 130 inches. Speakers were strategically placed on all four walls and beneath the screen. The walls wore 24'"x 36" black and white photographs of legendary Hollywood beauties. I saw a still of Marilyn Monroe. She was on a bed with nothing but a sheet to cover the things men wanted to see most. Next to it was a black and white of Sophia Loren and Clark Gable, which was next to a black and white of Elizabeth Taylor and Paul Newman. In the center of the floor, in front of the first row of seats, was a built-in touch screen remote control device.

The smell of buttered popcorn had me salivating. I looked to the left and saw a popcorn machine on a red wagon with red and white stripped wheels. A red awning covered the glass where the popper sat. Popcorn was still in it. There was even a soda machine, complete with a cup and ice dispenser, lids and straws. I walked over to the popcorn machine, opened the glass door, grabbed a handful and shoved it into my mouth. It was stale, but I didn't care. I wolfed it down and grabbed another handful. We walked down the stairs and sat in the leather seats. I said, "Portia's got a billion films. Which one do you want to watch first? I'm thinkin' I'd like to see *The Grasshopper* first. It was in a stack set aside from the rest."

"*The Grasshopper?*" Kelly repeated. "What's that about?"

"I don't know, but Jim Brown and Jacqueline Bisset are in it. So, we know it's something from the seventies. Jim was on top then."

"*Thee* Jacqueline Bisset?" Kelly asked. "Wet T-shirt Jacqueline Bisset?"

"One and the same," I said.

"What do you bet she's bangin' Jim in the film?"

"Probably so. Raquel Welch got her a piece of that in *100 Rifles*," I said, laughing. "Those films were shot when Jim ruled the world. Know what I'm sayin'?"

"I don't blame either one of 'em," Kelly said smiling. "I would've of got me a piece to of that too."

"Why do you suppose I wanna see that film?" I asked.

"Besides seeing Jim Brown in his prime?"

"Uh . . . yeah."

"'Cause you're wondering why a fifteen-year-old girl had the film in her special collection, right?"

"Right."

"And it wouldn't hurt to see if Ms. Bisset and Jim get their little swerve on in the film because if she thought the film belonged in the set aside stack, given that she likes the older boys, she may have let Joel Williams take her for spin too . . . following Ms. Bisset's example, of course."

"You are too good at this, Kelly," I said, smiling. "And get this . . . the disc is not in a professional case. The kind the studios put out. It's in a plastic one with masking tape on the back. That's how I knew who was in it."

"Bootlegged?"

"Probably," I said.

"And you're thinkin' a rich chick like Portia Barrington wouldn't need to buy bootlegged DVDs, right? She probably wouldn't know who to buy them from or where, right?"

"Exactly," I said. "Given the neighborhood this house is in, somehow I don't think the boy next door is selling them. Know what I mean?"

"So you're thinkin' what, Phoenix?"

"I'm thinkin' Portia Barrington's into something deep . . . so deep that it probably takes her into the 'hood. Probably drug dealers.

She probably thinks it's all so exciting. Rich, white girl runnin' around with black would-be gangsters."

"So what are you sayin', Phoenix?" Kelly said, smiling. "We white women can't wait to get our hands on a black gangster, or what?"

"No. Color is not the issue. Perhaps Gangsta Rap videos are in play here. Who knows? Again, no, I don't believe it's a color issue. I'm saying women can't wait to get their hands on a gangster, no matter what his color is, period. Being black or white, for that matter, has never been a deterrent for any hot-to-trot female who's got her mind fixed on getting what she *thinks* will fulfill her every longing. Am I right or am I right?"

"Can't say I disagree with your assessment."

"Then we're agreed," I said. "Portia's into something deep and it's probably drugs and drug dealers. Let's see if there's anything in the player."

I leaned forward and looked at the touch screen remote control. I found the word "play" and pushed it. The lights automatically dimmed. The curtains retracted to the wall. Seconds later, a hardcore porn film splashed onto the screen. I assumed Portia must have already been watching the film because the "actors" were already otherwise engaged, doing what porn "stars" do. The woman on the screen had two men in her. The camera angle showed absolutely everything. I supposed I should have been shocked that a fifteen-year-old girl who had lots of cash was watching hardcore stuff, but I wasn't. If we were right and she was into black gangsters and drugs, she could be heavily into porn too.

"Phoenix," Kelly said, laughing. "Don't ask me how I know this, but this is a British porn film. The name of the picture is *Uniform Behaviour*."

I took Kelly's advice and didn't ask her how see knew the name of the porn film Portia Barrington had last watched in her theater. I didn't have to. She couldn't wait to tell me about her collection of Anna Span films. She explained that Ms. Span was English and that she was the first female from the United Kingdom to direct skin flicks. She went on to tell me that Ms. Span's films were geared toward women and that women were visual too, just in a different way. I listened, but only because her expertise may have given me some insight into Portia's thought processes. So far, it turned out to be just as I thought. The fact that she left the disc in the player where anyone could find it, told me she either wasn't concerned about being caught with them, or that she was hooked and was watching porn so often she couldn't remember if she hid the discs after viewing them or not.

I thought there were more films because people who are into porn are really into porn. It's quite addictive according to experts. If addicted, one skin flick isn't nearly enough. I had stopped the film. Kelly and I went back into the bedroom and neatly turned it upside down. We found about ten more Anna Span adult films and lots of erotica and porn books. There were even *Playgirl* magazines, all of it where it could be easily found. Most of the material was in mint condition, like it was brand new. We found a large stash of the books and magazines in the linen closet, behind a tall stack of thick beach towels. The films were in a cabinet where the theater system was, just outside the entrance on the left-hand side. It was covered in hieroglyphics just like the wall. If Portia hadn't left it partially opened, we would have never found it.

We went back into Portia's bedroom to checkout her computer. I wanted to know what she paid for that home theater, so I went to the Elite Entertainment home page. I got the number and called them on my cell. According to the man I talked to, if I wanted the theater in my Arlington, Virginia home, they would bring all the material from Malibu, California and set it up for $150,000. I would have been stunned, but the $14,000 alligators in Portia's closet prepared me for the outlandish sum. I wanted to see her bank statements, her phone and cell records, everything. If she wasn't a minor, I'd check her income tax records too. $150,000 for a home theater is serious money for just about anybody. Lots of people didn't have homes that cost that much. But when a fifteen-year-old can buy it, probably with cash, I wanted to know where all the money was coming from.

We were both at the desk now, looking at her computer screen. I clicked on her favorite places file cabinet and discovered that it was full of kid stuff, like Disney Channel, Discovery, PBS, The KidsKnowit Network, Pogo, animals, et cetera. Out of curiosity, I clicked on the Disney website and a free porn site opened. The site was full of well endowed men. With the exception of the Pogo game site and one other site, all the links led to porn sites no matter what they were named. The other site she visited most often was a website called, The Jaguar Club.

When I clicked on the link, the home page opened. First, the eyes of a cat came out of the darkness. Then, we heard what sounded like a menacing tiger's growl and then a brown and white spotted jaguar materialized. Again, we heard a tiger's growl. Soon, expensive items materialized. First, an assortment of mink coats appeared and then diamond rings, Coach Purses, mansions, and ridiculously expensive cars, like a burgundy and black Bugatti Veyron, which cost a whopping 1.7 million dollars. The candy apple red Lamborghini that appeared next only cost a mere 1.6 million. Next, an assortment of sports cars appeared with price tags approaching a million dollars. After those, the Bentleys, Rolls Royces and other "moderately" expensive vehicles appeared along with the Hummer 2 and several Escalade trucks. Then, the site asked for a user name and password.

"Agent, Perry?" Mrs. Barrington called over the house intercom system.

"Yes." I said.

"You'll need the house and cell phone records, and her bank statements, yes?"

I looked at Kelly. She smiled, shrugged her shoulders and then whispered, "She *is* the District Attorney."

"Yes. We will," I said.

"Would you like me to bring them up?"

"No. We're done here. We'll be down in a few minutes."

"Okay. I'll meet you in the living room," she said.

"Mrs. Barrington . . . are you alone right now?" I asked.

"Yes. Why?"

"I'm wondering if you know any of Portia's user names and passwords. We've found a site I'd like to take a look at."

"Actually I don't, Agent Perry," she said. "Believe me, if I knew them, I would have checked out the Jaguar Club myself."

"Okay, thanks," I said, looking at Kelly. "We'll see you in a few minutes."

Chapter 4

Mrs. Barrington was waiting for us when the elevator doors opened. She handed me two manila envelopes with the house and cell phone records. She told us the records covered the last six months and that Portia's bank statements were in the cell phone envelope. She had written her and Mr. Barrington's office and cell numbers on the outside of each envelope. She also wrote Joel Williams' name and number near the top, right underneath Portia's cell number. Myles Barrington's office had ten landline numbers and six cell phone numbers. Mrs. Barrington told us that no one at his office is assigned a particular cell phone. They're in a rack at the office and whoever needed a phone simply grabbed the nearest one available.

I was initially interested in seeing the bank statements, but since Mrs. Barrington gave no indication there was anything there worth seeing, I focused on the day Portia was kidnapped. According to Jack Ryan, she disappeared June 8th. Then, I'd work my way back from there. We went into the living room where the command post had been set up and started examining the documents. I had given Kelly the cell phone records. She had the list of numbers that belonged to Portia's friends. The records were separated by date and time, numbers dialed, and incoming calls. The last and most important column had the length of the calls in hours, minutes, and seconds. It also had the time the calls were made. I immediately looked at that column. It would tell me who to contact first. Short calls could be wrong numbers or no one was at home. Almost immediately, I noticed that the longest calls came from Barrington's office and cell numbers.

The calls came at all hours of the day and night. Some of the calls were made as early as two or three o'clock in the morning and lasted for hours. I pulled out my cell and navigated to the calendar. It turns out that someone was making late night calls to Joel Williams' Crystal City apartment. The longest of those calls were on weekends. I cut my eyes to Kelly. She was busy looking at Portia's cell phone records. All of a sudden, I felt nagging prying eyes staring at me. I looked around the busy room full of people. The buzz of their endless banter filled my ears.

Near the door opening was Turquoise Barrington staring at me, like she was waiting for me to discover what she already knew. I looked at the phone records again, noting the length of the calls and the dates. I looked at my calendar again. The calls to Williams' apartment were being made nearly every night. I shuffled the records and discovered that the calls begin a couple of months ago. At first, the calls averaged between one and two minutes, but over time, the length increased to five or ten minutes. Then, they started lasting longer and longer. Some of the calls lasted from 9 o'clock in the evening until about 4:30 in the morning. I didn't like where this was going. Only people on their way to becoming new lovers talked that much at those hours.

I wondered when they hired Joel. I concluded that what Kelly and I had suspected earlier was indeed the truth. Myles Barrington's fifteen-year-old daughter and a man who worked for my husband were having a sexual relationship. And if not sexual, it was definitely inappropriate.

Oh . . . my . . . God!

I examined the number of calls to Joel Williams' apartment a second time and then looked at Mrs. Barrington again. She was nodding as if to confirm what I thought I had discovered. She was waiting for me to say something. I wondered if Mr. Barrington knew about the late night calls his daughter had been making to her chauffeur and bodyguard. I was thinking how could he not know? Some parents are in denial about their children's bad behavior and don't want to know the truth. But now that his child was missing and he had paid two ransom demands to secure her release, how could he not know of these calls? Besides all that, he was a defense lawyer. Checking her calls should have been the first thing he did. That's what I would have done anyway. If for no other reason than to find out whom she spoke with last. And I certainly would know where she's getting the kind of money it took to purchase that third floor theater. It annoys me that Portia's stepmother knew and her father didn't.

I felt Mrs. Barrington's lingering stare again. I knew she was watching so I decided to ask her a question with my eyes. I cut my eyes to Myles, who I could see over near the glass doors that led to the terrace. He was talking to someone. I couldn't see his face because his back was facing me. He must have arrived while Kelly and I were upstairs. I then cut my eyes back to Mrs. Barrington who was still looking at me. I held up the records and tilted my head toward her husband. She shook her head, letting me know that he didn't know what she knew or at least suspected. It was all circumstantial at this point, but deep down, my intuition was telling me that Joel Williams was banging Myles Barrington's daughter.

I lowered my head and shook it. I looked at Kelly. She had a grim look on her face too. She had discovered the same truth. I was about to say something when she said, "I know what you're thinkin', Phoenix."

I exhaled noticeably before saying, "What am I thinkin'?"

Whispering, she said, "You're thinkin': How could he let himself get into this mess, right?"

I just shook my head slowly, disgusted by it all. I'd never tell Kelly this, but the fact the Joel was black and Myles Barrington's daughter was white and way underage on top of that, made it worse for me. I understood that Portia was very attractive and looked older than her age. After the conversation I had with my husband this morning, I understood how men are socialized to be straight up whores. I even understood that she probably initiated the relationship, given that the calls were made to his apartment, not the other way around.

But what I didn't understand was why he didn't think about the company he worked for and how that would make us look. One of the most challenging aspects of owning an African-American company is getting white clients with long money. I mean most black people, particularly black men, know we have to do what we do cleaner and better than everyone else because we don't have the best reputation. I'm almost certain Joel knew this and yet he went up in a fifteen-year-old white girl anyway. I hate to say this, but, I would have felt a little better if he were banging Barrington's wife. At least she's of age and African-American.

I locked eyes with Kelly and said, "Tell me what I'm thinking, Agent McPherson. And if you can . . . make me feel better about what I'm thinking."

Still whispering, she continued, "I doubt that you're going to feel better, but the truth is this Phoenix. People never think that they're going to get caught up in the forbidden. They never ever think that far down the road." She laughed a little before saying, "Don't ask me how I know this, but from the length of some of these phone calls, I can tell you they were highly sexual in nature. Priming the pump, you might say. I wouldn't be surprised if some self-stimulation was involved to be honest with you. Eventually, they just had to do the things they had been talking about doing. Did Williams think about how young she was? At first, yeah, probably. But after awhile, the addiction told him what to do."

I laughed and then said, "The addiction, huh? Is that what they call it now-a-days?"

"That's what I call it," She said.

"Well if you ask me, I think the *Diction* may be the more appropriate term."

"It is the more appropriate term. Why do you think I'm still dealing with a man who refuses to marry me? The addiction, that's why. And you know how it is. That thing be good, Phoenix, especially if you shouldn't be in the situation to begin with."

"I know," I said.

"And I guarantee you neither of them thought Portia was going to get snatched. It never even crossed their minds. Why would it? That's why the tracks leading directly to their relationship, or whatever it is they're doing, were easily discovered. If she doesn't get snatched, we're not here. If she doesn't get snatched, who's checking phone records and bank statements? You know this, right?"

I nodded. "Yeah, I know."

"What are you going to say to Keyth? I mean he was the one who hired him, right?"

I looked at her and said, "I have no idea at this point. The good thing is we're probably off the case because of this."

Kelly laughed a little and then said, "Forgive me for saying so, but, now I can get back to my business with Sterling Wise. Now I can handle my own addiction. When you drop me off at the Willard

InterContinental, I'm seriously going to get my freak on. Who knows . . . if I put it on him right . . . he might break down and leave Tiburon and move here! If he does, I can move in with him and live like the Barringtons!"

"Uh-huh. Wishful thinking. I totally understand after seeing the theater and Portia's film. Me? I just need to get some sleep. I'll be satisfied with that, at least for now anyway."

"You want me to call our fearless leader and let her know the bad news?"

"No, I'll call Director Malone myself. Let's have a talk with Mrs. Barrington first. We need to find out when they hired Joel and who Portia's friends are. I'm betting her friends know where the money's coming from."

"Yeah, and I'm betting they know all about the Jaguar Club too."

We were on our way over to Mrs. Barrington when the house phone rang. The team sprang into action, grabbing their headgear. Clearly, they thought it might be our kidnappers.

Myles Barrington stopped talking to the man he was with and hurried over to the phone setup. One of our guys turned on the electronic surveillance equipment so we could listen to the call later. The call was coming from Portia's cell phone. Kelly and I grabbed headsets and put them on. I nodded to Mr. Barrington. He picked up the phone. "Hello," he said tentatively, like he was on pins and needles, expecting the worse news, yet hoping for the best; that it would be his darling daughter Portia calling to tell him she was free and where he could pick her up.

"Didn't I tell you not to call the cops?" A man's voice said. He was full of rage, like he wanted to kill someone. "And I specifically told you not to call the FBI, didn't I, Myles?"

Barrington looked at me nervously. I shook my head, telling him to call his bluff. I wanted to see if he really knew we were involved.

"I didn't call the cops," Barrington said unconvincingly. The stress was causing his voice to break.

"You didn't call the cops?" The man said, laughing hysterically. "You must think I'm a fool. We've been watching. You've got a whole slew of cops involved. And two of 'em are whores. One of the whores is black and the other whore is white."

I looked at Kelly who was looking at me. She was smiling as if she enjoyed being figuratively backhanded. I wondered what kind of kinky sex games she and Sterling were playing at the Willard InterContinental Hotel. I looked at our techies. They were trying to locate him. They shook their heads, letting me know they didn't have him yet.

"Well . . . Myles?" The man barked again. "Am I lying?"

Barrington looked to me for answers. I nodded, telling him to confirm what the mystery man already knew.

"You're right . . . you're right," Barrington said, nervously. "The FBI is involved now, but only because you took our money and didn't deliver our daughter."

I decided to intervene. I wanted to keep him talking to see what he was after since he already knew we were listening. "This is Special Agent Perry. Who am I speaking with?"

"I know who you are, *Phoenix*!" the man screamed. "And I know agent Kelly McPherson is listening too! You're both whores! I don't talk to whores! I bang 'em, drop a few dead presidents on their nipples, and keep it movin'!"

I was about to say something when the man yelled, "Shut up! I didn't call to talk to you, whore!" He paused for a second. "Myles!"

"I'm still here," Barrington said, like a man tied hand and foot with a dominatrix standing over him, forcing him to do and say disgusting things.

"Now you listen and you listen real good!" he said, still screaming. "Are you listening, Myles?"

"Yes, I'm listening."

"Good! I want you to know you just killed Portia! She's dead! Dead! Dead! Dead!"

"Oh, God, no!" Barrington screamed. "Please . . . give me another chance! I'll pay whatever you ask! I swear to God! Just don't kill her! Just don't kill my baby!"

"Too late, Dumbo! She's finished. But . . . I'll tell ya what I'm gonna do. I'll let you speak to her for the last time so you'll know that we do have her and she's still alive."

"Daddy?" Portia said a few seconds later. Her voice trembled, like she knew the end was near and there was nothing she could do to avoid the horror of it.

"Yes precious, are you okay?" Barrington said desperately. "Did he hurt you?"

"No, Daddy," Portia said. Her voice was shaking even more now. "I'm fine. I'm fine. Why didn't you pay, Daddy?"

"I did pay, sweetie!" Barrington said, reassuring her. "I paid twice already. And I'll pay a third and a fourth time if I have to."

"Why haven't they let me go?"

"I don't know. We're working on that right now."

"When are you going to come and get me?"

"As soon as I can, honey," Barrington said. "Don't worry. I'm going to take care of everything."

Portia was about to say something when she was suddenly cut off. It sounded like someone put a hand over her mouth.

In an extremely calm voice, a different kidnapper spoke. The voice was husky, like he had been smoking for years. "Don't lie to the girl, Mr. Barrington. She's all done. End of story. Finito."

"I'll have the money this evening," Barrington said. "I swear! I'll bring the money wherever you say! And I'll be alone!"

The calm kidnapper remained quiet for a few seconds, like he was considering the offer. It sounded like he took a drag of a cigarette, blew it out, and said, "That's all right, Myles. Keep it. We already got five hundred large outta you. We don't need the other five. We're both at fault on this thing—you and us. You know that, don't you? We got greedy and you got stupid. Now your darling Portia will have to pay for our collective mistakes with her life. So sad."

"Please don't do this," Myles begged. "You can let her go now. You don't have to kill her."

The calm kidnapper paused again, torturing Barrington with excruciatingly loud silence. Just before Barrington made another plea for mercy, he spoke again. "If you ever see your daughter again, it'll be piece by piece."

In the background, I heard Portia say, "No . . . please don't."

Then a gun discharged.

The line went dead.

Chapter 5

The call appeared to come from Portia Barrington's cell phone. I wasn't so sure. It was possible that the kidnappers had her Subscriber Identity Module, better known as the SIM card. The SIM card made it possible to put the card in a compatible phone of their choosing and we wouldn't know the difference because her phone number would show up. With the SIM card, he could use multiple phones if he wanted to. We would have triangulated his position and moved in, but as soon as the line went dead, he removed the battery and the signal disappeared.

The question surging through my mind was how did he know Kelly and I were involved? He could have easily guessed that the Barringtons, after having been duped twice, called the authorities. But knowing that I was running the show specifically? Somebody had to have told him.

I looked at Kelly. I could tell she was wondering the same thing. We looked around the room. It became clear that we were all wondering the same thing. Who had talked? Which one of the FBI's finest was involved?

Barrington broke the silence first. He was furious. "How did they know you were involved, Agent Perry?" His voice was still shaking.

I said, "Mr. Barrington, I have no idea. But we're definitely going to find out."

"Can I talk to you a second, Phoenix?" Kelly asked.

"Excuse me a minute, Mr. Barrington," I said and placed my hand on his shoulder.

Kelly and I left the living room and headed for the kitchen.

Mrs. Barrington called out, "Perhaps I can be of assistance."

I said, "Unless you know who the kidnappers are, or who told them who we are, I don't see how."

"I don't know who the kidnappers are, but they certainly know who you two are. How is that possible when we only called Palmer Davidson a few hours ago?"

"You're not suggesting former President Davidson is involved," Kelly said.

"No, I'm suggesting someone from the team that left here is," Mrs. Barrington said.

I looked at Kelly and then at Mrs. Barrington. As gently as I could, I said, "We appreciate you helping us with the phone records, the bank statements, and the porn Portia's obviously into, but Jack Ryan and his team are above reproach. I can't think of a more honest agent than Jack Ryan. He and his team have about fifty years' experience with these kinds of cases. They're the very best the FBI has to offer."

"And yet the best swimmers drown," Mrs. Barrington said emphatically. "Until Portia's home safe and sound, no one's above reproach, Agent Perry. Palmer trusts you and we trust Palmer." She looked at Kelly, put her hands on her hips, and continued. "Everyone else is a suspect, even you, Agent McPherson."

I could tell Kelly was about to rip her a new one so I stepped in quickly. "Mrs. Barrington, we're all feeling the stress of the threat the kidnapper made. But just as you trust Palmer Davidson, I trust Kelly fully and completely. There's no way either of us are involved in this thing."

"Can you say the same about the rest of your people?"

"Honestly, no."

"Then Jack Ryan and his team could be involved," She insisted.

"Highly unlikely," I protested. "But as you said, even the best swimmers drown." I didn't believe Jack would be involved at all, but the truth is, people flip all the time. "Please give me and my partner a chance to discuss what happened in private, okay? I promise the FBI will do everything it can to bring Portia home safe and sound."

"The FBI?" Mrs. Barrington questioned. "Are you saying you're not going to be on the case?"

I exhaled softly. I didn't want to upset her any further. "I'm afraid we'll have to step aside on this one."

"Why? Because Joel Williams works for you and he's having inappropriate relations with Portia?"

"Yes."

"Well, I want you two on the case. As I said, Palmer trusts you to handle this thing for us. I'll make a few calls and it'll be all settled." Mrs. Barrington flipped opened her cell. She hit a few buttons. I guess she was looking up a number. Having found it, she said, "Palmer Davidson, please." She paused a second. "This is Turquoise Barrington. Tell him it's very important." She turned around and walked back down hallway.

We continued down the hallway until we reached the kitchen. I stood in the doorway to make sure no one overheard our conversation. Kelly leaned against the granite countertop. Even though I had assured Turquoise Barrington that Jack Ryan and his team were not involved, she was right. As far as I was concerned, everyone was a suspect except Kelly. What concerned me most was that one of the kidnappers was way too cool a customer, which told me he was a thinker. He believed he had everything under control. I also believed that he was capable of doing exactly what he said.

I looked at Kelly and said, "Do you think Jack Ryan is involved?"

"Honestly, no, Phoenix. But you never know. If the kidnappers do have someone on the inside, they just seriously exposed them, right?"

I looked down the hall to see if Mrs. Barrington or anyone else was coming. No one was. I looked at Kelly again. "There are three other possibilities. One, Myles Barrington's involved. Two, Turquoise Barrington's involved. Three, they have the house bugged."

"There's a fourth possibility, Phoenix."

"What have I missed?"

"Both of the Barrington's could be involved *and* the house is bugged."

I checked the hallway again. "If they're both involved, the question then becomes, why would the Barringtons kidnap their own daughter? If they are involved, was that Portia's voice we heard? If not, did one or both of them kill Portia accidentally and all of this is an elaborate ruse to cover it up?"

"If that's true, that would explain a lot. We need to find out where the Barrington's got five hundred thousand. We need to see their bank statements. Did they take out that much money or not?"

"If they're involved, they most certainly did. If for no other reason to cover their tracks. Let's not forget they're both attorneys. They're smart people. If they're involved in this thing, and they might be, they have thought this thing through. And guess what else, Kelly?"

"I know. Portia's dead. The girl on the phone was an imposter."

"I'll call Director Malone and bring her up to speed while you match Portia's friends' cell numbers with her calls. That'll tell us which friend we need to call on first. One should be Reilly Vanderpool. According to Mrs. Barrington, she's Portia's best friend. I gotta believe at least one of her friends knows what's going on with Joel Williams. I don't think Portia could keep that totally secret. One or more of them probably know about the Jaguar Club too. Also, have one of the techies copy the clip of Portia. We'll play it for Reilly to verify its Portia."

"Okay, I'm on it," Kelly said and was about to leave the kitchen. She stopped and turned around. "Wait a minute. If they are behind this, why would Mrs. Barrington be so helpful? Why would she lead us to Portia's porn? Why would she lead us to Joel Williams and his relationship with Portia?"

I said, "Was she being helpful, Kelly? We were going to get the records anyway. And how long would it have taken to find the porn? I mean it was practically out in the open. Sure the *Playgirl* magazines and the erotica were hidden. But, come on, we would have found all that without her help."

"Then she's throwing us off a trail that leads directly to her?"

"Maybe. It's possible that she really is trying to help."

"Okay, I'll get the friends list."

"Before you do that, get a couple of techies to sweep the place. But don't tell anybody what you're doing."

Chapter 6

I flipped open my cell and called Director Malone. She answered after one ring. "Kortney, this Phoenix. I've got good news and bad news. Which do you want first?"

"If you're calling trying to get off this case, forget about it. I just got a call from Palmer Davidson and he says Turquoise Barrington wants you on the case regardless of your husband's involvement. Have you spoken to Keyth about any of this?"

"No."

"Good. Don't say a word. Jack Ryan will handle the Joel Williams situation. Do not interfere. You got that, Phoenix?"

"Isn't this against protocol? I shouldn't be on this case."

"You weren't supposed to be on your cousin's case in Las Vegas either, were you?"

"That was different."

"You're right it is different. This time you won't be directly involved with whatever's going on with Drew Perry. You'll be handling the Barrington case. And if it leads to your husband, then and only then will you step aside and let Jack Ryan handle everything."

"Fine, but you should know that we've got a serious leak over here."

"What do you mean?"

"I mean the kidnappers know too much. They know who the lead agents are by name."

"How can that be?"

"I'm not sure, but we think they may have the place bugged. Either that, or someone is sharing information with them."

"You think our people are involved."

"Turquoise Barrington certainly does."

"Keep me informed of your progress, Phoenix. Palmer Davidson wants constant updates."

My phone beeped. I looked at the screen. It was Jack Ryan calling. "Hold on a second. Ryan's calling in now. He may have something." I clicked over. "Yeah Jack, what's going on over there?"

"Get over here right away," Jack said.

"Is he dead?" I asked with dread.

"I'd rather not say what we found. Anyone could be listening and this will be a very delicate matter. Trust me on this."

"We're on our way." I clicked back over. "Kortney, I gotta run."

"What did he find?"

"He wouldn't say. That means it can't be good. I'll keep you informed."

A View to a Kidnapping

The kidnappers were sitting in a black Chevy van with tinted windows, patiently waiting for their prey to arrive at 96000 Ferry Harbour Court in Alexandria, Virginia. The luxurious mansion belonged to famed defense attorney, Myles Barrington and his second wife, Turquoise. They had been on the quiet road for nearly an hour, expecting their man to show any time now. A new day was dawning as the darkness surrendered to a lesser shade of the same, becoming deep blue as the sun slowly crept over the horizon. Using a top of the line fourth generation night vision bi-ocular, costing nearly six thousand dollars, Bud, the leader, had checked a total of two cars that neared the Barrington house.

Neither car turned into the driveway.

They had followed the man they were expecting for a few weeks and probably knew him better than he knew himself. They believed it was important to know as much as possible about all the players before they made a move. They had been to his home, searched it, and bugged it, looking for anything that would tell them who he was, if he could be an undercover cop, a federal agent, or had ties to organized crime. They wanted to clone his cell phone, listen to those calls, but he kept it with him at all times.

Bud, who was sitting behind the wheel said, "I looked in on my kid before I picked you up. She looked so peaceful; her tiny little thumb was in her mouth. Tough breaking her of the habit, ya know?"

"You gotta little girl. I've got a big girl and a little girl. The big one likes expensive gifts and trips. And we both gotta keep 'em happy, don't we?"

"A few more jobs like this one and I can retire and live the good life. I've got Ericka's college tuition all paid for. My retirement house in the Pocono Mountains is all paid for too. Wanna see?"

"You got pictures of the joint?"

"Printed them out this morning."

He took the pictures and turned on the overhead light. "Wow, partner. Nice place. Ya gotta have me, Kristen, and the kid up sometime."

"Sure. She'll love it."

"Yeah, and it'll save me a few bucks, too!"

"How much ya got saved, Norm?"

"Couple hundred thousand, maybe. But I've got a couple trips planned that's gonna eat deeply into that."

"Are you serious, Norm? A couple hundred? Is that all? With all the snatching we've been doing?"

He turned off the overhead light. "Kristen has expensive tastes. She loves the best that money can buy, ya know?"

"You know what I think of *Kristen*. She's a greedy little bit—"

"Don't call her names, okay, Bud. I don't like that, all right?"

"Okay, well, I just think she's using you, Norm."

"Well, I'm using her too, okay. The sex is outta this world."

"And when that's done, then what?"

"I move on, Bud. All right? Jesus! It's my life, all right! Don't worry about it, okay?"

"I've gotta worry about it. Her greed could get us caught. Greed makes people careless. Greed makes people stupid, Norm. We've discussed this. If you run outta money because of that little . . . well . . . if you run outta money and get desperate, you might get impatient. Make no mistake, the cops will catch you. And when they do, you'll have to cut a deal. The deal will include giving them me."

"It'll never happen, Bud. I'd never ever turn on you. You know that, right?"

"And you've been seeing her how long?"

"Two short years."

"Two short years is right, Norm. That's long enough to eat through all your profits, my friend."

"Hey, there'll always be kids to snatch. Always!"

"Does it ever bother you? What we do, I mean?"

"I don't let it. It's the parents' fault. In these times they gotta know guys like me are just waitin' tuh snatch somebody's kid. If they don't look out for their own flesh and blood, I will and make a nice take for the trouble. I gotta babe that likes diamond and pearls."

"Well, I'm ready to get out of the game. Just a few more jobs and that's it for me."

"You keep saying that, but you haven't stopped yet. 'Just a few more jobs. Just a few jobs.'" Norm mocked and laughed.

"I mean it this time. My retirement is swiftly approaching."

"Sure. Sure. In the meantime, me and Kristen will fly down to Sydney after this job and then we're goin' to Osaka, Japan. From there . . . who knows?"

Bud looked at Norm. "Japan, huh?"

"Yeah, Japan. Ya gotta problem with that?"

"Not if you take someone other than, Kristen."

Laughing he said, "Not a chance. I can't wait to get her long legs in the air in the land down under and then in the land of the rising sun."

As the green lit digital clock in the dashboard neared 5:30 am, a third pair of headlights turned onto Ferry Harbour Court and drove toward the residence.

Bud looked through the single lens device again and zoomed in on the approaching black BMW. The man driving the car was a bald brown skinned good-looking African-American male named Joel Williams. According to their surveillance, he was also a notorious lady's man. They had seen him in action at Union Station in Washington, D. C. Females from eight to eighty seemed to be mesmerized by his smile and flocked to him like birds after a morsel of bread—and him to them.

"He's here," Bud said.

Norm looked at the dashboard clock and chuckled. "Right on time again. I guess this guy don't know blacks are supposed to be late. Good thing we did our homework on this guy, huh?"

"Good thing."

"Big SOB."

"Gigantic."

"Nervous?"

"A little."

"Think he'll put up a fight?"

"Yeah. He's supposed to be a martial artist."

They laughed.

Bud said, "Yeah, but is he a Chuck Norris type or a Steven Segal type?"

"They all think they're Bruce Lee, don't they?" Norm said and laughed a little. "Maybe he thinks he's Wesley Snipes!"

"Yeah. Blade!"

"Ever wonder if people have the slightest inkling that when they meet us, it could be their last day on earth?"

"I doubt it."

"Then let's make sure he never sees it comin'. A couple small holes in the back of the head when he least expects it."

"Agreed. The SOB is in the way. It's not personal."

"Yeah. Why leave witnesses? It's only business."

As Joel Williams' car neared the Barrington estate, the wrought iron electronically controlled gate slowly swung open like arms, welcoming him. The engine roared as he whipped the shiny four-door fully loaded vehicle up the driveway, through the gates, past the rectangular swimming pool and along the paved path that led to the white brick Georgian Colonial. He drove into an open bay of a ten-car garage, parked, and got out of his car. He was quite tall and solid—at least six feet four, and powerfully built, weighing a lean two hundred and forty pounds.

He had played linebacker for the Miami Hurricanes in college and had aspirations of playing in the NFL, but whenever a beautiful woman showed prurient interest, he was powerless to stop himself, which led to his lack of commitment to the game that could have made him an instant multi-millionaire. He loved women more than the game and it kept him from being the kind of player he could have been. On draft day, all thirty-two NFL teams passed on him.

Fortunately, Joel was well liked by his coaches. They didn't believe he would get drafted, but they didn't want to dash the kid's dreams. So they let him sit through two agonizing days as team after team passed him up, round after torturous round. His coaches had a backup plan though; several of them had NFL connections. They pulled some strings and got him an opportunity to play NFL Europe football for the Amsterdam Admirals.

The sexual freedom that Amsterdam offered proved to be far too much temptation for Joel. The Dutch were earning a billion dollars a year from legalized prostitution, where bordellos were as available as a McDonald's restaurant in the western hemisphere. Joel's sexual proclivities became a consuming addiction, derailing another opportunity to fulfill his NFL dream. Although he looked like a professional athlete, he didn't have the goods where it counted most—between his ears, where the will to succeed determined success. He didn't have the discipline it took to be who he wanted to be.

After two years in Amsterdam, he joined the Marine Corps and served in the Gulf during Operation Iraqi Freedom. Now, he was pulling double duty as a chauffeur and a bodyguard for Myles Barrington's precocious fifteen-year-old daughter, Portia.

He opened the driver side back door of the BMW and took out a tan leather shoulder holster and put it on. Then he strapped on his backup piece which was in a Velcro ankle holster. He made sure both Glocks and three ammo clips were fully loaded. He probably wouldn't need them, but it was better to have them and not need them, than to need them and not have them was his philosophy. Finally, he grabbed a black double-breasted chauffeur's jacket and slid into it. He was now in full uniform, complete with breeches, an English Cap, and knee high glossy black boots. The outfit was outdated, but he didn't mind. He had worn uniforms all of his life and always looked good in them.

He quickly walked toward the black stretch Lincoln that was parked a couple bays over and got in. He put the key in the ignition and hit a button. The car started. He drove over to the mansion and parked in front of the six massive columns that framed the entrance and called Portia's cell.

"Ya, ready, kid?" Joel asked when she answered.

"How old do I have to be to no longer be considered a kid, Joel?" Portia asked, teasingly.

"It's just an expression, all right? C'mon. You'll be late."

"If I'm late, it won't be because I left home late. It'll be because you made me late. Ain't that right, Joel?"

"Not on a cell, okay?" Joel said sternly. "How many times I gotta tell you that. Anybody could be listening."

"I know. Ain't it cool?!" Portia said laughing.

"I'm not laughing Portia," Joel said. "Come on. You'll be late."

"Keep your pants on. I'm coming out the front door now," Portia said and then thought for a moment. She smiled as she got into the back of the limousine. Then, she locked eyes with Joel in the rearview mirror. "Uh, given our conversation last night, maybe you should take your pants down."

T he mammoth estate sat on 4.5 lush, green acres and boasted five large bedrooms and private baths, all with picturesque views of the private beach that hugged the Potomac River. The lavish property was worth 7.3 million dollars. Rumor had it that Barrington didn't pay one dime for the home, the land, the limousine, or the dock. It was given to him in a package deal six years earlier in the spring of 1999. The deal included an additional 2.7 million in cash for getting the son of a software magnet off on a slam dunk murder charge.

The trial rivaled the O.J. Simpson fiasco in that it was nationally covered and discussed at water coolers on a daily basis. Ted Kennedy, Mary Jo Kopechne, and the narrow bridge in Chappaquiddick were being revisited by anchormen and women as part of their opening monologues, spicing up the story, which created a never-ending buzz about the sensational case. Everyone wanted to know if another son of the affluent had killed his bride aboard a luxury liner by tossing her over the side on their honeymoon.

Prior to exchanging nuptials in an outlandishly expensive ceremony and reception, the couple had been in a stormy relationship that included loud public arguments and several mutual assaults. The arguments and the physical altercations served as precursors to wild satisfying makeup sex. They had broken up numerous times, but apologized sincerely, promising each other they would never let it happen again. But it kept happening and they kept promising.

The kid swore his bride fell to her death by accident. The honeymooners were drunk and foolishly wanted to pretend like they were Leonardo DiCaprio and Kate Winslet in James Cameron's blockbuster, *Titanic*, when the bride plummeted to her death. Barrington got the jury to buy the story and was handsomely compensated for the verdict. During the course of the three month trial, Barrington had been harassed and had received numerous death threats. He hired a couple of bodyguards, but when the trial was no longer a hot news item, the threats ceased.

However, a couple of weeks after he released his security team, Barrington's fears resurfaced when two teenagers, Eric David Harris and Dylan Bennet Klebold, better known as the Trench coat Mafia, went on a shooting rampage at Columbine High School in Littleton, Colorado. He was shocked at first when he learned of it, and considered getting armed security for Portia, who was nine at the time. After a couple of weeks passed, the shock wore off and he didn't think about the Columbine incident again. He thought it was an aberration that would probably never happen again—not in America anyway. His fears resurfaced a third and final time when another school shooting occurred two months ago.

A teenager had shot and killed his grandparents prior to going on a rampage at Red Lake High School in Minnesota. A newspaper article reported that a witness said he was smiling the whole time. The incident sent a chill down Barrington's back and fully awakened him to the startling trend. He signed onto the Internet and Googled: School Shootings. He learned that students all over the world were committing mass murder and then killing themselves, robbing the families of their sons and daughters and the justice they deserved.

Barrington combed through article after article and discovered that school massacres in the United States went back as far as May 18, 1927. The incident occurred in Bath Township, Michigan, when Andrew P. Kehoe blew up his home, the school, and his car while he was still in it, killing himself, the school superintendent, and forty five others. He further discovered that forty years after the Bath

Township episode, Charles Whitman, an architectural engineering student and former marine, went on a shooting spree and blew away 16 people at the University of Texas at Austin before the cops killed him. The thing that persuaded him to take action was that teen shootings were not limited to the United States; they had taken place in Scotland, Yemen, Germany, Russia, and several places in Canada.

After learning of so many school massacres, Barrington insisted that Bishop Ireton High, one of the best schools in Fairfax County, beef up its internal security. Final exams would begin the second week of June, which was a couple months away, but he didn't care. No one could predict when a kid was going to lose his mind, want to kill himself, and everyone who he thought ever wronged him, slighted him, disrespected him, or would not date him. Besides, summer school would begin a week later and regular classes would start the last week of August.

He spent a small fortune on state-of-the-art metal detectors and promised to get the other parents to make contributions for the safety and welfare of their children. He hired a private security firm immediately. The electronic surveillance equipment arrived in a matter of days, but it took about a month to build the hi-tech centralized command center. Three metal detectors were set up at one entry point to make the process go quickly. Faculty and students were required to be checked in by a uniformed private security firm.

Portia had complained endlessly, arguing that the school was only about nine miles away from their home. She told her father how embarrassing it was to have Joel escorting her to every class and sitting in the back of the room.

Barrington stood firm because too many crazy things were happening in schools. He argued that it was just a matter of time before some crazed student tried to blow up a catholic school. Preventive measures were best. Portia needed to be protected, whether she knew it or not. He did, however, make one compromise. When she wasn't in school, he gave her plenty of freedom to do all the typical kid stuff, like sleepovers, supervised home parties, and taking the Blue Line Metrorail system into Washington, D.C., to hang out and see movies with her friends. But being the typical teenager, she broke all her father's rules repeatedly.

T he deep, blue dawn was slowly disappearing as the limo made its way along the path, past the swimming pool. Birds were singing loudly, making a joyful noise. It was approaching 6 a.m. Bishop Ireton was less than ten miles away, but traffic at that time of the morning was often congested and moved along at a slow pace, standing still for long periods of time, as vehicles poured into Baltimore and Washington. In the beginning, the ride to school was a quiet one, no talking, no radio, nothing but piercing reticence. It would have remained that way if Joel hadn't broken the damn of silence with a question. He asked her if he could stop at the Starbucks on King Street.

Portia had told him he could if he allowed her to have a cup too. Her stepmother wouldn't let her have any of her special blends. Turquoise had told her the caffeine would make her nervous. He agreed and Portia got her first cup of French Roast Blend, the flavor her stepmother favored. From that day forward, Portia enjoyed being chauffeured by Joel. They got to know each other a little better each day they rode together.

She liked Joel. His stories about his college and NFL Europe days intrigued her and she quickly developed a crush on him. He liked her too and allowed her to talk him into letting her open her own door.

When the limo cleared the gate and turned onto Ferry Harbour Court, Joel pulled over and stopped. Portia opened her door and got out. Then she opened the passenger side front door and got in.

Joel pulled off and they headed over to Starbucks to get their morning coffee.

Chapter 7

Bud and Norm waited until the limo turned onto Kimbrelee Court before starting the vehicle and following them. They smiled when they saw Portia get out of the back and into the front. They knew what was about to happen. They had planted listening devices in his apartment and had heard their highly sexual conversations. They laughed uproariously when the limo sped up and slowed down, weaving in and out of traffic at an unpredictable cadence, and often coming within inches of colliding with other cars. Before long, the limo stopped at Starbucks. They watched Joel and Portia go in to get their morning caffeine boost. Minutes later, they came out smiling like they had a secret nobody knew but them. Portia returned to the backseat.

Their reconnaissance had paid off. So far, everything was going like clockwork. They had considered killing Joel in his apartment, taking the limo, and picking the girl up themselves. If they did that, too much could go wrong. Once Portia realized it wasn't Joel driving, she would no doubt scream and attract attention. They couldn't afford to be seen wrestling with her in front of witnesses. Someone might just try to help her and get their head blown clean off for their trouble and further complicate the whole caper. Besides all that, there were traffic cameras everywhere. A meticulous cop might check the videos and get a photo, the make and model of their car, and a license plate number.

The keys to a successful kidnapping, they believed, were information, timing, a real good plan, and above all, patience. Patience was the key to it all. Patience gave them time to think things through. Patience gave them time to investigate all the people involved. Patience gave them time to decide if snatching Portia Barrington was worth it. Patience led to perfection—perfect untraceable crimes that is. Kidnapping was their profession. They had snatched so many people; boys, girls, men, and women of all colors, and nationalities, whatever their clientele demanded. But whenever they got ambitious and snatched the children of the affluent, they exercised even more patience which was why they had never been caught.

They had listened to Joel and Portia's plans after her final exam. They knew she was taking the Metro into Washington, but she refused to tell Joel why. The oral sex she had given him on the way to the coffee shop was payment to shut down his incessant inquiries. After all, he was assigned to protect her from the time he picked her up for school until the time he brought her home. If anything happened to her, the fallout would be on his shoulders. But the kidnappers had to follow them anyway, just in case there was a change in plans they didn't know about. Everything had to appear normal so as not to arouse the suspicions of the cops, which is one reason why they didn't snatch her before exams. Another reason is that they would've had to kill Joel to get her. That would have ruined any possibility of getting the ransom money.

Besides all that, if they took her before she reported to school, the attendance office could call Barrington or his wife. They might get worried and call the chauffeur. When he didn't answer, they would call the cops and the security firm. The cops would put out an immediate Amber Alert and give a description of Portia, what she had on when she left the house, and what kind of car she was riding in. Do-gooders would start paying attention.

Once an Amber Alert went off, the cops would spring into action. They might pull over every limo they saw whether it fit the description or not. The cops knew that if the missing kid wasn't found in twenty-four hours, there was a good chance the kid was dead. A lot of loot was riding on the girl. Killing Joel before they had to wasn't worth the risk of losing the money, getting caught, and doing some serious time in a Federal Prison.

After calling the school the previous day and pretending to be a parent, they learned that exams started at seven and were finished by eleven. They had heard Portia tell Joel she had two exams. According to the attendance office, each exam could take as long as ninety minutes. There was no way of knowing what time she'd get out of class, but no matter what, she had to connect with Joel.

The limo stopped in front of Bishop Ireton. They watched Portia get out and prance into the high security school like she didn't have a

care in the world. She didn't know that her world would change
suddenly and permanently in just a few hours.

After dropping Portia off at school, Joel pulled back into
traffic and hustled over to Union Station for his regular
early morning rendezvous with Marsha Spivey, one of
several chicks on the side. They were only able to spend forty
minutes together because she had to get over to Frank, Husker, and
Meadows, the firm she worked for in Pentagon City. Being female in
a male dominated office meant she had to get there before the
partners and associates. Above all, she had to be professional,
meticulous, and more than competent at all times. To do otherwise,
would send the wrong signal to the partners. They might think she
wasn't ambitious enough to work the extra hours necessary to bring
in more clients, which would mean she wasn't partner material.
Therefore, being late was a message she couldn't afford to send.

Marsha Spivey had met Joel at the firm a little over two years
earlier when she had hired the private investigative agency he
worked for. The agency was best suited for the work she needed
done because they were professionals who prided themselves in
meeting their client's needs. The man who owned the agency was a
client she brought to the firm. Her attraction to Joel was instantane-
ous and mutual. Being married to the starting point guard of the
Washington Wizards did not serve as a deterrent for their desire to
plunder each other.

In fact it made it easy to begin the sizzling affair and hide it for
more than two years. It had gotten personal when they happened to
bumped into each other at a coffee shop in Union Station. To justify
her desire to see Joel on a more personal level, she told herself that
her husband had plenty of women on the road and that he had at least
one woman in every city. She decided that her ballplayer husband
had given the women "backstage" passes for easy access to his hotel
suites.

Proof of his philandering was vigorously sought, but never subs-
tantiated. Instead of accepting the fact that her husband was not
having an affair, she convinced herself that he was cheating; he was
just really good at it—better than a woman. What did it matter
anyway, she'd thought. It was the twenty-first century and women

were allowed the same whorish freedom as men, right? As far as she was concerned ninety-five percent of NBA players, were players indeed—the kind of players that gorgeous women parted their luscious legs for. If he wasn't taking advantage of his celebrity, that was just too bad. She was thirty-two, sweltering hot, and left alone much too often. She wasn't about to play the dutiful wife while he sowed his seed all over North America. She needed "medicinal" attention and Joel was the cure for what ailed her.

Joel approached Union Station from Massachusetts Avenue and drove the limo up the ramp. Tour buses were filing into the multi-tiered garage, unloading scores of eager passengers of various ages and ethnic groups. He was always lucky enough to find an open space in the tourist driven station. He parked the limo and then rushed down the escalator to street level and over to Au Bon Pain's to get croissants and strudel. From there, he made his way back over to the escalator and up to the Mezzanine level to get coffee from Café Renee's, which was where they bumped into each other. Then he found a table, sat down, and waited for Mrs. Spivey. Moments later he spotted her getting off the escalator.

Marsha Spivey was a stunning five feet ten inch Eurasian tax attorney. It was easy for him to spot her through the bustling crowd of shoppers and tourists. She was a walking advertisement, wearing a perfectly cut, black collared, red Liz Claiborne business suit offset by large black buttons, a red imitation turtleneck, and red and black Jimmy Choo heels. She had a red leather Soho Coach Satchel on her left shoulder and a briefcase in her right hand. Her hair was black and silky, long enough to ride the middle of her shoulders. Today it was slicked back and in a thick ponytail. She had a tight body and long elegant legs to die for. Her breasts, 34DD, cost ten thousand dollars each and worth every eye-popping penny. Her husband bought them for her seven years earlier in Beverly Hills when the Wizards were in town to play the Lakers.

Her face lit up when she saw Joel. She looked like a woman who hadn't seen the man she loved in six months. She wasn't sure how, but he made her feel so alive, so vibrant. It wasn't just the marvelous sex they had; it was something that she didn't understand, nor did she care to. He made her feel good about herself and that's all that mattered. She wanted the feeling he gave her to go on forever.

Chapter 8

Joel owned Marsha Spivey's heart and he knew it. There was no doubt about that. Deep down, he felt something for her too, but he wasn't quite sure what it was. Having loved so many women in his life, he didn't know if what he felt for Mrs. Spivey was the real thing or just another fantasy that would soon become a puff of smoke and vanish. That was one reason he always had more than one woman. He never knew when one relationship was going to go sour. His biggest fear was being without a woman. He hadn't been alone since he was thirteen.

As he watched her make her way over to "their" table, he smiled, remembering the favor Portia had given him earlier on the way to school. The favor made it possible to resist his desire to talk Mrs. Spivey into calling in and heading over to his apartment in Crystal City. He sighed deeply and put the idea out of his mind—at least for the time being.

Mrs. Spivey sat down. "Well, he finally left with the team this morning."

"So, we're on for tonight then as planned?" He said as he wantonly stared into her gray eyes.

"Definitely," she said, lovingly. "I was thinking about blowing off my morning appointments so we can be together."

"But . . ." he said, letting it linger in the air, knowing her ambition would never allow her to deviate from her desire to be seen as a viable partner.

"But I can't. A woman who sees herself as a partner can't blow off business."

"I know," Joel said quickly. "And I totally understand."

She reached across the table and placed her hand on top of his. She wished she hadn't brought the idea up. She didn't want to get his hopes up and then not deliver. She said, "Do you, Joel?"

He took a big bite of his strudel and said, "I do. I admire your drive."

If it were possible, her face lit up even more. "Thanks for under-standing. And thanks for not putting any pressure on me." She paused for a moment, lifted the flap on the lid of the Styrofoam cup, and sipped her coffee. "I'm leaving him, Joel. How do you feel about a more permanent arrangement? I'm sick of all this sneaking around, aren't you?"

He cupped her hand and looked into her eyes and said, "You know how I hate sneaking around, too. I've told you this many times. It was all we could do until now. So, yes, I'm all for something permanent, but only if you're absolutely sure."

She sipped her coffee again. "I am sure, Joel. I've never been more sure of anything in my life. I love you so much. Do you know that?"

"I love you too," he said sincerely. But the truth was he never expected her to seriously consider leaving her multimillionaire husband, a posh mansion in Prince George County, and the Bentley she loved. "Can you leave it all, Marsha? I mean that's a lot to give up for a guy who can offer you nothing that approaches what you already have."

"I've been thinking about that and the prenuptial agreement I signed," she said and took a bite of her croissant. "I can give it all up. Can you?"

Joel frowned. "What do you mean? Are you asking me if I can give up the things you have? I don't quite follow you."

"Well, I don't feel right messing around on him behind his back and then taking his money too. If you could have caught him cheating, that would be different. And I can't keep telling myself that he has someone on the side without proof."

Joel smiled.

"What?" She said, smiling too, but unsure why.

"Remember when I said I admire you a few moments ago?"

"Yes."

"I think I admire you even more now. Not many women would walk away with nothing when there were millions to be had; espe-cially with him being in a contract year and scoring 30 points a game and 12 assists. He's probably looking at a hundred million dollar contract next year. Do you realize that, Marsha?"

"Well, I won't be walking away with nothing. I'll keep my car and a little money, but that's about it. Besides, that's his money. He earned it. I'll earn my own millions. As a matter of fact, I'm even thinking about letting him keep the Bentley even though it's in the prenup. Maintaining one would be too expensive for an associate tax attorney. Besides, it doesn't look right to drive one and live in an apartment. I might just sell it and buy a house for us. What do you think?"

He took another bite of his strudel, sipped his coffee, and without looking at her, said, "I think you should you give him back everything he ever gave you, including the ring. I think that if we're gonna do this, we gotta do it right. We can't take his gifts, sell them, and buy a house. I feel bad enough. I mean, I can't steal his wife and his money. You know what I'm saying?"

Marsha quieted herself and thought about what he said for a second. Then she looked at him and said, "I guess you're right. It wouldn't be right to do that. I won't take anything, but I'm keeping the ring."

He laughed and said, "Okay, fair enough. Now . . . can you deal with a man who's less accomplished than you? Most women can't. They think less of a man who doesn't have what she has. In this so-called enlightened age, most women still think a man is supposed to have more and support her. So where are you on the issue?"

She stared at him for a few seconds and said, "I can, but can you deal with a woman who's more accomplished than you? Most men can't."

He looked her in the eyes and said, "To be honest with you Marsha, I don't know. But I do know that I want to try. I've known a lot of women and I can't think of any that I would rather be with."

Beaming now, she said, "So we're gonna do this?"

"Yes." He said, unable to keep from grinning. "When are you going to tell him?"

"I've been thinking about that. I think I'll tell him when he comes back from their West Coast road trip."

Joel's grin evaporated instantly and a pronounced frown emerged. "Why not now, Marsh? Why not tonight?"

"I may be an adulteress, but I'm not a cold-hearted bitch. This is not the sort of thing that should be handled over the phone, Joel. I may not love him, but I do respect him. If I can't be faithful to him, I can at least be honest with him."

"Okay, here's what you're gonna do. When he comes home, make sure you're not there. Pack your stuff well in advance and meet him at a restaurant. Make sure one of our guys from the firm is there with you. Give him back his house and car keys. Then have our guy escort you outta there. You never know how he's going to react."

"So we're really gonna do this then?"

"Only if you're *absolutely* sure."

"I am. Are you?"

"I am, too."

"Hi, Mr. Williams." Joel heard a deep smoky voice say when he entered his Crystal City apartment an hour or so after escorting Mrs. Spivey to her train. "We've been waiting for you."

Hearing a strange voice in his home startled him. Adrenaline surged. He saw two intruders looking at him. One was tall, about six feet eight inches—a real bruiser. He was wearing overalls; the kind that men who fixed things wore. The other one was short, very thin, also wearing overalls. The short one had a black and yellow taser gun. The tall one had an expandable steel baton. They definitely meant business.

"What did I do?" Joel asked, attempting to distract them, if only for a second. That's all he needed was one second; one moment of indecision and he'd take both of them out.

"Do?" the one with the smoky voice asked. "Does it matter?"

"You got the wrong man," Joel said, taking several steps forward, pretending to be afraid while getting to within striking distance.

The intruders looked at each other and smiled.

Smoky voice said, "He thinks we're amateurs, Norm."

While they talked, Joel moved closer to them, eying the room for effective throwing weapons. They were about ten feet apart. He'd have to distract one while he took out the other. He spotted a Remington pump-action shotgun sitting on the kitchen counter. It was too far away for any of them to make use of it. Moving ever closer, he spied a bowl of his favorite candy—jelly beans. He smiled inwardly when he noticed that the thin man was standing on a rug he bought in Amsterdam. He had the taser so he'd have to go first, Joel thought.

"Yeah, probably thinks we didn't check him out," Norm said. "Probably thinks we haven't been following him for a while now. Probably thinks we don't know he's a Bruce Lee wannabe, too."

"Probably don't know this taser'll stop him either, Norm."

"Yeah. He's a big one, huh, Bud."

They laughed again.

That was all Joel needed. While they were still laughing uproariously, he reached down and grabbed the edge of the rug and pulled as hard as he could. The shorter thin man was suddenly in the air; his feet were above his head and he lingered, it seemed, in suspended animation.

Norm stopped laughing and took a couple hurried steps toward Joel with the steel baton raised.

To Joel, everything was moving in slow motion. Out of the corner of his eye, he could see the thin man's slow decent as he grabbed the bowl of jelly beans and hurled them at Norm. The beans hit him in the face and blinded him long enough for Joel to bloody his face with rapid fire punches. Then he hit him in the chest with a powerful thrust kick that sent him flying across the room and into the armoire.

Glass shattered.

Quickly Joel went after the thin man who had dropped the taser. He was desperately crawling across the floor on all fours to retrieve it. He could see inside the overalls. Bare breasts were swinging freely. That's when he realized smoky voice was a woman. "Where you goin', huh, Bud?"

Bud was only a few inches away from the taser when she felt herself being hoisted up by the seat of her pants and the back of her collar.

Joel was planning to toss Bud into the big man called Norm. Just as he was turning to throw the thin man, he felt the cool steel of the baton crash into the back of his skull. A little dazed, he staggered and dropped Bud. Still off balance, but determined, he turned around to deal with Norm. Before he knew it, he had been hit with several stinging punches to the face.

He went down and rolled just as his Sensei had taught him in jujitsu class. When he came up, his Glock was in his hand, safety clicked off, and ready to fire. Suddenly he was in excruciating pain. He felt his wrist shatter from the force of the steel baton. He went down hard.

"Tried to tell you," Bud's smoky voice rang out. "Just so you know . . . you never had a chance, pal. But the effort was truly inspiring."

"Yeah," Norm said, wiping blood off his mouth. "That wrist's gotta hurt, huh, Joel?"

Joel's body shook as pain impulses filled his mind. While the bruiser and smoky voice shot pithy comments back and forth about his debilitated state, he slid his left hand down his leg, hoping to reach his backup piece while they were full of themselves. He thought that if he could just get to the piece, he could still come out of this thing, whatever it was, alive and get a measure of revenge for the broken wrist. He was almost there when he felt two electrodes enter his abdomen. Current surged through him. He convulsed uncontrollably before losing consciousness.

When he came to, he was gagged and tied to a chair with plastic straps. Pain registered again. He tried to speak but his words were muffled by the gag.

He heard Bud's smoky voice saying, "Somebody should have told you this is the wrong century for martial arts. You paid all that money to learn how to defend yourself and it was ineffective against a taser. For martial arts to work, the other guy can't stand across the room with a taser gun, pal."

Norm said, "Cooperate and you just might live through this."

Joel nodded.

The gag was removed.

"We just gotta few questions," Bud said, clearly in charge, running the show. "What's the procedure if something happens to the girl?"

"The girl?"

Bud and Norm looked at each other and shook their heads.

"Hey, I know lots of women, okay? I have no idea who you're talking about?" Bud picked up Joel's Glock and said, "The one you're supposed to be protecting. Portia Barrington. Now . . . no more games. What's the procedure?"

"Portia? What does she have to do with this?"

The butt of the Glock crashed down on the side of his head. "Focus Joel," Bud said, calmly then screamed, "Now answer the question!"

"You mean Marsha's husband didn't send you guys?"

Norm looked at Bud briefly and then returned his attention to Joel and said, "Marsha Spivey? You mean the twist you meet at Union Station every morning, whose husband plays the point for the Wizards? That Marsha Spivey?"

When Joel heard Norm tell him he knew all about his affair with Marsha, he knew they were professionals, which meant he was in serious trouble because professionals didn't leave witnesses. He knew he had to try to buy some time and get them to relax. If they relaxed, they might make another mistake. "Yeah . . . Marsha Spivey. Her husband put you guys up to this right? You're just saying Portia to try and trick me, right?"

Bud and Norm looked at each other again.

Bud said, "Do you believe this guy?"

Norm said, "Last time, Joel. This is about Portia Barrington. No one else. Okay, pal. Nobody. All right? We know who you are. We know all about your women. We know that as a rule, you don't bring them here. We also know Portia is coming here today. We know you're bangin' her, all right! That's why she's coming over. We do our homework, okay, pal! Now . . . what's the procedure if the girl comes up missing?"

"I call Barrington and my boss. They'll wanna know everything that happened from the time I picked her up at the mansion until I dropped her off at school."

Bud laughed and said, "Would you tell 'em what happened in the front seat on the way to school, Joel?"

Joel frowned. *How do they know?*

Norm said, "Yeah, we know about those early morning blowjobs the kid gives you in the limousine, too. From the way you drove that car this morning, apparently the kid was trained by a professional. What'll you think, Norm?"

"Apparently the kid's been givin' blowjobs an awfully long time. Who knows? The kid might've started givin' slurpies when she was ten or something. What'll you think, Bud?"

"Ya never know among the rich and shameless," Bud said and laughed heartily.

Shame suddenly sprang forth. Joel hung his head. He had forgotten that in spite of her looks, in spite of her adult conversation, in spite of her sexual experience, Portia Barrington was only fifteen-years-old. He knew he should have quit the gig the moment she started leaving sexually explicit messages on his voicemail, but her words intrigued him, beguiled him, and eventually seduced him.

"No need to hang your head, Joel. We know lots of guys like you. So hey, we're not here to judge you," Norm continued. "She's a nice looking piece of tail even though she's only fifteen. Looks like the actress from that movie that came out last year, *Confessions of a Teenage Drama Queen*. My girl, Kristen, loves that dopey flick. What's that chick's name?"

"Lindsay Lohan?" Bud offered. "My daughter loves that movie too."

Norm said, "Naw. The other one. The one with the dark hair. The smokin' hot one."

Joel said, "You mean Megan Fox."

"Yeah," Norm said, "Megan Fox. That's her. You like the young girls, huh, Joel? You perverted bastard!"

When Joel heard Norm call him a pervert, all of a sudden he felt enormous guilt and the need to justify the sex he had been having with Portia Barrington. "Listen, man, she came on to me. Okay? All right, man? She kept beggin' me to run up in her, man. I kept telling her no. I kept telling her it was wrong. But she kept calling me, night after night. I told her she was too young. That I could go to jail. She said, 'Not if I give you a Monica Lewinsky. President Clinton didn't go to jail. Why should you?' I started thinkin' about that and when she kept beggin' me to let her go down on me, I couldn't resist, man. I swear to God! It's all on tape if you don't believe me. I fought that thing hard for at least three days before givin' in."

Norm doubled over and roared. "Three whole days, huh, Joel? That's gotta be some kinda record for you, huh?" Joel remained quiet. "So how did you end up having sex with her?"

"You think this is funny, man? She had me all hemmed up. What could I do, man? It was either run up in her or do some serious jail time."

"You perverts gotta million excuses," Bud said and continued laughing.

"I'm not a pervert! Okay? I'm not! All right? Anyway, once she did her thing, she told me that if I didn't go all the way, she'd tell Barrington and he'd make sure I was in jail so long that I'd forget what it was like to be free. I figured if she wanted it that bad, what could I do? She had me over a barrel, man, ya know?"

"You think Barrington'll pay?" Bud asked, ignoring his excuse for statutory rape.

"No doubt. He loves that girl. He thinks she's innocent. He'll pay whatever you ask. I'm sure of it."

"Good. What about the FBI? You think he'll call 'em?"

"No."

Bud looked at Norm. They shrugged their shoulders.

Joel said, "I cooperated. You're not gonna kill me, right?"

Norm said, "Keep cooperating. We'll see."

Someone knocked at the door.

Bud put the Glock to Joel's head, cocked it, and whispered, "Ask who it is."

Joel looked at the digital clock on the microwave. It was approaching 11:30. He hoped Portia hadn't changed her mind. She had told him she had some things to do after exams and that she would be by later in the afternoon.

"Who is it?" Joel yelled out.

"Who do you think?"

Bud gagged Joel again before he had a chance to warn whoever was at the door, and then whispered, "The girl's early. The exam musta been a piece of cake. Let her in, Norm. It's show time."

Norm went to the door and looked through the peephole. He smiled as devilish glee crept across his face.

Chapter 9

As the door opened, Marsha Spivey was saying, "I decided to blow off the day for the first time ever and—" She locked eyes with the man who opened the door, stopped in mid sentence, and looked at the apartment number on the door to confirm that she was at Joel's place. She looked at the man again, stunned that Joel hadn't answered his door when she had heard his voice.

"You must be looking for Joe, right?" Norm said with a big disarming smile.

"Uh, yes . . . yes I am."

"Come on in. You must be Marsha. I've heard so many wonderful things about you," Norm said, gesturing as if he were welcoming her to a Christmas party she had crashed.

Marsha frowned, wondering why Joel would tell anybody about her and their relationship. Tentatively, she walked in, not quite sure what to expect, but curiosity compelled her to enter.

Norm closed the door and called out, "Joe, you're not going to believe who's here, man."

Marsha felt more at ease, but when she walked into the dining room and saw Joel bound and gagged, a loud gasped found its way out of her mouth. She turned to make a run for it, but ran into Norman Green, who might as well have been a brick wall.

"Oh, no you don't," Norm said as he grabbed Marsha by her shoulders. "The party just started and you're our honored guest."

"Have a seat next to Mr. Lover Man," Bud said.

Marsha tried to run again, but Norm had firm hold of her shoulders. He forced her to walk into the dining room and sat her down. Then he tied her up with plastic straps.

Marsha's voice quivered when she said, "How long has Mason known?"

Bud snatched the duct tape off Joel's mouth, knowing he would be far more convincing since Marsha had no idea what she had inadvertently walked in on.

"Don't worry, Marsha. This is about Portia Barrington. They're going to kidnap her. This has nothing to do with Mason or us for that matter."

Bud put the gag back on and nodded to Norm, which meant, they were going to have some fun with them until Portia showed up.

Joel struggled hard to get free until he heard the cocking of a gun behind his ear again. "Settle down," he heard Bud whisper. "I'll say it again. If you two cooperate, you just might make it outta this in one piece."

"What do we have to do," Marsha said as if she was about to drown in desperation. "I'll do anything you say. Only don't kill us."

"You'll do anything?" Norm asked, grinning like he had something specific in mind.

"Yes," Marsha said without hesitation.

Bud, uncocked the Glock, tapped Joel's bald head with it and said, "What about you Mr. Williams? Are you willing to do anything we want too?"

Joel shook his head violently and said something too garbled to understand.

Bud removed the gag again.

"You're gonna kill us no matter what," Joel screamed. "Why should we amuse you before we die?"

"What if I promise we won't kill you two?" Bud said, eying them both, attempting to see if Marsha would convince Joel to play along. "Will you do what we want then?"

"Depends," Joel said. "What do you want?"

Bud looked at Norm and then back at Joel and Marsha. Smiling, she said, "We like to watch."

"Watch?" Joel questioned. "Watch what?"

"Sex acts," Bud said. "That's what we're into. It gets us hot and bothered."

"Sex acts?" Joel said. "And you call me perverted?"

"Hey, Joe," Norm began. "I told you before. I'm not here to judge you. But if you wanna play it that way, we can always tell Marsha about your . . . shall we say . . . proclivities."

"*Proclivities*?" Marsha said. "What proclivities?"

"You don't wanna know, Marsha," Bud said. "That's between us and Joe, right, Joe?"

Marsha looked at Joel and said, "What's she talking about, Joel?"

"Nothing, babe," Joel said. "She's just messing with your mind. Just like she's letting you think your husband set all of this up and he didn't. Mason doesn't know anything about us."

"Then what's this all about?" Marsha asked, unable to accept what she'd stumbled into.

"I told you already. It's about Portia Barrington," Joel said. "They're going to kidnap her and we've seen their faces so they can't let us go. Don't you see, Marsha, they have to kill us because we can identify them."

"Not necessarily, Joe," Bud said. "What if we made it worth your while? What if we cut you in? What if we threw some of the ransom your way? No one has to know you two knew about it."

"I'm an attorney!" Marsha screamed. "I can't get caught up in this! It's against the law! I could be disbarred!"

"Marsha, Marsha, Marsha," Bud said, totally relaxed and in control. "No one ever has to know you were in on it. Nobody. We'll rough Joe up before we go. Make it look like he fought to save the girl. Nobody even knows you're here, right? All he's gotta do is play his part and you two get to live. No one will know about your thing together. All we're asking you guys to do is do what you do when nobody's watching. Only this time, you'll have a couple voyeurs watching. It's a small price to pay to live."

Marsha looked at Joel. She could tell he was considering their offer, but being an attorney, she knew that every deal was negotiable. "If I have to put on a sex show, become an accessory to a felony, I'm going to need a nice piece of the loot to become a part of this illegal venture."

Bud looked at Norm and smiled. Then her eyes returned to Marsha Spivey. "Are we negotiating, counselor?"

"Yes, we are," Marsha said confidently.

"Marsha," Joel said, "you can't trust them to keep their end of the deal. It's in their best interests to kill us and leave no witnesses. Why would they ever let us live and risk going to prison for the rest of their natural lives?"

"Because it's not in their best interests to kill us, Joel. They're kidnappers . . . not murderers. Kidnappers are in it for the money. Kidnappers don't kill unless they absolutely have to. And if they drop us, let's says . . . fifty grand . . . assuming they don't get caught, we'll have to keep our mouths shut or we go to jail too. We could use the money for a down payment on our own house."

"Listen to her, Joe," Bud said. "She's making a lot of sense."

"We can't trust them, Marsha," Joel said. "What's going to keep them from taking the money and leaving the country without paying us?"

"It's still win—win," Marsha said. "We get to live in either scenario. We either live and get the down payment for our house, or we live and give the cops a full description of who these two are. They're not going to kill us, Joe. Kidnappers don't kill."

Joel thought for a second or two and said, "Are you sure you wanna do this?"

"Yes," Marsha said, "but with two stipulations."

"I'm listening," Bud said.

"First, I need you to blindfold us. And second, I need you two to be absolutely quiet. I don't even want to hear you breathe. That way I can at least pretend that no one is watching."

Bud looked at Norm, smiled and said, "Deal."

"Hold on now, Bud," Norm said, "Fifty thousand is way too steep. I would be amenable to say . . . five grand each, but that's it. We don't even know if Barrington'll pay."

"I can't do it for less than forty," Marsha said, feeling more confident that she had saved both their lives.

"No way," Norm said. "We don't even know what we're going to get out of Barrington. I'm willing to go, let's say . . . fifteen."

"I'll consider thirty," Marsha said.

Smiling, Bud said, "We'll go as high as twenty, but no more."

"Twenty-five and it's a deal," Marsha said.

"No deal! You get twenty and that's it!" Norm said. "Otherwise, you're both finished. And imagine, Marsha, imagine being found dead in the apartment of a man that's not your husband. People look for any excuse they can find when a woman fools around on her husband. They try to find away to blame him for what she herself did. But when you're dead, you can't explain why you did what you did. Bud tells me that's how women get away with their nonsense, right, Bud? They can explain away any and everything they do and if they're pretty, the whole country'll feel sorry for 'em."

"That's right, Norm," Bud said. She looked at Marsha. "Never under estimate the power of female explanation with tears. Never under estimate the power of love. All you have to do is say you were miserable in your marriage and that you fell in love with Joe. You and I know we can justify anything if we tell the story right. But if you're found naked with a bullet in your temple, that's going to be hard to overcome, especially when the cops connect you two to the kidnapping. When that happens . . . all bets are off. Take the twenty grand, let us watch, and buy your new house. What do you say?"

Fifteen minutes later, they were all in the master bedroom. Bud and Norm stood in the door watching a very naked Marsha and Joel plunder each other like it had been ten years since they had been together.

The couple was so into their loving making it was as if they were oblivious to their captors' wanton gaze. At first, they found it difficult to do it, knowing Bud and Norm were watching. But once the kissing and fondly began, being blindfolded and hearing only their own breathing, they quickly gave into their carnality as their bodies demanded more stimulation.

Bud and Norm watched as their bodies moved at a fierce pace. They listened as they howled like there was a full moon lighting a midnight sky. When they realized the couple was approaching the peak of excitement, they pulled out their pistols and screwed on sound suppressors. Then they quickly moved into position on either side of the bed and pointed pistols at their temples and waited for them to climax. When Joel and Marsha were at the heights of their orgasm, while they were still screaming, they pulled their triggers.

Pop! Pop!

Sudden silence filled the room.

"Bud, you think we have time for a quickie before the kid gets here?"

Bud looked at her watch. "Yeah, but it's gotta be real quick, okay? I'm talking Speedy Gonzales quick, all right? It's a little after twelve. The girl's gotta be done with her exams by now. She could be here any minute."

Norm pulled Bud close and kissed her hard on the lips. She kissed back. Then he took her by the hand and walked quickly to the adjacent bedroom. As they moved through the doorway, Bud grabbed the doorknob and closed the door, giving a very dead Joel Williams and Marsha Spivey some much needed privacy.

Bud kissed Norm again and said, "From now on, I want you to call me Brooke when we do it, okay?"

It was 10:30 when the Metro Yellow/Blue line stopped at Crystal City Station. Portia Barrington was sitting on the train, still wearing the school's required uniform, a white polo shirt and a beige skirt. It had taken considerably more time to get to the train station and into the city than it took to complete her two exams. She aced both multiple choice exams in twenty minutes, but Mrs. Rosenhaus, her contemporary history teacher, refused to let her take her second exam until 8:30, which was when the 7:00 exams officially ended. Otherwise, Portia would have gotten into the city two hours ago. She had a number of things to do and the two hours she lost were invaluable.

The doors retracted.

She stepped onto the platform and made her way over through the turnstile, up the escalator, and then through the underground mall. She loved riding the metro system. It was preferable to being treated like a coddled celebrity, having her door opened when she got in and out of the limo. The royal treatment had made her an easy target for other, less fortunate students, whose parents didn't make the kind of salary Myles Barrington made. She never forgot what it was like when her father was defending a man that the whole country thought was guilty of murder. As she passed shop after shop, her mind regressed six years.

She was in the third grade at the time and the kids who teased her were merciless, calling her "murder child". The faculty had done its best to shield her from the teasing, but they couldn't be every-where. The kids took full advantage of lavatory breaks and recess. Her cheeks were wet nearly every day for almost six months. The damage done to her psyche had been so traumatic that years later, she vowed she would do whatever she had to do to never experience it again.

She knew her father thought she was the epitome of virtue and even though she was far from it, she did everything she could to keep him thinking she was still the "good" girl she had been the first nine years of her life. Because of the teasing she'd suffered at nine, the last two years of her life were forever altered when she deleted her virginity at thirteen. The in-crowd girls at school, who were heavily influenced by the reported behavior of highly visible celebrity women, had convinced her that she could never be a part of their inner coterie until she was one of them, hymen less, via penile ingress.

Although what they wanted her to do was in direct opposition to what her parents had taught her, she wanted to be accepted, needed to be accepted. If being accepted by her peers meant she could no longer be a virgin, so be it. Having made the decision to "do it", she needed a willing participant. She chose her seventeen year old cousin, Sean.

She always thought Sean was hot even though they were first cousins. She didn't know what the word "incest" meant at the time and even if she had, it wouldn't have made a bit of difference. Sean was so cute, so adorable; she loved being in his presence. And he knew absolutely everything there was to know—at least that's what Portia thought. She'd had a crush on him since she was ten years old. She had told him about her dilemma at school and he listened attentively.

He told her how foolish it was to want to be a part of a clique that didn't have her best interest at heart. She rejected his advice and continued the pursuit relentlessly. The more she pursued him, the more he rejected her and didn't want her around. He finally told her that if she kept pestering him about it, he'd tell her parents.

The rejection made her pursuit all the more tantalizing. There were a number of boys her age that would have been eager to deflower the young maiden, she knew. But she wanted what she wanted. She was going to have Sean no matter what, even if she had to resort to blackmail. The threat of telling her parents was totally unacceptable. There was no way she was going to let him have the goods on her, to quell her, to quiet her.

Her response to the threat was to get the goods on him and in so doing, force him to do what she wanted. Nobody was perfect, she knew; even Sean. So she watched his every move closely. She followed him around the mansion, unbeknownst to him, hoping he would commit some act, some larceny that would give her the leverage she needed to be like all the other girls. She spied on him every time they had family gatherings, parties, and sleepovers. She soon realized that she may not ever catch Sean doing something for which he could be blackmailed. That's when she decided to create a scenario of temptation that he just might fall for. And if he did, she would have him.

P ortia thought the timing had been absolutely perfect. The summer was nearly over and what she wanted more than anything was about to happen, if her plan to seduce her first cousin succeeded. With sincere eyes, she apologized to Sean and begged his forgiveness for asking him to be her lover. He fell wholeheartedly for her trick. He loved his little cousin and it had bothered him that he couldn't be close to her anymore. When she offered the apology, he smiled and accepted it without a second's hesitation.

They'd had a great time together, playing board games, horse-shoes, volleyball, and swimming with family and close friends. As the heat of the day blazed on, she kept getting Sean ice cold glasses of Country Time Pink Lemonade, his personal favorite, and other soft drinks, knowing his kidneys would eventually send him a message he couldn't long ignore. She waited patiently for her rat to nibble on the "cheese" she'd carefully put on the trap.

After about four glasses of lemonade, Sean had to go.

Portia decided she had to go too, albeit for different reasons.

The closest bathroom available was the first floor master suite, where her father and stepmother slept. They walked along the pool together, chatting about who would win the monopoly game they were currently playing.

The game that Portia was trying to win had nothing to do with Boardwalk. Hers was a high-stakes game of blackmail and seduc-tion—in that order.

After relieving himself, Sean couldn't resist the urge to examine the belongings of his famous uncle. While looking at his aunt's expensive jewelry, he saw Myles' wallet through the mirrored dresser. It was on the bed, right where Portia had placed it when he went into the bathroom. He walked over to the bed, picked up the wallet, opened it, and counted seven crisp brand new hundred dollar bills. He looked to the left and then to the right, checking to see if anyone saw him. His heart was threatening to explode. Seeing no one, he quickly peeled off three hundred, stuck it in his pocket, and practically ran out of the room. He had no idea that Portia was hiding in her stepmother's walk-in closet, and had recorded it all on a camcorder.

Later that night, Sean did twenty laps in the pool. Portia watched. Nearly everyone had left and those who hadn't were either in the house stuffing themselves with delicious food, drinking intoxicating beverages, engaging in political and legal conversation, or watching television. Sean got out of the pool and toweled himself and then headed for the pool house.

When Sean entered to change into his clothes, Portia scanned the grounds, making sure no one was around. In a few minutes it would happen. She looked around once more before opening the pool house door. Sean was nude. She stared at his cheeks for a while and then she locked the door and leaned her back against it.

Surprised to see her, Sean grabbed his towel and covered his genitals. "What do you think you're doing?"

With her back still against the door, she took in an eye full of his ripped abdomen and deep muscled chest. She could hardly contain her delight and the anticipation of what was about to happen. She was so stimulated by the thought of breaking the rules, and doing the naughty things she had continuously imagined, that her mouth watered and she swallowed hard before saying, "You're going to do it to me, Sean."

"What is *wrong* with you, Portia? Didn't I tell you not to bring this up again? Didn't I tell you I'd tell Uncle Myles, if you did?"

Calmly, almost serenely, she said, "Yeah, you did. But you won't be telling Daddy anything."

Stunned by her sudden bravado, he frowned and said, "Give me *one* reason why I shouldn't go tell right now, *Portia*. Just one reason."

Portia smiled mischievously and breathily whispered, "I'll give you three hundred reasons, Sean." She waited for the wheels to turn in his mind, the revelation of having been found out and being caught red-handed. When the moment of realization dawned, it felt so good, so satisfying. The pursuit had been well worth it, especially since he was going off to Yale in another month or so.

Sean knew he should have been firm when he refused to engage in carnal knowledge with his thirteen-year-old first cousin and face the music for his theft. But the truth was that he had been denying his own desire for the girl. He knew it was wrong and had tried to do the right thing. Now, though, there was no reason to reject the pleasure he had savored since she made the initial offer months ago. He knew nothing of consequence would happen for stealing a few hundred dollars from a very rich uncle, especially if he told the whole truth, that being that Portia had been pursuing him sexually, and had threatened him with blackmail. Instead, he let lust decide the matter.

An hour later, Portia was forever changed. She walked out of the pool house a different person, with a different perspective; a powerful one, now understanding what the power of knowledge could bring her. Before leaving, she made sure Sean knew that he would have to perform regularly, until he went away to college. She never told Sean that the wallet and the money in it was hers all along.

Since then, she has had numerous other lovers.

All of them much older than she.

All of them knew exactly how young she was before the act was consummated because she told them. When the men she selected realized how old she was, their expressions let her know they knew to stop, but not one man ever did. She soon realized that their desire to stop themselves, yet being unwilling or unable to, was an incredible aphrodisiac.

Chapter 10

To stop the sudden flow of images past, Portia inserted the plugs of her iPod into her ears and turned it on. Her head bobbed as she listened to Usher's *"Yeah"* blast its rhythmic beat. The music served as a distraction, quieting her conscience, which was screaming at her, begging her to stop making decisions that would haunt her for the rest of her life. But it was too late for her, she thought. It was too late to change the path that she was on; a path that would one day lead to ruin and perhaps, her destruction. She had engaged in every imaginable form of taboo sex before her fifteenth birthday. She had performed so many despicable acts that she didn't see the point in stopping. Otherwise, what she was about to do wouldn't make any sense. Besides, she was nearly at her destination now. It was almost time to perform—again. And she would. She was about to meet her lover at the Gateway Marriott.

The book bag strapped to her back contained two sets of sexy lingerie she had ordered online from the Victoria's Secret website. The black nylon bustier with a black lace garter was for the man waiting for her in the Presidential Suite of the hotel, but the purple babydoll halter was for Joel Williams, who she would be visiting shortly after she handled her first piece of business at the Marriott. But first, she needed to make a deposit at her bank before heading over to his apartment.

She walked through the lobby and made her way over to the elevator and up to the Presidential Suite. Tears were moistening her cheeks as she stood outside the door. Her conscience was now louder than the music she was listening to. Even though she had turned the music up, it could not drown the guilt that was threatening to consume her. She wiped her eyes and brushed away the tears. Then she took a deep breath, forced herself to smile, and knocked on the door. A few seconds later, it opened.

The man who opened the door was clean-shaven, had a full head of dark hair, and was nearly thirty years older than her. His skin was dark olive. He was wearing a white tuxedo jacket with black slacks and a black and white bowtie. He was scowling when he said with a British accent, "What took you so long?" He looked at his Rolex. "I've been waiting for two hours, darling."

Portia smiled when she realized who he was being that morning. They had played many sex games and he always played powerful or dashing men he'd seen in his favorite films. Some of which were, Rhett Butler, Sonny Corleone, Maximus Decimus Meridius, Achilles, and Tony Montana. Today, he was James Bond—007. "Oh, James, that's so sweet of you. Can't wait to get the goodies, huh?"

"I checked into the suite last night. The hotel desk clerk told me I couldn't check-in before twelve, if someone occupied the suite. So, I came over here early this morning with nothing to do and no one to screw."

Portia sauntered up to him and kissed his cheek. Doing her best impression of Miss Moneypenny, she said, "Don't be mad, 007. Blame Mrs. Rosenhaus. The old bag wouldn't let me take my exam until 8:30. I finished my first exam a little before 7:30. I went to her class right away, but she's a stickler for the rules. What could I do, lover?"

"Check out time is twelve, darling. But they're going to let me stay until three. Can you stay that long?"

"Sorry babe. I got an hour. Two tops. That includes clean up time." She looked at her watch. "I need to be outta here by noon; no later than 12:30." She saw the aggravation in his eyes and said, "You remember that slinky little Victoria's Secret outfit you told me you wanted to see on me?" His eyes filled with lust. She took the black bustier out and showed it to him. "This is all for you. I promise it'll be unforgettable, okay?" She smiled again. "Now . . . you did bring the money, right?"

When he imagined her in the sexy outfit, a wide grin emerged. "Yeah, I brought the money. This better be worth every dime."

"It will be lover."

"Put it on. I wanna see you in it. And then you know what I'm going to do?"

"What?"

"I'm gonna tear every stitch of it off you."

Portia laughed and said, "That's going to cost you a little more."

"And I'll willingly pay it," he said.

"Just so I'll know what accent to use, which bond girl am I playing this time?"

"Dr. Holly Goodhead from Moonraker," he said and then laughed hysterically. "The name fits you, my dear. Now run along and don't keep me waiting much longer. I've gotta get to the bank too."

It had been five years since Brooke Ursula Davis and Norman Green were forced to leave the police department. They had both resigned after an investigation by Internal Affairs was launched when drug money disappeared from a major bust. The dealer's attorney told the D.A. that close to a million dollars was missing. The money was never recovered. They had refused to take a polygraph test. Bud and Norm had been good cops for eight and ten years respectively, but when cancer ravaged Bud's mother and her medical bills spiraled out of control, she became desperate to get her mother the best treatment available.

Norman Green's reasons for stealing the money were altogether different. He was a spendthrift who always spent more than he had and was over his head in debt. He also gambled more than he should in an attempt to satisfy his girlfriend who loved to travel to exotic locales first class. His bookie promised him that if he didn't pay up, and soon, he would send a few guys to take it out of his ass until he did.

The solution to both their problems was sitting on the table along with several kilos of cocaine. Bud had looked at Norm, almost pleading with her eyes, asking him, without saying a word, if he would go along with her taking a portion of the cash. He knew what she was thinking and nodded. They weren't worried about other cops on the scene knowing. Lots of cops were not only on the take, they were shaking down dealers regularly. Cops didn't rat on cops. It was the law of the jungle. Unfortunately, Bud and Norm thought the dealer wouldn't talk either. If he did, he certainly wouldn't incriminate himself by mentioning the money.

When no one was watching, Bud had grabbed ten tall stacks of greenbacks, put them in a garbage bag, and walked out the front door. No one stopped or questioned her. They both knew that once they took drug money, there was no going back, but they had no idea just how out-of-control their lives would become by committing a single crime. Being law enforcement officers and ripping off a known hood like Robert Tarantino for a cool million had turned them both on.

Later that same night, their smoldering five-year affair began in an empty parking lot of a movie theater—in the squad car. As cops, they could always get away for a romp without suspicion. Their affair worked well because Bud was a lesbian who had a live-in girlfriend. They adopted a little girl that they both adored. To everyone who knew them, they were the nicest couple in the neighborhood, but Bud's girlfriend had no idea she was struggling with her sexual identity. Norm, on the other hand, had a live-in girlfriend too. And they too, had a daughter.

After months of investigation, they were suspended without pay. Internal Affairs was threatening to suspend the other officers on the scene too. Bud and Norm were told that if they didn't resign, they would be fired. And if they fired them, the department would have to fire every officer that was in the house at the time of the bust. Their union representative urged them to fall on their swords because the other officers hadn't taken a dime of the money. They couldn't afford to lose their jobs protecting them with their silence, especially since they had house notes and college tuition to pay. Bud and Norm eventually left the force and took security jobs.

The presiding judge dismissed all charges against Tarantino when the Internal Affairs report came in. Although he was free, Tarantino was still out of a million cash and the confiscated cocaine. He knew Bud and Norm took the money, but they were untouchable as long as they wore the shield. He waited, paying strict attention to what would happen to them. Six months later, when the heat was off and they were no longer cops, he and a few of his friends paid them a visit. Most of the money was already spent by the time he caught up with them. So they owed him—big-time! Tarantino made them an offer they couldn't refuse. He told them they had to work off their debt or die—their families too.

Chapter 11

Portia Barrington inserted the key Joel had given her into the lock and entered his Crystal City apartment, which was right across the street from the Gateway Marriott. A salacious grin emerged when she heard what sounded like intimate sexual murmuring. She knew it was Joel and another woman, but she was unmoved by it. She just shook her head wantonly and then thought, *"The more the merrier. This is gonna be wild."* She let the sound of them guide her to the master bedroom. She listened at the closed door, but realized the sound of delicious sex acts wasn't coming from there.

For a short moment, she wondered why Joel and his lady friend weren't in there. Occasionally, Joel would take her to a room other than the master bedroom, but mostly, they did it where he slept. The sound of intimacy pulled her further down the hall to the bedroom adjacent to the master. The door was open. She looked in, expecting to see Joel and the lady he was with, but she was surprised, stunned even, that it was a man and a woman she'd never seen before. The man was ferociously delivering his package with fervor, like he was a Federal Express employee fearful of losing his job. The woman's feet were flatly pressing against the headboard, which rang out a consistent beat as it slammed against the wall, threatening to blast through it.

Portia knew she shouldn't watch, but she couldn't help herself. Her eyes were transfixed; her heart pounded enthusiastically, taking it all in, receiving voyeuristic pleasure impulses as her twin portals observed the bawdy spectacle. Watching the live sex act set her private place ablaze. The heat caused her to melt. The sound that came from somewhere deep within them added to the screening. Hearing them was like having just the right music for an Oscar winning film. Had it been Joel and a woman, she would have immediately disrobed and joined the hedonistic romp. Instead, she moistened her middle two fingers and stuck them down her panties, vicariously joining the couple as they all approached the final curtain, the peak of ultimate physical fulfillment.

When their howling dissipated and their breathing slowed, Portia said, "Where's Joel? He's expecting me."

Simultaneously, Bud and Norm swiftly whipped their heads in the direction of the voice. They had been so into their love making that they hadn't bothered to close or lock the door. And now their prey was not only there, but she had gotten an eye full of their unrestrained debauchery.

"Close the door!" Norm shouted angrily.

"I just wanna know—"

"I don't give a damn!" Norm said. "Close the door! Now!"

Obediently, Portia did as she was told, thinking Joel would tell her everything when he returned.

Totally shocked Portia was there and had been watching their powerful thrusts, and listening to their orgasmic sighs, Bud and Norm scrambled to their feet. They put their clothes on as quickly as they could, embarrassed that they had let their lust get the better of them while they were on a job.

When she saw the door opening, Portia was hoping it was the woman coming out, but it was Norm. She could see inside the room again. The woman was almost dressed. She looked at the man again. He was about to say something, but Portia cut him off. She didn't want him to scream at her again. "I'm sorry. I shouldn't have watched. Could you tell me when Joel is coming back? He has to take me home."

Norm smiled and said, "I'm sorry I yelled at you, kid. It's just that we didn't know you were here."

"I understand," she said. "Where's Joel?"

Seconds later, Bud came out of the room. She looked at Norm and tilted her head to the right, telling him to get the syringe. Then, she looked at the young girl who had caught her doing nasty things and said, "You must be Portia. I'm Brooke."

"Hi, Brooke. Will Joel be back soon? I have to get home."

"Joel is here, honey," Brooke told her.

"He is?"

"Yeah. Follow me."

They walked a few feet down the hall and stopped at the master bedroom. "He's in here, honey," Brooke said. "He told me to wake him when you arrived."

Portia smiled and opened the door. She gasped when she saw what looked like a bloodbath. The sheets were no longer white. Joel was naked and on top of a woman. She stood there, shocked at what she was seeing, but was unable to stop looking, and unable to scream. Her eyes bulged. She put her hand over her mouth and took a few steps backward.

"See, Portia. He's here. Just like I said."

Hearing Brooke's voice snapped Portia out of the fog she was in. She turned to run, but ran right into Norm, who grabbed her and lifted her off the floor. She screamed. Her legs flailed against the air as she struggled to break free, but his embrace was too powered. She could hardly breathe.

"Give me the syringe," Brooke said. He handed it to her. "Now hold her still."

She inserted the needle and pushed the drug into her vein. Soon Portia was no longer struggling. They rolled her up in a rug and took her to their van.

Chapter 12

The smell of death lingered in the air when Kelly and I entered Joel Williams' apartment about an hour after Jack Ryan called me. The place was crawling with forensic people wearing booties and surgical gloves. I now knew what Ryan didn't want to tell me over the phone. Joel Williams was dead. Two terrible things immediately came to mind. First, Mr. Williams would never answer our questions. Second, my husband had hired him and now his ass was on the line because of it. The rich were always able to purchase whatever kind of justice they wanted. With Joel dead and unable to vindicate Drew Perry, I figured Barrington would be going after my husband and our private detective agency.

Kelly said, "Where's the party?"

"Master bedroom," Julie Campbell yelled out. "Two stiffs. They each have a single bullet wound in their temples. Small caliber weapons. They were shot while they were having sex." She laughed and said, "Looks like he shot before he got shot, know what I mean, Kelly."

"Tell me the second stiff isn't Portia Barrington," I said, after locking eyes with her. Even though hearing cops laughing at a murder scene was nothing new, I wanted her to see how serious I was. None of this was funny to me. A young girl had been abducted and more important than that, my husband had to be questioned and there was nothing I could do about it.

"We've identified the woman as Marsha Spivey," Julie said, no longer laughing.

My eyes bulged a little when I heard the woman's name. "Mason Spivey's wife?" I asked.

"One and the same," Julie said. "Apparently Mrs. Spivey and Mr. Williams were seeing each other when Mason was outta town."

"Where's Mason now," Kelly asked.

"The team's in the air," Julie said. "They're on their way to Utah."

"Where's Ryan and Boyd?" I asked.

"Ryan's in the bedroom and Steven is on his way over to Drew Perry to question the owner," Julie said, attempting to soften the blow she had just delivered.

I tried not to show just how afraid I was. I knew how the game was played. If something happened to Portia Barrington, if she didn't live through this thing, the guns of judgment would point directly at my husband. There was so much I wanted to say at that moment, but I too, was being scrutinized—every move. My investigation had to be conducted by the numbers. I couldn't be seen as an impediment to an active case. As long as I was involved, I could at least have a look at all the evidence and draw my own conclusions.

Kelly and I entered the bedroom and saw Joel Williams and Marsha Spivey in the missionary position. There was the normal buzz of perpetual conversation going back and forth. Photographs were being taken. Evidence was being collected. But we didn't see Jack Ryan.

"Where's Ryan?" I asked.

"In the next bedroom," one of our guys said. "Either Williams was bangin' Mrs. Spivey in every bedroom in the apartment, or there was another woman here very recently."

I didn't say a word. Kelly and I just left and went to the next bedroom. Ryan was in there by himself. He was looking at the sheets through a pair of ultraviolet goggles. I closed the door, looked at Kelly, and nodded. She knew to do what I couldn't.

Kelly said, "Where do you get off sending Steven over to Drew Perry without our permission?"

Ryan was no amateur. He took off the goggles, smirked at Kelly, and then faced me. "Agent Perry, questioning the man who hired Williams is standard procedure. You know this. And besides, you don't want to get mixed up in this thing if we find more than what we've already found."

Chapter 13

J ack Ryan was right about it being standard procedure to question my husband, I knew, but still, I couldn't help feeling the way I did, like I was pursuing my husband for a crime I knew he did not commit. If my husband was guilty of anything, he was guilty of hiring a man he hadn't thoroughly vetted. Another thing that bothered me was that of the three CARD team members assigned to the case, Steven Boyd was sent to question Keyth. He was best known for his interrogation technique. Behind that boyish grin, Steven was an absolute shark. He had a way of making victims feel comfortable while he siphoned off vital information they didn't know they were revealing. His victims were always stunned when he arrested them.

While I was sure Keyth hadn't done anything wrong, I was very nervous nonetheless. Steven could probably get my husband to reveal how often we have sex and that of all the positions we've tried, doggy style was my favorite. I would not want that piece of information floating around the Bureau. FBI agents can be merciless when it came to teasing each other.

"You said you found something else," Kelly said to Ryan, taking the heat off me.

Still looking at me, Ryan said, "Agent Perry, I really don't think your husband has anything to worry about. And believe it or not, by sending Steven, our best guy in these matters, protects your husband."

"So that's why you sent him there, Ryan?" Kelly said, "To protect Keyth?"

Ryan's eyes never diverted from mine when he said, "Yes, Agent Perry. That's exactly why I sent him there without telling you. If you would have made one call, even if it was to check on your children or to set a lunch date or whatever, it could be construed as impeding the investigation. And believe me, our guys will check both your cell phones. We're thorough that way. I believe things are exactly as they seem. We've already gotten pressure from the top to step aside and let you run the show, which makes no sense since we have far more experience at this sort of thing. Once it was revealed that the girl's chauffeur worked for you and your husband, that alone should have gotten you booted off this case, but even that wasn't enough for the brass.

Then, I get a call from our people at the Barrington mansion saying that the kidnappers knew who you and Agent McPherson were. You'd think that would be enough to remove you. The brass says you're running the show until they say different, which is a total mystery to me. All I can say is that you must know some big-time people with some serious juice because they're violating their own procedures. Assuming that's the case, that someone is running serious interference for you, it's better that Steven checks out your husband's story. If the kidnapper carries out his threat of killing the girl and this thing blows up in everyone's faces like these things tend to do, the brass won't be able to protect you then. And since there's no paperwork on you being in charge, I'm sure it'll all come crashing down on the CARD team's head—namely me."

I wasn't the least bit surprised that the techies had called Ryan and apprised him of the lasted developments. I'm sure they resented my presence too. We can all be territorial in that way. Nevertheless, I believed Ryan, but still, I had to be careful until Steven Boyd cleared Keyth of any wrongdoing on his part. I wasn't going say anything about Drew Perry to the CARD team unless it was absolutely necessary. I briefly cut my eyes to Kelly, telling her to continue our investigation.

Kelly said, "What have you found, Jack?"

I reached out for the goggles Ryan was holding. He handed them to me. I looked at the bed and saw the semen stains. I took off the goggles and retuned them to Ryan. Then I walked around the room, examining everything, looking for evidence. Silence was filling the room. I looked at Ryan, he was still looking at me, waiting for my personal response, I guessed. I said, "I believe there's a question on the table, Agent Ryan. Please answer it." Then I continued snooping.

Jack finally looked at Kelly and said, "We found tapes of explicit phone sex between Williams and Portia Barrington."

When Ryan said that he had found sex tapes of Williams and Portia, I breathe a sigh of relief because I knew then that Williams, whoever he was, had gotten caught up in a very bad situation with the girl just as Kelly had said at the Barrington mansion. I was convinced my husband would be cleared. Plus that bit of info may have exonerated Williams too, I was thinking until Ryan dropped the next proverbial bombshell.

"Agent Perry," he began, looking at me again as if he knew I was feeling good all of a sudden and wanted to shatter my glasshouse. "I'm afraid we're not exactly out of the woods where your husband is concerned. Not yet, anyway."

I looked at Kelly and she said, "Why is that? Williams was smart enough to keep tapes and Portia's phone records proves she was calling him late at night and talking to him for hours. He may be guilty of having sex with her, but he's not apart the kidnapping. What's the problem?"

Ryan looked at me again, paying strict attention to every muscle in my face, ready to gauge my reaction to what he was about to say. "Well, Agent Perry, I'm sure your husband will be absolved of any wrong doing, but we also found numerous DVDs of Williams and other men having sex with what appear to be underage girls in upscale apartments. Penthouses to be exact. And guess what else?"

He waited for an answer.

I raised my eyebrow, expecting yet another bombshell.

"The Penthouses are within the building."

The rest of the air went right out of my balloon. I got the feeling that Ryan was enjoying himself as he parceled out vital information bit by precious bit. Well, I wasn't amused. I wanted to slap the grin he was trying to hide off his face and hoped he'd try something so I could kick his ass. And then he'd know who was in charge of the case.

"The building belongs to a man named, Jericho Wise," Ryan continued. For the first time, he looked at Kelly and said, "His current address is in Tiburon, California, an expensive suburb of San Francisco."

Ryan's cell rang. He looked at the caller ID, and then looked at me for the briefest of seconds. That's when I knew it was Steven calling.

"Yeah?" Ryan said.

While Ryan took his call, Kelly and I silently stared at each other for a few seconds. Kelly's jetsetter boyfriend, an attorney and sports agent, lives in Tiburon too. His last name is Wise also. By looking at Kelly when he revealed that bit of information let us know that Ryan knew who Sterling Wise was and where he lived. He probably knew even that wasn't going to get us kicked off the case so he just made sure we knew he knew.

A fter a cursory examination of some of the incriminating DVDs the CARD team found in Williams' apartment, I noticed that the DVDs were in plastic cases like the one I found in Portia Barrington's bedroom. The DVDs were tawdry to say the least and that's sugarcoating it. The men were tipping the girls hundreds of dollars in cash. I was thinking that if a couple hundred was the tip, how much were they paying for being serviced?

From what we could tell, in addition to having sex with an underage girl and being in possession of films that clearly depicted teenage prostitution, Williams was also burning multiple copies of studio quality DVDs. His third bedroom was full of DVD burners, at least twenty, and the walls were lined with thousands upon thousands of movies. For a second, I thought I was in Blockbuster.

As I perused his enormous collection of films, which was meticulously in alphabetical order, I saw one of my favorite Bruce Willis pictures, *Tears of the Sun*. I found a copy of *The Grasshopper*, which confirmed where Portia had gotten her copy. I picked up a bootlegged version of *Ice Station Zebra* and pushed it into his DVD player and was astounded to see that Mr. Williams had the nerve to illegally sell movies that still had the FBI warning on them. The warning clearly stated that copying and distributing copies carried up to a $250,000 fine and five years in jail. A flame ignited in me. I was thinking how stupid could this man be. I mean if you're going to bootleg, why copy the FBI warning and implicate yourself further? The criminal mind never ceases to amaze me. Few criminals ever stop to think their crimes through to a logical conclusion before implementing them.

Truth be told, much of my anger stemmed from the fact that Williams was African-American. What burnt me up even more was that my husband had hired him. I probably shouldn't have been, but I was thoroughly embarrassed. I was the only black person in the room. In fact, I was the only black person that had anything to do with the case except for Mrs. Barrington, who thankfully, had been very helpful so far. Then I wondered if Williams could stoop so low as to have Portia selling DVDs for him.

We also found hidden cameras and recording equipment. It turned out that his apartment was under constant surveillance. The dining room, living room, kitchen, and all the bedrooms had hidden cameras in them. The only rooms impervious to the recording eye were the bathrooms. I guess Williams had at least one line he wouldn't cross. Yet, when we looked for the DVD that might have shown us what happened on June 8th, it was missing. According to a voice recording on the 7th, Portia was supposed to come to his apartment after exams for one of their escapades. The disc of the 8th would have shown us who the players were and exactly what happened that day.

I had noticed the security cameras when we entered the building so I sent one of our guys down to the lobby to get the security tape of the 8th. He returned empty handed. He told us that the tape was missing and that Eddie O'Bannon, who worked that day, had quit on the 8th. Our guy ran Mr. O'Bannon's name through the computers and discovered that he was a part of a street gang named the Chiefs. The litany of crimes in his jacket was a mile long, starting when he was ten years old.

Normally something like that would have been expunged, but on his eighteenth birthday he was serving time in a state penitentiary for manslaughter. The crime was still on his record. He had just gotten out of Norrell prison three months ago and was in a work release program after having done a ten-year stretch for selling crack. We did, however, have his most recent address, but with a missing white girl, and two decaying bodies in an apartment full of state-of-the-art recording and surveillance equipment, I got the feeling Eddie O'Bannon was in the wind. In the recesses of my mind, I thanked God, Portia wasn't blond to boot. If she were, the media would have a field day with this.

I had our guys canvas the building, as we desperately tried to find whatever morsel of information was available, but of the few tenets who answered their doors, none of them knew anything. Kelly and I canvassed the penthouses. There were ten of them. Again, after knocking on nine doors, no one answered. They could have all been at work, but I doubted it. I think they had been tipped off by the doorman. It's nearly impossible to have illegal activity going on in the building without the doorman knowing of it. People had to sign in and out of the building. If Mr. O'Bannon flew the coop all of a sudden, he had to know who had entered the building that day. If he knew that much, he probably knew what happened in Joel Williams' apartment. He may have even been in on the kidnapping.

I exhaled and pushed the doorbell of the last penthouse. I didn't expect anyone to answer, but I knocked after waiting about twenty seconds. No one else had answered so knocking on this door was more of a formality than anything else. I was dog tired and I needed to lie down. Truthfully, I almost hoped no one answered. It was approaching 8:30. I couldn't wait for my day to end so I could go to bed. I had been up for over forty-eight hours. My eyes were red and watering. Just as we were about to leave, we heard a woman say, "Just a minute."

A surge of energy reinvigorated me. I was thinking: finally, someone who might be able to answer some questions. The door opened and a statuesque blond with big fantastic brown eyes said, "Yes? Can I help you?" She was clothed in dark olive skin. Her accent was Italian, her beauty exceptional. She looked like she was on her way to the gym to workout. Or maybe get a man's attention. A pink camisole leotard covered her sensuous curves. Her breasts were so perfect that I wondered if they were real. Gray leg warmers hid her calves and ankles. A matching headband and sneakers added to her nicely pieced together ensemble. Her hair was slicked back and in one long braid. A leather Coach Satchel was slung over her shoulder.

We flashed our credentials. I said, "I'm Agent Perry and this is my partner, Agent McPherson."

"Yes, what can I do for you, Agent Perry," the woman said.

She wasn't the least bit surprised that the FBI was at her door. I didn't think so anyway. She said my name like she'd heard it before.

I got the feeling she had been expecting us. Had the doorman warned her? I wondered. Perhaps that's what kept her from answering the door sooner. "Please don't be alarmed," I said, "but there was a double murder in the building and I was wondering if you could answer a few questions."

Again, no surprise registered. She didn't even flinch. I would think that a double murder in a secure building would have at the very least frightened her into asking which of her neighbors had been killed. Instead, she folded her arms and said, "Don't you need a warrant to ask me questions?"

I looked at Kelly. She was thinking the same thing. The woman knew something but she didn't know enough not to answer her door. I said, "May we come in, please?"

"You need a warrant to come in here, do you not?" she asked.

I looked at Kelly again and then refocused on the woman. "If we could just come in for a few moments, Ms. . . . ."

She exhaled hard like we were getting on her last nerve. "Agent, Perry," she said my name like she was annoyed and then looked at her watch. "I'm on my way to the gym and my masseuse will be here within the hour. I really don't have time for this and I don't know anything about any murders in the building. I live alone and I keep to myself."

I heard Kelly exhale hard. I glanced at her again. Her face was twisting, like she was on the verge of one of her famous eruptions. She was tired too and getting more frustrated with each succeeding response from the mystery woman. What she was about to say would only make matters worse, I could tell, so I reached out and touched her arm, hoping she would settle down. Then I said, "Well, could you just tell us if you were home on Wednesday, June 8th last week?"

"I'm sure I was, at some point," she said. Then she closed her door and started walking. "What time?"

At least she was talking now, I thought. Walking with her, I said, "May I ask what you do for a living, ma'am?"

She locked eyes with me and squinted to let me know she wasn't going to answer that question either. "What time of the day, Agent Perry?"

I was about to respond when Kelly barked, "Are you a U. S. citizen?"

Her face was twisted into an angry scowl. "Don't you need a warrant to ask me that?" she snapped back.

I could feel Kelly's energy. She was about to lose control. I said, "Kelly."

"No," Kelly said, looking at me. "I'm sick of this." She looked at the woman. "Listen, you can either answer me, or I can call the people from ICE over here," Kelly said loudly. "I guarantee you'll answer them." Her anger was calculated in that she wanted to see if the woman knew what ICE meant.

The mystery woman was unmoved by Kelly's not so subtle threat. She continued walking down the hall until we came to a set of double doors. She slid an electronic card in the slot and a green light lit up. She opened the door and went in. We followed. There was fresh fruit, coffee, several juices, croissants and bagels available on a long counter. She popped a slice of fresh cantaloupe into her mouth. She looked at Kelly and said, "Help yourself to some of the fruit and refreshments, Agent Perry."

The mystery woman had just politely backhanded my partner. I looked at Kelly and smirked. She hadn't offered me anything at her hotel when I picked her up that morning and I hadn't eaten all day. Still smiling, I put several pieces of pineapple, cantaloupe, and two croissants on a paper plate. Then, I poured myself a cup of orange juice and followed her through a set of double doors that led to gym.

Mirrors covered all four walls of a vast rectangular room. Olympic weights and barbells were everywhere. Nautilus treadmills, steppers, and other exercise machines were plenteous. The mystery woman placed her satchel on the floor and then went straight to the balancing bar and lifted her right leg onto it and stretched. After she stretched her left leg, she sat on the floor. Both legs were flared out east and west of her slender shoulders. She put her forehead on the floor and breathed in and out a few times. I was amazed at her flexibility.

I started working on the pineapples first. They were so fresh that I continued eating them one after another until they were gone. I said, "Thanks for the fruit, ma'am. Now . . . we just have a few questions. I realize you're busy, but so are we. We're trying to find out who killed one of your neighbors and you don't seem the least bit concerned that not one, but two murders took place in this building.

You can save us a lot of time in the investigation if you cooperate. Otherwise, I'll have to take you in for prostitution. I'm not here to bust you and I know you don't want me to do that. That's bad for business. Besides, your *masseuse*, as you call him, will be here within the hour."

That got the mystery woman's attention. She whipped her head towards me and said. "Agent Perry, I know my rights." She looked at Kelly. "I am a naturalized citizen of the United States. I am not concerned about Immigration and Customs Enforcement." She looked back at me. "If you must know, my name is Francesca Ferrari. I was born in Pompeii, Italy, but I was raised in Milan. I've been in the U.S. for the last seven years."

"And you sell yourself for a living," Kelly said, for effect.

"Kelly," I said, playing along with the good cop bad cop routine, "why don't you go downstairs and question the doorman again. Let him know we know he called Ms. Ferrari and see what you can get outta him. Make sure our guys get the phone records for his station to see who else he called." I looked at Francesca to see her reaction to my next sentence. "He may have called Mr. O'Bannon too. I'll be downstairs in a few minutes."

Ms. Ferrari gave no indication that she knew O'Bannon. Her eyes followed Kelly as she was leaving the gym. When the door closed, she rolled her eyes and then looked at me. "I know Joel and his lady friend are dead."

I ate a piece of cantaloupe and then locked eyes with Ms. Ferrari, searching them for any hidden truths she was not yet ready to reveal. "How did you know he was dead?"

She put her forehead back on the floor, breathed deliberately, before saying, "Is it a secret, Agent Perry? You've got agents knocking on all the tenets' doors, do you not?"

I smiled. "So you got a call from the doorman then?"

"Again . . . is it a secret?"

"How do you know Mr. Williams?" I asked, avoiding her question.

"We were friends," She said.

Chapter 14

Before I left the gym, I told Francesca Ferrari that I had guessed that she was a courtesan the moment she refused to tell us what she did for a living. I explained that women who earn enough income to live in a building like this were generally well educated and very proud of their accomplishments. I further explained that only two kinds of women hide who they are; women who work for the CIA and women who sell themselves. I often wondered what the difference was since both were in the same business. She smiled and admitted that she had a masseuse, but he had already come and gone. She was flying to the Caymans to do some "business".

Ms. Ferrari told me that she and Joel had gotten involved within a month of him moving into the building. She had hidden her profession from him for a while because she didn't think it would get serious. When it did move to the serious stage, she felt he should know the truth. When I asked her if Mr. Williams ever had a key to her penthouse, she told me he had, but returned it. She went on to tell me that they remained friends, but the romance ended, which hurt her deeply.

Ms. Ferrari told me she traveled a lot, sometimes for weeks at a time, depending on what her client wanted, which would explain how Mr. Williams would have been able to use her penthouse for trysts with underage girls. I didn't tell Ms. Ferrari my suspicions, but I assumed that if they remained friends, she may have told him she was leaving and for how long. I figured Mr. Williams set up hidden cameras in her penthouse. Then it occurred to me, if he was recording men with underage girls, he had also been recording Ms. Ferrari. Maybe he got off on that too. Maybe he was selling those DVDs as well. I didn't let on, but while she was in the Caymans, I was going to have our guys check the penthouse out to see if there were hidden cameras in there.

I took the elevator back down to Mr. Williams' floor. I went and grabbed a hand full of the taped phone conversations he'd had with

Portia. They were on CDs. Then I went to his third bedroom and took about five of the DVDs in plastic covers. Kelly was sitting on the coach. Her mouth was wide open and her head was completely relaxed and titled back. She was fast asleep and snoring softly. I frowned. She had a lot of nerve sleeping while I was still working. I hit the leather on the coach with my open hand. It made a loud slapping sound. Kelly nearly leapt out of her skin.

"Wake your ass up," I said, laughing. "If I'm working, you're working."

Kelly swallowed hard, and gathered herself. "What I told you in Vegas was true."

"Which was what exactly," I said.

"You really can mess up a wet dream," she said, both yawning and stretching.

K elly and I made our way over to the elevator and took it to the underground garage. I kept thinking about the three ransom demands. With all the revelations we've had so far, I was more convinced that the ransoms were blackmail. Yet, it made absolutely no sense. If it was indeed blackmail, what did they have on Barrington? More important, why would Barrington tell us it was a kidnapping if it wasn't? And was that really Portia Barrington's voice we heard? If it wasn't Portia, why would Mrs. Barrington go along with all of this? Why would she give us inside information on Portia? Was it to appear that she was cooperating when she really wasn't?

The elevator doors opened. I was still deep in thought when I heard Kelly yawned again and then say, "So did Francesca tell you anything we can use?"

"Yepper."

"Like . . ."

We got into the car. "She used to date Joel Williams and he had a key to her penthouse," I said and started the ignition. "They were still friends. She also confirmed that she's a working girl and that she's often gone for weeks at a time."

I shift the gear to first, eased off the clutch, and pulled out of the garage.

"And you think Williams is using the penthouse when she's gone, huh?"

I nodded a few times and then said, "She's leaving for the Caymans tonight. Our guys'll check out her place in the morning."

"So what's bothering you, Phoenix?" Kelly said, smiling. "You didn't get a warrant or something?"

I rolled my eyes. "Of course they'll have a warrant. I'm wondering about the ransoms, Kelly. Why would they ask for three ransoms?"

"Something is definitely fishy about it. That's for sure."

I looked at Kelly and said, "This is going to sound crazy, but what if they wanted Barrington to call the Bureau? Maybe that's why they kept asking for more and more money. They had to know Barrington would eventually call us, right?"

"Yeah, so?"

"Well, why did they want him to call the Bureau? I mean we're talking about kidnapping charges. That's serious time in a federal pen. Kidnappers want money as quickly as they can get it. And they hope to God you believe them when they promise to release or kill the person they've kidnapped."

"And you're thinking . . . what exactly?"

I exhaled hard and looked her. "Remember when the guy on the phone said he was going to kill Portia? I think he needed a reason to kill her. And if he needed a reason to kill her, that was the plan all along. The question then is why did he want Portia dead? Why the game if he was going to kill her all along?"

"To cover up something else she was into?"

"Exactly. See, if they kill her because Barrington brought the cops in, we don't dig into her life. It would be a kidnapping gone bad."

"Since they don't want us digging into the girl's life, that's exactly what we have to do, right?"

"Right! And guess what else you have to do?"

"What?"

"Find out what's going on with Sterling's brother, Jericho."

Kelly exhaled hard. Then with dread, she said, "Don't remind me. I wanted to forget he owns the building that Williams was killed in."

All of sudden, Kelly was frowning. I said, "What?"

"Didn't you say Francesca Ferrari was going to the Caymans?"

"Yeah . . . so?"

"Jericho owns the Renegade Hotel and Casino in the Caymans, remember? When Coco Nimburu was trying to kill him in the Denver airport four years ago when we first met Sterling, he told us he didn't want our protection. He said he'd be safer with his brother in the Caymans, remember?"

"Vaguely," I said. "It was a brief meeting that took place four years ago. You're hoping Ms. Ferrari's stint in the Caymans is just a coincidence, right?"

"Yeah, but I get the feeling that all of this is connected, Phoenix. And if it is, and we have to go after Sterling's brother, that'll probably end our relationship."

I pulled up to the curb of the InterContinental Hotel. Kelly just sat there in the seat. Her eyes were closed. She was shaking her head slowly. "So how are you going to play it tonight with Keyth?"

She opened the door and got out. She looked at me and I said, "I don't know for sure. Who knows what Steven got outta him."

"Nothing incriminating, I hope."

"You and me both. My first plan is to get some sleep. I'll figure out a way to bring it up in the morning somehow. That's the plan anyway."

"All right. I'll talk to you in the morning."

Chapter 15

W hen Kelly closed the door, I picked up my purse, looked through it, and found the first of the CDs of Portia and Joel talking. I slid it into the CD player and pulled away from the curb. The conversations were innocuous at first. Portia was telling Joel how she didn't like him at first and how she used to hate having a chauffeur. Then she started getting personal, telling him how she didn't really care for her stepmother. When Joel asked her why, she refused to say. When Joel asked her if it was because she was black, Portia denied it and explained that she couldn't very well dislike Turquoise because she was black and yet be friends with him and he was black. When Joel pressed her for information, she changed the subject and then got off the phone.

The next time they spoke was a couple days later. Joel told her it wasn't a good idea to be calling him. It didn't look good and that it was inappropriate. Portia told him he was the only real friend she had. She said he was the only person who really listened to her and that she didn't have any friends and that none of the girls at school liked her because she was smart. When Joel asked her how the boys felt about her, she told him they all liked her. Joel then said that was the problem. Then he hesitated, like he knew he shouldn't say what he was about to say.

Both of them were silent for awhile. Maybe a full minute. I got the feeling that their relationship was moving to a whole other level. An inappropriate level. Then Joel said, "Listen Portia, you're a beautiful girl, okay. All the girls are jealous of you, that's all."

I could tell Portia was smiling from ear to ear when she said, "You really think I'm beautiful, Joel?"

"Yes. I wouldn't lie to you about something like that." He paused a second time, contemplating what he was about to say. Again, I got the feeling he knew he shouldn't say another word, but he did. "If I was a teenager, I'd definitely be interested in you."

Portia laughed and said, "If you were a teenager, I wouldn't be interested in you."

After another long pause, Joel said, "Really? And why is that?" He sounded like his ego had been wounded. I knew then that he was teetering on the edge of dropping his guard and allowing himself to slip on very thin ice.

"I only like older guys, Joel," Portia said.

"Really? And what would you know about an older guy?" He laughed. "You're only fifteen."

"I may be only fifteen, but I'm not a virgin," she said as if she had to both defend herself and prove something to the man she had set her sights on. "Daddy thinks I'm still a good girl, but I'm a bad girl. A very bad girl. I love being bad, Joel. Do you want me to show you how bad I can be?"

"Portia . . . listen . . . this has gone far enough, okay. I think it's time you found some friends your own age. Seriously, okay. You're only fifteen years old. You have your whole life ahead of you. The last thing you need is to be involved with older men. Trust me, okay."

"Age is just a number, Joel," Portia said without hesitation, like she had said it before, perhaps to the older men she had alluded to. "If you're worried about getting into trouble, I'll never tell on you. Never! No matter what. And you don't have to worry about me getting pregnant. I'm very careful. I don't want a child either. Like you said, I have my whole life ahead of me and I have plans for college and everything. I don't see what's so wrong with having a little fun, do you?"

"No, I don't. I just think you should have it with boys your own age, not men my age. There's something kinky about that to be honest with you."

Then Portia said, "Yeah, I know. Ain't it cool?"

"Okay, that's enough. Don't call me anymore. Talk to your friends and if you don't have any, get some. Now, goodnight." He hung up.

I let out a sigh of relief, thinking good for you, Mr. Williams.

The phone beeped before the next message played. "How you doin', Joel? This is Pastor Moreno of Living Word Holiness Church. I got another list of movies I need." He rattled off a long list of films he, his wife, and his congregation wanted. The phone beeped again. According to the date time stamp, two days had passed. It was Portia again.

K elly walked into the Willard InterContinental and made her way over to the elevators. She pushed the up button and waited. The doors parted. She stepped in. As it rapidly ascended, she thought about how she would broach the Jericho Wise subject with Sterling. It was a slippery slope because Sterling didn't talk about Jericho much at all. He talked in detail about his mother, Brenda, his dad, Benjamin, his younger brother William and William's deceased wives, Francis and Terry, his Aunt Johnnie, and nearly any other member of his family living or dead. But the only thing she knew about Jericho was that he was filthy rich and lived a life of luxury in the Grand Caymans. Whenever she tried to find out more about him, Sterling would change the subject as if Jericho was a CIA operative or something. Everything was hush, hush where he was concerned.

Now though, she had a job to do. She had to make inquiries that she knew Sterling didn't want. She was in love with him and up to now, she had respected his wishes and he had respected hers. She didn't like to talk about her daughter, Blaze, for reasons she was unwilling to divulge. Sterling never pried. He thought it strange that a mother didn't like talking about her daughter, but that was it. He had told her his Aunt Johnnie was off the hook too, yet he had no problem telling her all the details of her life in New Orleans in the 1950s and beyond. He had no trouble talking about his entire family, which had made Kelly very curious about Jericho and his Vietnamese wife, Pin (Peen).

The elevator doors parted again. Her nerves were starting to fray as she approached the Abraham Lincoln suite. She stood outside the door and listened, hoping that Sterling would be asleep so she wouldn't have to say anything until morning. That way she'd have at least eight hours of peace with him before the inquisition began. She put her ear to the door to see if she could hear anything. Sterling was on one of his cell phones talking, probably to one of his many clients.

Sterling's phone constantly rang at all hours of the night. At first, he refused to turn it off, even if they were making love. She had found the interruptions very distracting especially since all the clients had different ring tones. It seemed like every few minutes, she'd hear a chime, a klaxon, a bell, a cow, et cetera. The chimes seemed to know when she was at the cutting edge of orgasm. It was very frustrating for her. Sterling explained that his clients made it possible for him to live in Tiburon and to fly back and forth cross country to see her. Nevertheless, to accommodate her, he turned the ringer and the vibrator off while they made love and talked afterward. But when the talking was over, and Kelly was asleep, he turned the phone back on and checked his messages. He often left her in bed alone to attend to his clients' needs.

She stuck the keycard into the slot and waited for the green light. She walked into the room. Sterling put his right index finger in the air, letting her know he would be done as soon as he could, which meant it could be another hour, perhaps two, because as soon as he was finished with one of his football player clients, one of his basketball player clients would call. Every one of his clients thought they were Michael Jordan or Tiger Woods or somebody of that stature, which Kelly would have understood. After all, those guys were not worth tens of millions, they were worth hundreds of millions. If they were calling, the orgasm could wait. But what bothered Kelly was that Sterling treated all of clients like they were Michael or Tiger. After all they paid for cruises to Australia, and Tahiti; and first class flights to Cancun, and Japan, et cetera.

"Will you listen to me, Shaun," Sterling was saying. "Uh-huh . . . uh-huh . . . yes I realize that, but listen, we gotta get these women to sign confidentiality agreements now. Yeah, I know you *think* you can trust them, but you can't. Sure you can trust them now, Shaun, but listen, man, you're married . . . no, I'm not judging you. I'm just dealing with the reality of the situation. You've got major endorsements galore. Everybody loves you right now. What do you think'll happen if it gets out that you're bangin' 30 different women, all at the same time? And half of those are the wives of the guys on the tour. Okay, so it's only seven wives! Do you really think the number is going to matter to your sponsors, Shaun?!"

Kelly mouthed, "How much longer?"

"Just a few minutes," Sterling mouthed.

"I've had a very rough day and I'm tired. I'm going to take a hot bath and then I need to talk to you, okay?"

Sterling nodded and continued his conversation. Kelly sat down and listened for a few more minutes. She could pretty much tell what the client was saying based on Sterling's aggressive urgings.

"I'm sure you don't have to worry about the wives. After all, what the hell are they going to say, 'I'm bangin' him too?!' It's the single women you gotta worry about, Shaun. The single women! Why? Are you serious, man? Because they all think they gotta shot to be your wife . . . yeah, yeah, I know . . . but it doesn't matter that you told them you love your wife and that you're not leaving her. They all still think they gotta chance with you. And if nothing else, they love flying first class to all the places you go, staying in five star hotels. That's the exciting part of the affair, see? Okay, okay, let me ask you this . . . do they know about the other women and the wives you're bangin'?

Kelly just sat there, shaking her head, fascinated by the conversation.

"Uh-huh, that's exactly what I thought. All it takes is to get caught with one of them. Just one and you're through . . . finished. And because you're the All-American boy, the thing'll be huge . . . you're the Peyton Manning of NASCAR, Shaun. Your sponsors are gonna run for cover. Why? Are you serious?! Because women are the big buyers in this country, Shaun! That's why! And it doesn't matter that a lot of them are married and would want you to get up in them if they ever met you. They'll be pissed that you shattered their dream of at least one man having the strength to be faithful to his wife. Uh-huh, well, you can pay now, or pay incredibly later.

"Yeah, they'll sign it. Of course they will, especially when you tell them you're going to have to end the relationship if they don't . . . right . . . right. And see, Shaun, once you get caught, and all the women see that they were not the only one, they're going to come after you in the media like you wouldn't believe. And understand this . . . once it comes out, the media is going come after you exclusively. They're not going to condemn the women at all. They'll make them out to be the victims of a mega celebrity whose voracious sexual appetite led him to deceive not only his wife, but 30 other unsuspecting women.

"They won't say one word about the women knowing you were married or that you specifically told them you loved your wife and you were not leaving her for them and that they accepted the relationship with those stipulations . . . uh-huh . . . yeah don't worry, I'll handle the paperwork and the women. Just give me their numbers and I'll get them to sign the agreements. That way you'll be covered . . . okay, okay . . . I'll talk with you later. All right . . . all right . . . bye.

"Oh, and Shaun . . . one last thing . . . cut your single friends loose . . . especially the celebrities. Yeah, yeah, I know, but they're single and you're not. They can do that, but you can't. Listen to me, man, we're talking about some serious money here. Today . . . if you're single . . . nobody cares if you're bangin' two or three woman at a time. The public could care less that you're the pitchman for this or that. But if you're married, forget about it. Think Derek Jeter, man. Jeter has dated lots of women but nobody says a word. Why? Because he's single, man. Well at least think about it, okay? All right, call me back if you need to. Bye."

Sterling clicked off his Bluetooth and looked at Kelly. She wasn't smiling. He thought she was upset because he was still working. He kissed her and said, "It's been a busy day. I thought I would be finished by now, but it's been call after call after call since you left this morning. Have you eaten since breakfast?"

"No. We've been busy all day too with the kidnapping."

"Why don't you go ahead and take your bath and I'll order something to eat, okay? We can talk during dinner, okay?"

"Okay. Order me soup and salad. I'm going to soak for awhile and then I'll be out.

"Sure you don't want me to soak with you?"

She forced a smile. "Maybe later."

Chapter 16

I hit the garage door opener. The door retracted and I drove in. Keyth's pearl white Infiniti SUV was parked. I had the feeling he was up waiting for me. I'm sure he couldn't wait to tell me about his exciting day and how Steven Boyd questioned him like he was a suspect in Joel Williams' murder. I really didn't want to have any conversations. I was too tired, which meant that I would not have the patience required to talk about why he hired Joel in the first place. Any answer he gave wouldn't be good enough at this point. I was thinking, why get into it tonight? We should both sleep on it and give it a whirl tomorrow when we've both had enough sleep and would be less irritable.

I looked at the dashboard clock. 10:15. Then I grabbed the next CD and slid it into the player. I wanted to hear the next conversation Joel had with Portia.

"Joel . . . I know you're there," Portia was saying. "Will you please let me apologize in person before I see you tomorrow when you pick me up for school? Please, Joel. I feel so bad for what I said. Please let me apologize."

I heard what sounded like the receiver being picked up. "Hello," Joel said.

"Hi, Joel."

"Make your apology and don't call me here or on my cell again, okay? If you do, I'll have to tell your dad what you're doing. I don't want to do that, okay. So please stop this."

"Okay, I promise. This'll be the last call I ever make. To be honest with you, I don't see what the big deal is. I didn't do anything wrong and neither did you. All I did was tell you that I wasn't a virgin and that I like older guys. Can you at least explain to me what was wrong with sharing that information with you? You're the first person I've ever told that. And after the way you responded, I'll never tell another soul any of my secrets. I thought a person was supposed to be able to tell a true friend the intimate details of their lives. But I'm so sorry I told you the truth. I'm sorry I didn't lie to you and confirm what most people think of me . . . that I'm innocent and pure as the driven snow. I'm sorry you thought so highly of me. I didn't intend to give you the impression that I was perfect like you."

"Hey, I'm not perfect, okay? I never said I was perfect."

"Well, you sure act like it now."

"What do you mean by that? I act like it now?"

"Well, you told me that when you played college and NFL Europe football, you had lots of girlfriends, didn't you?"

"Yeah, so?"

As I listened, I was thinking this kid is truly slick. She had successfully gotten him to pick up the phone and talk to her even though he told her not to call him again. And now she had him on the defensive when in fact, he had done the right thing by cutting the conversation short and telling her to never call him again. He had even told her to get friends her own age. Now she was trying to equate a fifteen-year-old girl's sex life with older grown men to his college and NFL Europe days. I shook my head and continued listening.

"Yeah, so? Are you telling me you didn't have sex in college and when you played professional football?"

"So what, Portia?"

"So what? So you're saying you were a virgin when you entered college? Is that what you're telling me, Joel? If so, I understand where you're coming from. It would make sense to me then. But, if that's what you're telling me, if you were a virgin when you entered college, that fact would mean that you lied to me, wouldn't it? So is that what you're telling me, Joel? Is it?"

Joel answered her question with his silence.

Portia continued, "Didn't you tell me you lost your virginity to an older woman when we were on the way to school in the limo, Joel? Didn't you tell me you had sex with your high school football coach's wife? And that she was thirty-three and you were only fourteen? Didn't you tell me that? Or were you lying to me?"

Joel exhaled hard and said, "Listen . . . I should have never told you that. But don't forget that you asked me why men could have sex with lots of different women and it was okay, but women couldn't, remember? You had asked me why men thought women, who did the same things they did, were whores. That's when I told you about the coach's wife. I was telling you she shouldn't have treated her husband like that. What I did and what you should do . . . what a lady should do, is altogether different, okay? I thought I was helping you, Portia. That's all."

"Oh I get it. You're invoking the double standard rule, right?"

Joel was quiet for a few seconds and then in a much less commanding voice, he answered, "No, it's just that it's not something that you should be doing, okay?"

"So then it's do as I say and not as I did then?"

"Listen . . . that was a situation I got caught up in. It wasn't right. It changed me forever, okay? It still affects me today. That relationship is probably why I have so many different women and not just one now."

"So basically, you have an excuse is what you're telling me, right? Let me ask you this . . . how many times did you have sex with her, the coach's wife? Once? Twice? Three times? Or did you keep doing it with her until you left for college? I bet you kept doing it with her until you left for college because you enjoyed it so much, didn't you? And then when you got to college, you started having sex with your professors, didn't you? You started having sex with your professors because they were older and you had developed a taste for older women, didn't you?"

"I never said I was perfect, Portia," Joel said, like the wind had be taken from his sails of righteousness.

"Yet you judge me for telling you that I'm attracted to you and that I would love to be with you. It's no different than what you yourself have done! And you did it with your coach's wife to boot! For four years! It must have really been something to do it with her that long, huh? But I'm the scum of the earth and you're Gabriel the Archangel. But okay, Joel. Judge me if you like, but know you did it long before I did. We're the same. No different. The same."

"Are you through, Portia? I sincerely hope you are. I've listened to you. I've heard everything you've had to say. Now . . . don't call me again to talk about this stuff. I'm serious. If you call me again, it better be to let me know there's been a change in your schedule. It better be something important. Otherwise, I'll have to tell your dad about this stuff."

"Daddy won't believe you," Portia said laughing. "And he'll fire you for even suggesting something like that."

"Thanks for letting me know. I'll just have to let my boss know what's going on and he'll assign me to something else."

"You'll still get fired because my dad is important to your boss's business. He'll tell your boss to fire you or he'll let all his clients and associates know what you did and they'll drop Drew Perry."

Loud silence filled my car. I was hoping Joel would be strong. I was hoping he wouldn't give into her demands.

"I'll tell you what, Portia. That's a chance I'll just have to take, okay? You do what you have to do. But if you call here again, I'll do what I have to do. Now, goodnight!"

He slammed the receiver into the cradle. The phone beeped again. Joel picked up the phone and screamed, "What, Portia!"

"I'm sorry, Joel," she said and sounded sincere. "Don't be mad, okay, please."

"I'm not mad, okay. Just stop calling me. You're way too young for me. Way too young."

"So if I was older, we could then?"

Another long pause filled my car and it caused my heart to race. What was he doing? Was he about to give in? Was he about to continue the course he was on? It sounded like it. I continued listening and started shaking my head.

"Are you there?" Portia asked.

"Yeah, I'm here."

"So how old would I have to be to make love to you, Joel? Just tell me that and we can get off the phone."

Joel exhaled hard and said, "Portia . . . I need my job, okay? And I know Keyth Perry doesn't want to lose any clients over this bullshit."

"If you answer my questions, I promise I won't say anything to my dad, okay? I swear I won't. I'm just curious. I just want you to tell me how old I'd have to be to make love to you. That's all I want to know."

"That's the last question you're going to ask me?"

"It depends on your answer."

"Eighteen."

"So if I was eighteen, we could do it?"

"Only if you promised not to tell anybody. Not a soul. People talk to damned much. And if people knew I was bangin' your brains out every night, there would be a big mess."

I sat in my car shaking my head. Portia Barrington was a skilled manipulator and Joel Williams was a sincere fool. At that point of the conversation, Joel had made a huge mistake, but probably didn't know it. Or perhaps he did and just didn't care. Or perhaps the abuse that he suffered at the hands of the coach's wife had forever altered his moral compass as he alluded to. It sounded like that early encounter with an authority figure at fourteen had disfigured his sexual psyche.

"Oh, so you'd bang my brains out, huh, Joel?"

"Hell yeah, but you too young, otherwise I'd be all up in it. I'd have you climbing the walls."

"Um, you're making me wet. Keep talking."

"What the hell am I doing!?" Joel screamed. "Goodnight, Portia!"

"Okay, I'll let you go, Joel," Portia said in a sultry voice. "Just so you know, I started masturbating when you said you'd bang my brains out."

"Really?"

"Yes. You wanna listen for a while. I'm almost there. You can hear me if you want."

"Goodnight, Portia."

"You know what I like doing more than anything?"

"What?"

"Sucking a big fat cock!"

It sounded like Joel hung up the phone. I looked up and saw my husband standing in the doorway. He was just standing there watching me. I guess he wanted to see what I was doing.

"You coming in or what?" he said,

"Yeah. I'll be right in."

Chapter 17

I let out a loud sigh when I walked into the house. I was glad to be home. I set my purse on the kitchen counter and opened the refrigerator. I grabbed the orange juice and poured myself a glass. I couldn't wait to shower and get in bed, but I knew that wasn't going to happen for awhile because I felt my husband's daunting stare and I knew what it meant. He wanted to talk about the Steven Boyd interrogation. At least that's what I thought until he said, "Savannah is becoming more moody than usual. She's always wanted to spend more time with you and you've been making promises that you haven't kept. I understand that you love being with the Bureau, but it's time for you to start participating more in her life before it's too late."

My husband was basically accusing me of being a terrible mother, and an absentee parent. I took offense to that and got defensive right away, which is precisely why I didn't even want to talk about the Barrington kidnapping until tomorrow when I'd had sufficient sleep. Without thinking I said, "So what are you saying? Your mom isn't doing a good enough job?"

Keyth took a deep breath and held it, stifling the rage I saw in his eyes. After our brief stare down, which lasted for a long minute, he said, "I realize your father had to be both mother and father while you were in Beijing, but it isn't my mother and father's job to raise our daughter. It's ours. Not just mine and *my* family's job. It's yours too."

"I know that, Keyth!" I said, nearly shouting.

"If you know that, Phoenix, why don't you act like?! You're her mother. Savannah's only mother. She'll never have another."

I exhaled hard, feeling naked before him. Then I folded my arms, and said, "I'm aware of my inadequacies, Keyth. You don't have to remind me every single day of how poor a mother I am. I promise I'll put the time in with Savannah after this case, okay? Just let me get some rest. Let me clear my head. I don't want to argue."

"So you're the victim? Not Savannah?"

"You can be so melodramatic sometimes, you know that?"

"So when Luther gets her pregnant in another few months, that'll be okay with you, huh?"

"Keyth, my daughter is not having sex! I said I'd help after this case and I will."

"Your daughter, as you call her, isn't pregnant today, but tomorrow will soon arrive."

"It's your job to keep her from getting pregnant, not mine!"

"It's my job, Phoenix? It's our job. I'm putting in my time. What about you?"

"My father raised me by himself. And I remained a virgin until the day we recited our vows! What's the problem?! Can't handle your end?"

Keyth took another deep breath. And then another before saying, "Phoenix, I realize you never had your mother to raise you and you never really developed maternal instincts, but you're not going to sacrifice Savannah so you and Kelly can run around the country playing cops and robbers!"

That really hurt, but instead of showing him how vulnerable I felt after hearing his assessment of what Kelly and I did, I dug my heels in deeper and said, "So that's what you think of me and my job? I'm just running around *playing* cops and robbers, huh? I'm *playing*?"

I knew what Keyth meant, but I felt as if he was attacking me. I had to defend myself or be devoured. I knew he would feel bad about saying I was playing cops and robbers, so I used it against him, knowing he would back up off me and change his tone, which is what I wanted. Portia Barrington didn't have anything on me. I knew how to manipulate my husband when it suited me and now was a good time. He was right, but I couldn't admit it. His truths pierced my heart, which meant they were spot on. Only the truth hurts when we hear it. That's why we avoid it. Knowing the truth means we have to do something about the truth we've heard. I generally chose manipulation. It worked well for me.

"I didn't mean it the way it sounded," he said, falling into my carefully laid trap. "I'm just telling you you're about to lose your daughter if you don't get seriously involved in her life and I mean right now. This very instant!"

I frowned and said, "Why . . . did something happen today?"

"She quit the tennis team today, *Phoenix*."

Stunned, I said, "What? Why? She loves tennis."

"Not anymore."

"Did she say why?"

"No."

"Did you ask her?"

"Yes."

"And she didn't tell you?"

Keyth exhaled hard and said, "What did I just say, Phoenix?"

"I'll talk to her in the morning before I leave, okay?"

"No it's not okay. Talk to her right now. For all we know, you'll get another call and you'll have to leave again. This needs to be handled right now. And you . . . not me . . . need to handle it."

Looking for a quick solution to our daughter's problem, I said, "You think she's on her cycle?"

Something inside Keyth ignited when he said, "You think she'd tell me that?! Come on!"

"I told my father everything."

"So this is about you and Sydney and the twelve years you two spent together in Beijing?" He glared at me. "Why don't you ask her if she's on her period, Phoenix?"

"Fine, Keyth. Let's go talk to her now."

"Let's? No, you go talk to her."

"You know I'm no good at that."

"You weren't any good at kung fu the first time you stepped on the mat either, were you? But you kept practicing until you mastered the art. If you can practice the same kick more than a thousand times to perfect it, to master it . . . master this . . . if for no other reason . . . so that you'll have peace of mind when she goes off to college."

I looked at my watch. 10:35. "Is she still up?"

"Yes. I told her you'd be up to talk to her in a few minutes."

Chapter 18

A t my husband's urging, I made the long trek through the house and up the stairs. I'm not sure why, but I hated this part about being a mother. It's so much better when Keyth talks to Savannah. That's how it was with my father. I think the father-daughter relationship is so important. In many ways, it's more important than the mother-daughter relationship; especially when a young girl reaches puberty. Like I told Keyth, I told my father everything. We had the most wonderful relationship. I just wanted the same for Savannah. To me, it's a father's job to be an example of what a man should be in his daughter's life. It's his job to teach her about men, how to avoid fools, and how to choose a good man.

As I approached my daughter's bedroom, I hesitated. I so hated this part. I felt so inadequate. Nevertheless, Keyth was right. I didn't master kung fu in one day. It took twelve long years of practicing daily to master all the techniques. And it has taken a lifetime of discipline to master chi, control, and power. I suppose that if I had put in the time with Savannah, I wouldn't be standing outside her door now, wondering what I was going to say to the daughter that I loved so much. I could hear her playing John Madden Football on the Playstation I bought her for Christmas a couple of years ago. I took a deep breath and blew it out. This was so stressful, I swear.

I walked into the bedroom and said, "Hi, sweetie."

"Hi." She said.

She was playing with the '89 San Francisco 49ers, which reminded me that Kelly was supposed to talk to Sterling about his brother. I wondered how that was going. The other team was the '84 Chicago Bears. Both teams had won the Super Bowl those years. Savannah wouldn't have a sense of NFL history if it wasn't for her father, I'm sure. I picked up a controller and said, "You mind if I be Jim McMahon?"

"It's not going to help you," She boasted with a bright smile that reminded me of my deceased father.

"We'll see," I said. "So how's everything?"

"Fine," she said, and hit the button for the coin flip.

She had chosen heads, but it came up tails. I decided to take the ball. I hadn't played the game in awhile, but my competitive spirit wanted to kick her butt even though I knew I didn't have a chance. I smiled when the game started. The game was in Chicago, at Soldier Field, and it was snowing. I was going to give her a healthy dose of Walter Payton and eat up a lot of playing time.

"Your father told me that you quit the tennis team," I said to break the ice.

I handed the ball to Payton and ripped off a sixty yard run. It felt good. Part of my strategy to win was to run my plays after I asked a distracting question.

"I don't want to play anymore," she said and chose her defensive play.

"Why? Did something happen? Are the girls on the team jealous of you?"

I handed the ball to Walter again with one second left on the play clock. The 49ers were in the backfield so fast that it was as if they knew what play I had call. I lost five yards on the play. I decided to go with the flea flicker next. I said, "So, nothing happened between you and the other girls?"

My daughter was flipping through screens so quickly that I got the feeling she wasn't thinking when she said, "Not with the girls."

"Not with the girls?" I questioned. Again I waited until there was only a second left on the play clock, which was frustrating Savannah. Kids are so impatient. I would use that to help me win the game. I snapped the ball and handed it to Walter. He ran with it and then turned around and pitched it back to quarterback Jim McMahon. I hit a wide open Willie Gault for a 35 yard touchdown. I couldn't contain my glee.

Savannah said, "Don't get too excited. You got lucky. It won't happen again."

That was something she'd heard her father say to her many times when she scored on him. I would often hear them playing together in the basement. Those two were so into the game that you'd think they were sitting in the stands of a real stadium watching a real NFL game.

I said, "I know it was luck. Sometimes it's better to be lucky than good. That's what my dad used to say when we played games together."

"I miss grandpa," Savannah said.

"Me too," I said.

While I was responding to her, she snapped the ball and Joe Montana threw an 85 yard touchdown bomb to Jerry Rice. Savannah looked at me, smiled, and said, "It's all in the wrist, mom." Then she laughed hysterically.

"So, the problem is with the coach, huh?" I said.

"Do I have to play tennis?" She asked.

"So, the problem is the coach then?" I asked a second time. "I thought you liked . . . what's her name again?"

Savannah frowned when she said, "Ms. Tobias."

I knew then that it wasn't tennis she didn't like. It was her coach. She used to speak so glowingly of her. I started to wonder just how out of touch I had been. I had forgotten the coach's name. I bet Keyth knew though. He usually kept up with that sort of thing. He made sure he was at all the matches, and her piano and violin recitals. Another pang of guilt shot through me. "She's your English teacher also, right?"

"Uh-huh," she said.

She scored another touchdown. My questions were no longer serving as distractions. I started rationalizing immediately. I had missed so many of her firsts. Just last weekend, while Kelly and I were in Las Vegas, I had missed her first kung fu tournament; a tournament I sponsored to attract new students. She and Luther Pleasant were the only black sash's to compete. My cousin had gotten killed and my Aunt Ruth needed me. I was obligated to go.

Savannah was so hurt by it that she wouldn't even hug me when I left for the airport. I decided right then that if she didn't want to play tennis anymore, fine. It really didn't matter what the reason was. She was already into kung fu, fencing, piano, and violin. That was more than enough to keep her busy. Besides, she was a straight-A student. If she didn't want to play anymore, she didn't have to.

Chapter 19

I woke up to an alert klaxon that doubled as my alarm clock. God, I wanted to hit the snooze button. I turned my head and looked at the digital time keeper. 6:00. I turned it off as quickly as I could so as not to wake my husband, but he was already awake. He had that certain look in his eyes that all women recognize immediately. He wanted to get up in me again. I had given it up before we fell asleep and now he wanted some more. I kind of laughed and said, "Come on. Don't worry about taking care of me. Just get it so I can shower and get out of here." Well, I didn't have to tell him twice. I think he was up in me before I finished speaking. I was hoping for a quick wham bam, and it was, but I think I enjoyed the romp more than he did. Never underestimate the morning quickie!

It was 6:30 by the time I finished showering. I hadn't gotten as much sleep as I wanted, but I felt refreshed, recharged, vibrant even, and raring to go thanks to my horny husband. Keyth and I passed each other when I left our adjacent bathroom. He told me his mom would be there at about seven when he left. When we kissed, I felt his hardness pressing against me. He wanted some more, but I didn't have the time. Otherwise, I would have. Hell, we could have stayed in bed all day long if the Bureau wasn't so disruptive to our conjugal visits.

I told Keyth I was looking forward to riding him later that night when I came home and to make sure he was awake to get what I was going to put on him. I always try to give his mind something to feast on in my absence. I like giving him something to dwell on for the day. I make phone calls and tell him how hot I am for him or that I'm going to wear my leopard bra and panties. I like tickling his mind, creating a sexually charged atmosphere, priming the pump, you might say. It keeps things interesting, new, and hot between us. And now that I've heard fifteen-year-old Portia Barrington's method of phone sex, I would probably try that too. I love my husband and my marriage, and the kids we've created together. I don't want to lose even one aspect of them.

I left my amorous husband and went straight to my daughter's bedroom. As I climbed the stairs, I remembered that I used to look in on her whenever I left the house and again when I returned. I would watch her sleep in those days. I don't know how it happened, but somewhere along the way, I started slacking off, leaving the domestic stuff to my husband, thinking, I guess, that it had worked for me and that it would work for Savannah. I couldn't have been more wrong.

As I approached her room, I could hear her practicing the violin. I laughed when I heard the tune she was playing. If was from our favorite film, *The Godfather*. The door was open. I stood there, watching, listening, enjoying the tune, but enjoying my daughter's love for music even more. She was truly talented. I realized that unlike my father who missed nothing of my developmental years, I had missed the most important things in her life and that I could never ever get those moments back. I wouldn't even have the memory of them to reflect on when I grew old.

Except for her kung fu uniform, I noticed that she was ready for school. Her hair was combed, and her school uniform was neatly laid out. Matthew Henson Academy was one of the best schools in the area. The kids who elected to attend had to go to school year round. I assumed she was still in her kung fu uniform because she practiced for an hour every morning before going to school. She often meditated for fifteen minutes afterward.

Savannah's eyes were closed as she played. Then, as if she felt my invading presence, she opened her eyes and saw my reflection in the dresser mirror. I smiled at her. She didn't miss a beat of *Sicilian Pastorale* when she turned around. She continued playing the Nino Rota melody as if she was playing it just for me. I was beaming. I was so proud of her at that moment. She finished the tune and I applauded.

She said, "I heard you coming up the stairs while I was meditating. I know how much you and dad love the movie so I played it for you."

"You heard me coming up the stairs?" I questioned. "I was quieter than an insect."

She smiled and said, "Obviously, not quiet enough."

I returned her smile and said, "You are obviously excelling at everything you put your hands to. I'm so proud of you, Savannah." I hugged her and she hugged me back, which was a huge turnaround from the previous week when I had to leave before the tournament. While I didn't say anything to her, in my heart, I knew she was practicing her kung fu regularly to keep pace with Luther Pleasant, her friend from school, who was a better practitioner of the art. I did the same thing with my master's son. He was better than me at first, but I used him as a measuring stick to excel. Savannah seemed to be doing the same thing. I felt good when I left her room.

Just before I entered Sydney's room, I could hear the snap of punches and kicks. I realized that he, too, was up, and in his kung fu uniform practicing before school. They say the apple doesn't fall far from the tree. Evidently, I had passed on my loved for the art and my discipline as well. After doing a perfectly balanced spinning round-house kick, he saw me, and ran to me. He was trying to keep pace with his sister. A little competition never hurts. In fact it often helps push us to higher heights we didn't previously think we could reach.

"Morning, Mommy," he said. "I love you."

I smiled and said, "I love you too. Time to get ready for school."

"Okay," he said. "Will you be home for dinner?"

"I'll try," I said, knowing there was a fat chance of that now that the Barrington kidnapping was probably worldwide news because of Myles Barrington's celebrity. Due to the latest development, I expected Kortney Malone's call for an immediate update as to what happened and how the media found out.

Chapter 20

The call I was expecting from Kortney Malone never came. Normally, when the media got a hold of case as big as this one, she calls to either chew me out for something, or to encourage me. Yet, on a case that has now drawn the attention of the national media, she hadn't called. It was quite puzzling. I didn't know if that was a good thing or a bad thing. Maybe she hadn't seen the news, I thought, and then quickly dismissed it. I figured that since Palmer Davidson was involved and he was a personal friend of mine and the Barringtons, and had appointed her to the position of director when he was in office, she was going to stay on the sidelines as much as she could on this one.

Palmer could still help her advance in the world of politics if she was so inclined, but she would have to play ball and be a good soldier in its never ending war. After all, she still had her position as director because his former vice president was now sitting in the Oval Office and they were very close. Rumor had it that Davidson was still running the country incognito. If true, he would be our first four term president since Franklin Delano Roosevelt.

I called Jack Ryan from my cell while I was in the heavy morning traffic on the way into Washington. I told him that since he was better suited to running a kidnapping, that he should get over to the Barrington mansion and basically babysit them until the kidnappers called back while Kelly and I did what we do best, which was checking out all leads. With rancor, Ryan explained that his team had been there all night. I got the feeling he was pissed off because I slept in my own bed and he didn't.

I felt like mimicking a child crying, but I didn't. Instead I said, "Rank has its privileges."

I knew it would get under his skin. He said something under his breath that I couldn't understand. I think one of the Barringtons came into the room or something. He must have gone outside or something because I could hear birds tweeting all of a sudden. I guess he had to get one last dig in. He responded with, "The fact that you didn't know to either stay the night or assign someone to from the very beginning is yet another reason you never belonged on this case in the first place."

I explained that I was tired and couldn't think yesterday because I hadn't had any sleep for nearly seventy-two hours. His response to what I thought was a legitimate excuse was unsympathetic to say the least. Ryan didn't care about my lack of sleep. All he cared about was doing whatever it took to get the girl back and to comfort the parents in any way possible. If that meant pulling an all-nighter so the parents would feel comfortable, that's what an experienced agent would have done without being told to do it.

When Ryan finally got off his soapbox, I rolled my eyes and said, "Did the techies find any hidden cameras and bugs?"

"Yes. We found both."

"Great and you swept the entire house?"

Ryan breathed hard into the phone. I got the feeling that I had gotten on his last nerve, which to me was a reasonable strategy since I was out gunned in the childish shootout.

"Yes, we found both. I've got Boyd trying to track down the manufacturer. From there, we could probably find the store they were purchased from and if we're lucky, the fool used his credit card. If he did, we'll have him."

I smiled and said, "There are at least two, not one, kidnappers. An experienced agent like you should have remembered that." Then I hit the end button while he was still talking.

Chapter 21

T he air conditioning the hotel offered felt good when I entered through the lobby doors. I think the temperature was already over 80 and it wasn't even noon yet. Washington felt like the swamp that it was rumored to be when the founding fathers decided it would be the Capitol City. I walked into Café du Parc, which was located on the Pennsylvania Avenue side of the hotel. It was about 7:30. Kelly was waiting for me, sipping her coffee. I slid into my seat, placed Portia's phone records on the table, and offered an enthusiastic, "Good morning."

"Morning," She said, smiling.

I said, "I take it things went well with Sterling last night."

The aroma of the hazelnut in the coffee Kelly was sipping was so alluring that I considered ordering a cup while I waited for the details of her conversation with Sterling to come pouring out of her. She was about to say something when the waitress came over. I ordered quiche, strawberry crepes, and herbal tea. When the waitress left, I looked at Kelly, expecting her to tell me how it all shook out with Sterling.

"I'm going to withdraw from the case, Phoenix," Kelly said without looking at me and sipped more of her coffee.

"Went that well, huh?" I said, laughing, attempting to add a bit of levity to the situation.

"Yes and no," She said smiling.

"So what happened?"

"Long or short version?"

I looked at my watch. "We *are* on the taxpayer's dime."

"Okay, I'll cut to the chase," she said, still smiling. "I asked him about his brother and how he got his money. What you've got to get is that Sterling basically comes from a working class background. His family originated in New Orleans. He and Alex Haley have a lot in common in that they both know the intimate details of their family's history of the first African being brought to these shores. Sterling can regal you for hours with stories about the matriarch of their family. A woman named, Ibo Atikah Mustafa. I mean he can go on and on about his family's history, but when it comes to Jericho Wise, he wouldn't give up any details. Nothing. Zip. Nada. I pushed him to talk and he pushed back, then we got into this huge argument over dinner." She exhaled and continued, "To make a long story short, we both apologized and my legs ended up in the air half the night."

I laughed out loud and said, "So basically you're telling me your interrogation failed, and you didn't get much sleep after being up for almost three days."

"That and he called his brother and told him the Bureau was asking questions about his business affairs, which is why I'm getting off this case."

"He called his brother and told him in front of you?"

"Yeah. He wanted me to know he was calling him. It was his way of letting me know that anything I had to say in his brother's absence might as well have been said in his brother's presence."

"And you've never met his brother?"

"No. I've been seeing Sterling for four years now and I've only met his younger brother William, and selected members of his family, but not the whole family because I'm white. Apparently, some of the women in his family don't play that. That's what he says anyway. It may go all the way back to some of the stories he told me about Ibo Atikah Mustafa. Who the hell knows?"

I said, "And you're sure you want off the case?"

"Face it, Phoenix, neither one of us should be on this case at this point and you know it. Kortney knows it. Turquoise Barrington knows it. And I gotta believe Palmer Davidson knows it. Yet here we are, right in the middle of a very messy case where the lead investigators are compromised in that they have personal stakes. It's insane."

"It is insane," I said. "Did Kortney call you?"

"No. You?"

"No. It's a curious thing, isn't it? She's gotta know this case is all over the news by now, don't you think?"

"Yep."

"Did you see Greta last night?"

"My legs were in the air, remember?"

I rolled my eyes and said, "So were mine, but I somehow managed to keep up with current events before I put them there. I don't know about you, but I'm working a case that requires constant vigilance."

Kelly laughed and said, "I was working too, Phoenix. Having my legs up in the air is just one of the perks. Call me Mata Hari, if you like."

Smiling, I said, "Wasn't she executed?"

Kelly changed the subject back to Bureau business when she said, "So Greta was talking about the kidnapping last night, huh? I gotta believe Kortney had to have seen the broadcast. She's quite the news hound, particularly when it concerns her beloved Bureau."

"She had to have, Kelly, yet she hasn't said a word about the coverage. And to top everything off, Marsha Spivey is murdered along with a principle suspect. And we're still on the case? That's off the hook!"

"Maybe her legs were in the air last night too," She said laughing.

"Well if they were, the television was on and tuned to the news the whole while. I'll bet she was either watching the screen, or she was riding him, probably so she could watch the screen at the same time."

"Will you do me the favor of calling our fearless leader and breaking the bad news to her?"

"Sure," I said and flipped open my cell. I hit the contacts button and found her personal number. The line was ringing. "Morning to you too, Kortney. So you saw that, huh? Well I was expecting a call. Uh-huh, I see. Well Kelly wants off the case because her boyfriend is the brother of the man who owns the building Williams and Spivey were found in." I looked at Kelly and said, "You knew that already, huh?" Kelly's eyes bulged a bit. "And you're not worried about any of this getting out? Okay. Yes. Yes. Okay. Was he serious about that? Okay, if you say so." I hit the end button.

"Well . . . what did she say?" Kelly asked anxiously.

"She told me to tell you that if you're retiring or resigning, she'll accept your credentials and your weapon, but if you just want off the case, forget about it. You're in until the bitter end, just like she is. Palmer's calling the shots and everybody's ass is on the line, including hers. And if Portia isn't found—dead or alive—in another 48 hours, we all might be finished at the Bureau."

Kortney had explained that Portia Barrington was Palmer Davidson's goddaughter and that he was very unhappy with the way the investigation had gone so far. He told her we were to use the full power of the Patriot Act to find her. That meant we were to suspend Habeas Corpus and start kicking in doors and kicking ass in general, consequences be damned. The Patriot Act basically gave us carte blanche to do whatever we needed to do to find the girl, which meant that the kidnappers were now classified as terrorists.

The reclassification was almost plausible when you consider the number of ransom demands and the hefty sums of money they had already collected. It could be argued that the "kidnappers" were using the money to support terrorist activity. I wanted to find the girl probably as much as Palmer did, but I was ambivalent about what the former Commander in Chief wanted us to do. My plan was to only resort to the Patriot Act when absolutely necessary. I hoped it wouldn't be.

The waitress brought my breakfast and then she poured more of the hazelnut blend into Kelly's cup. Before I started eating, it occurred to me that Portia's friends probably knew she was missing by now, even if they hadn't seen any of the news channels last night. I looked at Kelly and said, "If someone killed me, and you didn't know who had done it, would you go to work the next day or would you stay at home and mourn my death?"

"Phoenix, you're my best friend ever and I love you. As you know, I've never really had any women friends and if something like that happened to you, I think I'd need lots of time to mourn your passing. I really do? Why do you ask?"

I started working on the quiche before saying, "I'm wondering how close Reilly Vanderpool and Portia are. I know Mrs. Barrington said they were the best of friends, but that doesn't mean they were."

"What's your point?"

"The quiche is excellent. Would you like some?"

"No, I'm fine."

"Suit yourself," I said and put another forkful of quiche in my mouth. "I'm wondering what Reilly is doing right now, assuming she knows Portia is missing. Did she go to class today? I'm pretty sure the summer session has started at Bishop Ireton. I guess I'm trying to figure out if we should go to the school or to her home first. What do you think?"

Kelly sipped her coffee. "Why don't I call their home and find out." Then she picked up the manila envelope that contained the phone records and took out its contents. She scanned the document.

"Go right ahead," I said and started working on the strawberry crepes. "I see why you enjoy coming here so often. You and Sterling seem to have finally hit your stride. That is as long as you don't ask him questions about his brother."

After Kelly found Reilly Vanderpool's number, she flipped open her cell and dialed the number. I could hear the phone ringing. "Hi, this is Capitol City Air Conditioning. We're offering a special this weekend due to the incredibly high heat index. Is this the Vanderpool residence? Oh, great I have the correct number. Am I speaking with the lady of the house? Oh, this is her daughter, Reilly?" She looked at me and smiled. "And how old are you Reilly? Please tell me you're at least eighteen. Sixteen, huh? I'm sorry we need an adult's approval for this special. When will your parents be home? Okay, we'll try to call back then." She closed her cell and sipped her coffee.

I sipped my tea and said, "I hope you blocked your number before you called."

Kelly rolled her eyes and said, "I most certainly did, thank you." She sipped more of her coffee and thought for a few seconds before saying, "As for Sterling and I . . . well we're still together, but I think I want more."

"More from him? More from the relationship? What?"

Kelly raised her hand to get our waitresses' attention. Then lifted her chin, telling the forty something woman she needed more service.

When the waitress arrived, she said, "More hazelnut, Mrs. Wise?"

She was about to pour more into Kelly's cup when she said, "Yes, but I'd like it to go, please."

"Sure, no problem." She looked at me. "Can I get you anything else?"

"No, thank you," I said.

She looked at Kelly. "Will we be billing this to your suite?"

"Yes and give yourself a nice tip, okay?"

"Thanks, Mrs. Wise, and please visit us again soon."

I laughed under my breath.

"What?" Kelly said.

"Mrs. Wise?"

"I never said we were married. The staff just made the assumption because we come here so often. Besides, it's easier than having to explain that I'm doing sinful things."

I finished off my breakfast and said, "I thought doing sinful things was acceptable these days."

"I suppose. But deep down, a girl wants to be an honest woman."

I didn't respond. I just watched her, trying to gauge what was going on with her and Sterling. They have had an up and down relationship for years. I'm sure part of it is because he lives in California. And the other part is because he doesn't want to get married. I had given her my opinion a number of times, but this time, I wanted to keep my mouth shout, which was incredibly difficult, but I was winning the battle.

All of a sudden Kelly said, "I love him, you know."

She had said it as if a spirit was channeling through her. I was stunned because she had never said she loved Sterling. At least I don't remember her saying she loved him. She had always told me that it was just sex and when she was tired of it with him, she would move on. Again, I won the battle of the tongue.

Chapter 22

The valet brought my car and held the door open for me. And then he hesitated for a few seconds, waiting for a tip. I reached into my pocket and pulled out a five. He took it out of my hand and left without a thank you. I got the feeling that the tip wasn't enough for the young man. We got in and felt the cool air blowing. Just before I pulled away from the curb, I got a call from Keyth. He wanted to know what I wanted for dinner. I told him he would do just fine. I also told him that if I had any energy after that, I'd love to have steak and shrimps. We both laughed and said, "I love you."

Kelly said, "How do you and Keyth keep the romance going?"

"You don't want to know. And besides, I don't want to argue with you about the way I live my life."

"I promise I won't argue with you. Now tell me, please. I really want to know."

I glanced at Kelly for a quick second as we headed over to Alexandria, which was where Reilly Vanderpool lived. It would take about thirty minutes or so once I merged onto I-395 south, depending on traffic. I looked at Kelly again. She looked desperate for answers. As I merged onto the interstate, I tried to decide if I wanted to have what I thought would be a futile conversation that could very well lead to an argument. After looking into her eyes for a few more seconds, I said, "My beliefs are my beliefs. And your beliefs are your beliefs. Let's leave it at that."

"Who am I to argue with success?"

I checked all three of my mirrors before zipping into the far left lane. I kicked it up to 85 and pushed the cruise control button. I could feel Kelly's burning eyes staring at me, demanding that I discuss a subject that I wanted no part of. I turned my head and looked at her for a second and then returned them to the road. "Okay, fine. My husband and I love each other, but I know there are lots of other women who would be willing to love him too because he's intelligent, thoughtful, charming, employed, and handsome. Most women who don't have a man of their own would find those traits hard to ignore and try to take him from me. That's how the average American woman thinks nowadays. It's chic to bed another woman's man these days. Never mind that AIDS is still on the hunt for the foolish of heart.

"In fact, things are so upside down in this country right now that another female could know Keyth was married to me and she wouldn't give a damn about me, my family, or herself even if he told her dumb ass that he wasn't leaving me for her. That's how desperate some of these women are. So to avoid that nonsense, or at least try to, I'm quick to apologize when I'm wrong, which as you know is hardly ever," I laughed out loud and continued, "And when I'm home, I give him all the attention he needs. I listen to him, I respect him, and I give *him* the last word." I looked at Kelly for a quick second. "I said I give *him* the last word. I also do my best to make him feel like the other woman would if she could get her hooks in him."

"But that sounds so one-sided, Phoenix. That's so antiquated. You're so much stronger than that. You sound like a submissive Muslim woman, not a sophisticated American woman."

"It is antiquated, Kelly. I have no problem acknowledging that. But let me add this: everything old isn't necessarily bad. It's the so-called new things that are causing families to disintegrate, not the old. And let's not forget you're asking me how you can keep *your* man. I'm not asking you." I paused for a few seconds to get her response, but she didn't offer one. "I'm submissive to my husband and I have no problem acknowledging that either. Believe it or not, submission is the key to peace in every situation. Selfishness and wanting your own way is what's causing you and Sterling problems. You want your way and he wants his way. The "me" first mentality is destroying many relationships along with the family unit. Even-tually, it'll destroy the country itself."

"Oh, come on, Phoenix. You don't submit to Kortney all the time, do you? Didn't you pretty much force her to give you time off so we could find out who killed your cousin in Vegas a couple of weeks or so ago?"

"Yes, but I never said I was perfectly submissive. Not being per-fectly submissive in no way changes the fact that I am. My family should always come before my job. I've gotten away from that, but I plan to get my priorities together as soon as we finish this case. But at the same time, I'm very strong and you know this. Everything has a natural order. My name is Phoenix Perry, not Phoenix Drew-Perry. I took my husband's name. No one forced it on me. That was my choice from the very beginning. I wanted to be his wife. I wanted to have his children. I chose to live a certain way because that's how I was reared and it works for me and my family.

"Yet, I have all sorts of power within the framework of my family. I make most of the decisions. Keyth has the final say, but he defers to me almost every time because he recognizes my intelligence and my ability to make sound choices. He knows I don't do things frivolously. I tell my children what to do and I expect what I say to be done in the manner in which I prescribed. I'm in charge of the cases we work. I'm in charge of my mind and my body, but I still understand how I fit within the framework of any group I'm a part of. I know how to take orders and I know how to give them without being overbearing. When I worked for you, did I not do as I was told? Of course I did. Yet, you would never consider me a weak woman for submitting to your authority or the Bureau's, would you?"

"No."

"The bottom line is, if it came down to it, I could easily kick Keyth's ass and he knows it. But just because I could, doesn't mean I should cut his balls off with my words or my actions and in so doing, supersede his authority unless he does something that would warrant action to the contrary. Most American women don't believe in being feminine anymore. I still do. That's what's going to win Sterling over, Kelly. Your femininity is your greatest gift. It isn't your weakness.

"It's generally the other woman's femininity that attracts men and husbands in particular. The other woman lets your man be a man, which is all he wants to be in the first place. A man doesn't think like a woman because he's not a woman and he doesn't want to be a woman. We're the ones trying to figure out what we want. The men know what they want, but we try to make them want what they don't find attractive, which is a woman with a masculine attitude. Homosexuals aside, men want women, not men. Don't forget your biology, Kelly. Men and women are lock and key relationships. We are not single celled amoebas. We need each other. Opposites attract. Likes repel. Again, look to the natural order of things to win Sterling's heart. Ask yourself, why men seek out other women?"

"That's an easy one. They do it because they're dogs."

"Fair enough, but what does that make us?"

"Huh? What do you mean what does that make us?"

"Come on, Kelly. Think! Who are the men sleeping with? Other men? Or other women? I mean, I've never heard a man say, 'I'm through with women'. Men will never ever be through with women; especially feminine women. But men will always be through with a particular kind of woman. If you want something more with Sterling, find out what kind of woman he's interested in settling down with."

"I see what you're saying."

"Do you see, Kelly? I mean seriously. We're our own worst enemies when we buy into the "all's fair in love and war" foolishness. But then we blame the men for doing what we in essence approve of. Not all of us, but too many of us are involved in the madness, sleeping with our sister's man, our cousin's man, our husband's father or uncle or brother. When you consider what way too many women have allowed themselves to become, I don't think anyone can deny that America has become a prototypical cesspool of illicit activity, but we let the men shoulder the brunt of it because they're easy targets.

"It's time we start looking at ourselves for allowing much of what's going on between the sexes now. It's time we raised the level of our standards—personal and otherwise. Or at the very least establish some standards and boundaries. What's funny to me is, the same things you call antiquated and outdated, used be every woman's minimum standard. Let's face it, we've gained our liberation and our independence, but in the process, we've lost our shame as women. All the relationships we used to nurture by nature are paying the Grim Reaper's toll. And as a woman, you know that when a woman loses her shame, she's capable of doing anything, or accepting anything. That's when she starts to think your man is fair game."

"That's so one-sided, Phoenix."

I checked my mirrors before switching lanes. Then I switched lanes and took the off-ramp.

"Listen, you asked me how I do it. I told you and you've rejected it. Now, I'll answer what you didn't ask, which is how does my husband keep the romance going? He does the same things I do. When he's happy, he makes me happy. When I'm happy, I make him happy. Sterling, and no other man, wants to come home to a nagging, argumentative wife when he could be having sex with a woman who doesn't on the regular. Think about it, Kelly." I parked the car, but I kept it running so we could continue feeling the cool air. I said, "Now . . . how do you want to play Reilly Vanderpool?"

"By ear," she said. "We don't know what the kid knows. When we find out, let's go with what never fails. Good cop, bad cop."

"Just in case it doesn't work, call that Captain in the Arlington department that has the hots for you. What's his name again?"

"Charlie Downs."

"Give him a call and see if he'll let us bring her there to scare her. Good cop, bad cop may not work. The kids are pretty sophisticated these days. But if we take her in, she'll break."

I turned off the ignition and we got out of my car and walked up to the front door. I lifted the brass knocker and let Reilly Vanderpool know she had visitors. Just before I knocked a second time, the door opened. I recognized her right away. She was one of the girls in the DVDs. I looked at Kelly. She recognized her too, but neither of us let on. She smiled and said, "Hi. May I help you?"

I could see why older men risked all for the young woman in front of me. She was quite stunning and she had what looked like beautiful Mediterranean skin. Her hair was thick and full of rich luxurious curls. I wondered if her mother or father was Lebanese. Her breasts were firm and looked like they didn't need a holster, 36C, I'd say. She had a Scarlett Johansson smile and sparkling white teeth that were shielded by full lips. I said, "Reilly Vanderpool?" She nodded. We held up our credentials. "We're federal agents. I'm Phoenix Perry and this is my partner, Kelly McPherson." I could see she was shaken upon hearing that, but she had tried to hide it. "May we come in?" I continued and entered the premises without her permission. I didn't think a sixteen–year-old would try to stop two FBI agents from entering the house the way

Francesca Ferrari had, especially if I acted like I didn't need her permission.

"What's this all about?" Reilly said, nervously. She was still trying to be tough.

Kelly immediately went into her bad cop routine to put her on the defensive while I looked for weaknesses in her character and listened for inconsistent statements. "Why are you so nervous, Reilly? Is there a boy here with you or something? And why aren't you in school?"

All of a sudden Reilly smiled again. "You called me about an hour ago pretending to be some lady from Capitol City Air Conditioning, didn't you?"

I knew right then this wasn't going to go well. I looked at Kelly and she knew too. But we had to roll with it.

"And you know there's no boy here," Reilly continued. "I'm here alone. This is about Portia Barrington, isn't it?"

"What are you so nervous about then?" Kelly said, firing another shot. "You had to know we'd be here to ask you some questions about the kidnapping."

"I'm not nervous," Reilly said, full of confidence now that she had seen through our little game.

It was my turn. "I'm not sure you understand the gravity of the situation, Reilly," I said politely. I'm wondering if there's someplace we can talk so I can explain just how much trouble you could be in if you don't cooperate."

"I'm really not supposed to have anyone in the house," Reilly said and laughed in our faces. "And I know you don't have a warrant. If you did, you wouldn't have bothered calling first. You would have just came and kicked in the door."

"Fine," Kelly said. "I think we should have this conversation downtown anyway."

"What's the charge?" Reilly said, still smiling. She was enjoying our exchanges.

I said, "I don't think that'll be necessary, will it Reilly? We just have a few questions and then we'll be out of here. You're parents don't even have to know we were here. But, if you want to play hardball, we'll have to take you in, fingerprint you, and put you in with girls who would love to do all sorts of nasty things to you and make you do those same nasty things to them. If we have to take you in, we've gotta call your parents and everything. You don't want that, do you?"

Reilly Vanderpool didn't even flinch when she said, "Sounds like a wild time to me. Let's go." Then she put both arms out, daring us to cuff her and added, "The good cop, bad cop thing isn't working."

I knew right then that we had to call her bluff just as she had called ours. I pulled out my cuffs. She started laughing and said, "So you're going to take me in?"

I cuffed her hands behind her back and said, "You seem to think this is a joke, but it isn't. You're best friend has been kidnapped and you don't seem to give a damn."

Her smile evaporated. "You can't do this to me, I'm a minor."

Kelly locked eyes with her and said, "You're the second teenager that said that to me this week. The other one was a sixteen-year-old serial murderer." She snapped out her baton, put it under her chin, and lifted her head with it. "Just so you know I beat his ass with this before I cuffed him. If you don't show us some respect, I'll have to use it on you and say you resisted arrest." She stared into her eyes for a few more seconds. "Now let's go, Ms. Vanderpool."

W e let Reilly Vanderpool cool her heels in an interview room while we sipped tea and coffee as we observed her through the two-way mirror. She had asked for her phone call and a lawyer, but I told her she wasn't entitled to one because she wasn't under arrest. I hadn't Mirandized her either, but she quoted every one of her rights perfectly like she had been practicing for the day we'd show up. I knew that few teenagers had patience, which is why we put her in the interview room by herself. I knew she would start to get bored, then antsy, and then angry, mainly because she didn't have anything to do. She had to sit in that room and be alone with her own thoughts. I believed that would be a terrible prospect for a girl who was selling her natural goods. Far as I could tell, she had no idea that we knew about the prostitution ring.

Kelly said, "So how much longer are we going to let her sit in there?"

"Until she can't stand it any longer," I said. "She's a smart girl. She's probably trying to figure out how she's going to get out of this. We'll arrest her for prostitution in a little bit and let her call her parents. I don't think she even has a lawyer. And I don't believe for a second she's going to call Myles Barrington and ask him to bail her out."

"She can go court appointed."

"That's what I'm hoping for, Kelly. They're backed up with lots of cases. They won't be in any hurry to get this kid out. Now if she calls her parents, that'll be a different story. The parents can afford a good attorney, but, they're going to know about the prostitution, Joel Williams, the films, everything. This kid needs a bucket of ice cold water thrown in her face to wake her up to the consequences of the kind of life she's living. Part of that is our responsibility. Then when we've shaken her enough, we'll get to the truth."

"Sounds like a plan," Kelly said. "So how did it go with Keyth last night?"

"It went okay, I guess," I said. "Steven Boyd didn't bother to tell him that Williams was dead. Boyd told Keyth that Williams had applied for the Bureau and he was just doing a preliminary background check. I guess he was trying to feel him out. Perhaps Ryan was right. Maybe he was trying to protect me."

My cell rang. I looked at the caller ID and said, "Speak of the Devil."

"Ryan?" Kelly asked.

"Yeah," I said and then answered the call, "Agent Perry."

He sounded angry when he said, "Are you two ever coming back here? Some of us would like to go home too."

"I thought a smart operator like you could figure it out on your own. Just rotate shifts if you think you have to babysit the Barringtons."

He was quiet for a few seconds and said, "Do you know something I don't, Agent Perry. If so, please share it. We're supposed to be a team of professionals, remember?"

"Now how could a small time agent like me know more than professionals who have more than fifty years' experience combined?"

"Let's have what you got. That is if you have anything at all."

"You're going to disagree. So just stay there just in case my inexperience proves to be an Achilles heel."

I figured one of the Barringtons must have been in earshot because he was talking through clenched teeth when he said, "We don't have the luxury of just sitting around here if you have something solid. Spit it out and I'll decide if it's worth pursuing."

"You'll decide?"

"Well, I'll give you my professional opinion. Now . . . what do you have?"

I looked at Kelly and said, "Don't tell the Barringtons this, but I think Portia's dead."

"Okay, tell me why," he said hesitantly.

"Because the kidnappers asked for three ransoms for one reason and one reason only."

"And what would that be, Agent Perry? I'm sittin' on pins and needles."

"He needed an excuse to kill her. They never called back, did they, Ryan?"

He was quiet for a few second before saying, "No, they didn't."

"And they won't be calling again. No need to. They got five hundred thousand already. Why leave a witness. Besides, this thing is about prostitution. Teenage prostitution and Portia knew too much. You saw what was on the films and you heard at least some of the tapes of Portia and Williams. Clearly, she was no angel. And if you carefully check out her room, you'll discover all sorts of nasty things that point to Portia's complicity to certain crimes."

"Why didn't you tell me this yesterday?"

"Frankly, because you're arrogant, Jack. And you're disrespectful. Furthermore I don't appreciate the way you and your team talked to me yesterday."

"What was all that business about working together and being united in front of the Barringtons?"

"We weren't in front of the Barringtons at Williams' apartment, were we? Now that I've brought you up to speed, you decide what to do with the Barringtons. Kelly and I are about to question a suspect. Have Mrs. Barrington give you a copy of Portia's friends' addresses and phone numbers and tell Steven to interview them all. If he likes, he can have Agent Campbell go with him. But tell them, no screwing on the taxpayer's dime. They can do that on their own time." I hit the end button. Then I looked at Kelly and said, "Let's go talk to Reilly."

Chapter 23

We walked into the interview room. I handed Reilly her purse and told her she could make her phone call if she still wanted to. Normally, we'd let her use a phone in the precinct, but we wanted her to use her cell. When we had gone through her purse, we found a pink cell phone, but it was turned off. We tried turning it on, but we needed the four digit code to unlock the phone and check her contacts page. We were hoping she would unlock her cell and make the call in front of us. Then when she did, we could see her contacts. However, we had to play her just right so that she wouldn't be suspicious. I handed her the purse.

Reilly took it, smiled, and said, "What? More good cop, bad cop?" Then she laughed at us again.

I said, "You can make your call now if you still want to."

Puzzled, she said, "If I still want to? You mean I can go?"

"No, you can't go just yet. We've got a few questions. The law says we can hold you for seventy-two hours on suspicion if we want. That's what we're going to do if you don't answer our questions. So you can call your lawyer, if you really have one. Or, you can call your parents and let them know where you are if you like. But if you just answer a few simple questions, you can walk out of here free as a bird in twenty minutes. And your parents won't ever have to know you were here. It's up to you."

She thought about the proposition for a few seconds. Then she said, "What do you want to know?"

"Thanks, Reilly," I said. "I only have a few questions. Before we get started, can I get you anything? A Coke, water, anything?"

"No, I'm fine."

"Okay, let's get started. You said you were aware that Portia Barrington is missing?"

"Yes."

"When did you find out she was missing?"

"It was on the news last night?"

"When was the last time you saw her or spoke with her?"

"The last day of exams."

"Wednesday, the 8th of June?"

"Yes."

"And you haven't heard from her since?"

"No."

"How long have you two been best friends?"

"Since the eighth grade."

"Well did you two have a falling out or something?"

"No."

"You two are best friends and you don't talk to each other daily? Portia's been missing for three days and you say you two haven't had a falling out. I find that hard to believe, Reilly. Agent McPherson and I are best friends and we talk every day. Portia's been kidnapped. We're trying to find her. Tell us the truth. What happened between you two?"

"Nothing," Reilly said, and looked away.

Ms. Vanderpool had been looking me in the eyes when she responded to each of my questions, but when I asked her what happened between her and Portia, she looked the other way. That in and of itself doesn't mean that something happened to disrupt their relationship, but it meant that she knew something that she wasn't willing to talk about.

I looked at Kelly. She didn't believe a word of it either.

As if she knew we were about to ask some very tough questions, she reached into her purse and pulled out her pink cell phone. She looked at me and said, "I think I want to make my phone call now."

I had to play this just right so I said, "What's the problem?"

"No problem. I just think I should have my lawyer here now."

I looked at Kelly and then again at Reilly. "Go ahead, but they're simple questions. You don't need a lawyer, but it's up to you."

She looked me in the eyes as if she was trying to figure out something. Then she turned on her cell and made the call. "Chris . . . I'm in the Arlington Police Department. I need you to come and get me out. Uh-huh. Uh-huh. No, they haven't charged me with anything yet. Okay. Okay. Bye."

She put the phone on the table. I looked at it. We both had the same idea. I reached for it and so did she. She was able to grab it before I could. I looked in her eyes again. She was scared to death. Then she started hitting buttons.

I said, "May I see your cell phone?"

"Sure, Agent Perry," She said, handing it to me, smiling all the while.

I hit the contacts button, but all the names, numbers, incoming and outgoing calls had been erased. For her to do that without hesitation, I assumed she had everything backed up on her computer.

I looked at Kelly.

She nodded slightly, letting me know she agreed with me.

It was time to drop the bomb on her before whoever she called arrived.

I said, "Now what would make you erase every number in your phone, Reilly? What are you hiding?"

"I'm not hiding anything," she said defiantly, trying to appear brave, but she came off like a frightened little girl.

I said, "We can help you get out of the trouble you're in."

"I'm not in any trouble."

I exhaled and said, "Reilly, we know you're into prostitution. We know you're selling yourself to older men."

"No, I'm not!" She screamed, as if screaming somehow authenticated her claims. "I would never do anything like that."

What most people didn't get about lying was that you should never get angry about a false accusation. Getting angry about a lie only makes you look guiltier. Acting as if you're outraged by a statement that has no basis in truth, should have a calming effect because you're probably guilty of something you're not being accused of. Everyone has secrets and because you're being accused of something you didn't do, as opposed to something you did do, should put you at ease. Poor liars don't know this simple truth, which is why they get caught and eventually tell everything they know. Now that I had successfully gotten Reilly riled up, it was just a matter of reeling her in before whoever she called arrived.

I looked at Kelly and nodded.

She left the room.

Then I looked at Reilly and said, "Yes you would sell yourself and you have done it many times. And so did your best friend,

Portia." Here's where I began to improvise to get the truth. At this point, all I had to do was accuse her of something she was innocent of and she would provide the answers we were looking for. I was shaking my head when I said, "It's over, Reilly. You were the one who got the whole thing going. And you got your best friend Portia involved. If she dies because of you, you'll be an accessory to the crime. We're talking thirty years minimum of hard time with harden women who are going to eat you alive your first day in. And you'll have 10,949 days of abuse left."

Reilly started crying. "I didn't get Portia involved. She got me involved. Portia got all of us involved."

I fought off burgeoning delight, knowing I had her now. She was mine.

Kelly rolled a cart in with a television and a DVD player. She plugged it in and then returned to her seat.

I said, "Reilly Vanderpool, you're under arrest for solicitation and obstruction of justice."

Kelly Mirandized her.

"I didn't do anything wrong," Reilly said through unrelenting tears.

"All of who?" Kelly said. "Portia got all of who involved."

"I want immunity," Reilly said, wiping her eyes.

I looked at Kelly and tried not to laugh.

Then I handed Reilly a box of tissue and said, "Sure, we'll give you immunity and witness protection too." I remembered Portia's computer and the link: The Jaguar Club. It was worth a shot so I went for it. "We know about the Jaguar Club, too, Reilly."

Reilly stopped crying and looked into my eyes. "You do?"

I had to wing it a little now. "Yeah. It's all on DVD. We found them in Joel Williams' apartment." I handed the DVDs to Kelly. She put the first one in. "You and your friends are sleeping with older men for a ton of money. Again, we have you on DVD. Take a look at this, Reilly."

When Reilly saw herself on screen she cried all the more, covered her face with her hands, and screamed, "Turn it off! Please turn it off!"

I nodded to Kelly. She hit the stop button.

"Do I need to show you the others?"

She shook her head rapidly. The tears continued their slow decent.

"How many girls are in the club and what are their names?" Kelly asked.

"It started out as a dare a year or so ago," Reilly began. "Portia had bragged about having sex with older men during a sleepover. She told us we didn't know what we were missing because we were doing it with boys and not real men. When we were in the kitchen, I asked who she had done it with. She wouldn't name names, but she did tell me she had done it with a rich guy and that he was a wonderful lover. She asked me if I wanted to try it out. At first, I said, 'no', but later, I changed my mind. I made her swear she wouldn't tell the Jaguars. I made her swear that it would be our secret forever."

"What's his name?" I said.

"I can't tell you that!" she yelled. Then she calmed down and said, "I'll end up like Portia."

I looked at Kelly. We both knew the gamble was about to pay heavy dividends.

I said, "What do you mean you'll end up like Portia? Do you know what's going on? Do you know where she is or who took her?"

"I don't know which one, but I'm sure it's one of the men that we see. Portia loved to blackmail people. I think she was blackmailing one of the men and he killed her."

I said, "Portia's still alive. I heard her on the phone yesterday. Her parents confirmed that it was her voice."

"He's going to kill her because he can't let her go."

"Why?" Kelly asked, "What does Portia know?"

"I wished I'd never gotten her involved," Reilly said.

I said, "I thought you said she got you involved."

"She did, but I told her two years ago, she couldn't be a Jaguar unless she lost her virginity. She wanted to be in the group so badly that she blackmailed her cousin Sean into sleeping with her. And after that, she was never the same. It wasn't long before she completely took over the Jaguar Club. All the girls started listening to her and doing what she said. She had something on all of us."

"What did she have on you?"

"She recorded me having sex with the older guy. After that, she made me get the other girls to do it so she could get them on tape too. She told me she would give me my recording back if I helped her. I knew I shouldn't have done it, but, I was desperate. I couldn't let her keep that recording of me and . . ." she hesitated and then went on, "It was the same thing we did to her only worse. She told us that if we didn't do what she said, she would put the videos on the Internet. Then she said that we could make a lot of money if we went along with it for a little while, just a few times to see if we wanted to be a real club and not suckers."

Shaking my head, I looked at Kelly. "A fifteen-year-old madam." I looked at Reilly again. "Who's in the club? Who are the girls?"

"Skylar Harris, Keira Everhart, Sabrina Mathias, Caprice Gunnar, and Kai Romero."

I said, "So a total of seven girls?"

"Yeah . . . when you count me and Portia."

"Do you know who the men are? Do you know their names? How does this work? How much are they paying?"

"We don't do names. They don't know ours and we don't know theirs. We don't know anything about them other than they have lots of money to spend."

"What do they pay?"

"$10,000 an hour. $50,000 for the night. A weekend is negotiable. Portia took twenty percent of everything, including tips. I found out later, after I had gotten involved, that the man I'd had sex with that first time had paid Portia $10,000 and she didn't give me a penny of it. She scored a total of $60,000 off all of us before we ever saw a dime. When we confronted her about it, she said, 'I'm entitled to a finder's fee.' Then she told us not to worry about the first score, we'd make more than we knew what to do with."

More tears ran down her cheeks.

Kelly probably didn't mean to ask, but she was astounded, as was I. She said, "What do you do for that kind of money."

"Absolutely everything. I'm so ashamed," Reilly said, and covered her face while she cried into her hands. "At first it was straight sex for a few thousand. But then, after the easy money started rolling in, we were having threesomes, girl on girl, oral, anal, whatever they wanted. Before we knew it, the clients were paying $10,000 an hour.

"How do you get your money?" Kelly asked.

"Electronic transfers."

I said, "We can protect you, Reilly, but we have to know who to protect you from."

"Maybe you could, but you couldn't protect everybody I know, could you?"

Kelly and I looked at each other. She had a point. There was no way to protect everybody she knew.

"Why can't you just put me in protective custody now?"

"We could but that wouldn't protect your family and friends. And it would signal the people you're protecting that we know something about them and their activities."

Captain Downs entered the interview room and said, "The girl's attorney's here."

"Thanks, Charlie," Kelly said. She looked at me and said, "That was fast."

I said, "Don't say anything to anybody, Reilly. As far as you're concerned, you never talked. And you asked for your attorney right away. Stick to that no matter what and you'll be all right until we take you into protective custody."

Reilly stopped crying and took a vanity mirror out of her purse. "My eyes are red. Anybody got any Visine?"

I had some in my purse. I handed it to her. She put some in. Then she touched up her makeup. "How do I look," she said, looking at Captain Downs.

"Beautiful," he said. "You ready?"

"Yeah, sure. Let's go."

My cell rang as Reilly Vanderpool was leaving the interview room. Jack Ryan was calling. I hoped he had something important for us.

Chapter 24

"Yeah, Jack, what's up over there?"

"Myles Barrington wants us outta here. He thinks the kidnappers haven't called back because we're here. Nothing we can do if he doesn't want us here. We're gonna pack it up and take off."

"Okay. Go ahead and go. We're on our way there, but don't tell Barrington we're coming. And Jack, put a couple people on Reilly Vanderpool's house. She gave us some valuable information. I'll fill you in on it later. It may be nothing, but the kid's scared to death."

"What did she give you?"

"Are the Barringtons anywhere near you?"

He hesitated for a second. "No. What do you have?"

"As I said earlier, this thing is about teenage prostitution. There are seven girls that we know of. It appears that Portia is a teenage madam with a penchant for blackmail. There's big money on the line and there's at least one banker involved. He's doing the wire transfers."

"You've got to be kidding me, Phoenix."

"I wish I were, Jack. If we find and flip the banker, we're that much closer to getting Portia back in one piece."

Still skeptical, he said, "Do you have one shred of proof on any of this?"

"Other than the DVDs, no, but why would Reilly Vanderpool lie about something like this? She didn't come to us to confess, I had to sweat it out of her, Jack."

"I'll put Campbell and Boyd on the girl, okay?"

I hesitated before saying, "Jack, put somebody else on the girl."

"Why? What's wrong with using them? I trust them both with my life."

"I don't think it's a good idea to put those two on Reilly. If something did happen, I don't want lovers guarding her. And if something happened while they were on duty, who knows what the fallout would be when the media finds out that not only did the

Bureau assign two agents that are sharing a bed during their off duty hours, they've been allowed to work cases together for years. I don't have to remind you that I shouldn't be on the case myself since Williams, as you stated, technically works for me. If that comes out, the director won't be able to protect me. Then she'll have to come after you, Jack. She won't have a choice."

"I disagree, Phoenix. My people can handle themselves while they're on duty. I have no reservations about them working together. If I did, I would have made one of them transfer a long time ago. I stand behind them one hundred percent."

"Duly noted. Now put somebody else on her! That's an order, Jack. As for Boyd and Campbell, you told me yesterday that having Boyd interview my husband protects me. I'm protecting them. Tell whomever you assign to Vanderpool that they are not to have any contact with the girl until they hear directly from me."

"I understand, but—"

"I've made my decision. End of story."

I hit the end button and called Reilly Vanderpool's cell. "Hi Reilly, Agent Perry here. I'm sending a couple agents to watch your house, okay. Don't be alarmed. They'll be there to protect you and your family. No, they won't say anything to your parents. They won't even come to the door. They'll be watching the house just in case you're right, okay?"

Chapter 25

Kortney Malone called my cell while we were on the way over to the Barrington mansion and confirmed what Jack Ryan had told me. Barrington was willing to pay another ransom if he had to. She told me to continue the investigation, but to be discrete. I told her Kelly and I were on our way over there and that I could probably talk to Mrs. Barrington. She told me to be discrete a second time. I also told her that I had told Ryan to assign two agents other then Boyd and Campbell to protect Reilly Vanderpool. She understood, but she didn't acknowledge that she knew about their relationship.

By the time we made it there, all our guys were gone. Mrs. Barrington told us that her husband had gone to the office because sitting around waiting for a call that might never come was driving him insane. She went on to say that Barrington wanted us out of his home just in case the kidnappers were still watching the house or something. He was hoping that there was still a chance to get Portia back, even though they had promised to kill her and send her back to them in pieces. According to Mrs. Barrington, finding the surveillance equipment made her husband more uncomfortable. The idea of strangers being in his home and planting them there in first place completely unnerved him.

I assured her the kidnappers would not know we were there because our guys had found the bugs and the camera and that staking out their home was too much of a risk. Then I asked, "How do you think they got in?"

"I have no idea." Mrs. Barrington said.

"Forgive me for asking, but is there any chance Portia let them in? Do you think the kidnappers could be a couple of the men you saw her with?"

"It's entirely possible, but I don't think it would have been them."

"Why not?"

"Grown men having sex with an underage girl is one thing, but planting a camera and listening devices in our home and kidnapping Portia took lots of planning. Perverts are not that sophisticated, Agent Perry. They would have to have inside information. They would have to know what school she was going to, what time we were at work, where her chauffeur lived, lots of stuff. That's too much stuff for a couple of perverts. But assuming a pair of perverts did do all of that, would they ask for a second and a third ransom? I sincerely doubt it, Agent Perry. I've put my share away, so believe me, I know."

I said, "How were you able to come up with the cash so quickly?"

She lowered her eyes to the floor before saying, "Palmer says we can count on your discretion so I'll just tell you the truth, okay?

I nodded.

"On occasion, Myles accepts cash from clients."

"Cash he doesn't tell the IRS about?"

I didn't mean to ask her that. It just slipped out.

Mrs. Barrington didn't respond at first. She just looked at me for a long while and then said, "Agent Perry, don't probe too deeply into Myles' financial affairs, please. Try to focus on the kidnapping."

That last line sounded like an order.

I looked at Kelly. She was starting to realize the same thing.

It was all starting to become clear as to why it was so important that I remain on this case. Barrington had probably told Palmer about the undeclared money. I was put in charge because I owed Palmer my career. Never mind that we had thrown the Bureau's code of ethics out the window.

I looked at Mrs. Barrington again. "But the money is central to the case."

"Then talk to Myles about it!" She snapped.

That was definitely an order.

I exhaled and said, "Just how much money undeclared money does he have lying around?"

Mrs. Barrington exhaled hard. Then she crossed her legs and folded her arms.

"Fine," I said and switched gears. "Have you had any maintenance done to the house . . . electrical service . . . air conditioning . . .

telephone service . . . anybody that doesn't normally come into your home?"

"I already told agent Ryan this. But, no we haven't. No one at all."

A female voice said, "Cable Company come."

I turned around. A heavyset Spanish woman was standing in the doorway of the living room. I looked at Mrs. Barrington.

"Come on in, Maria," Mrs. Barrington said pleasantly. "When was this? And why didn't you say something before."

Maria looked afraid, like she thought her job was on the line. I wondered if she was an illegal. If so, that too would explain why Kelly and I were still on the case. Palmer knew he could depend on me to keep that little item under wraps too.

"No one ask Maria, Mrs. Barrington," she said, looking at the floor. "I did not think Cable Company take Portia. Now . . . not so sure."

"When were the men here," I asked.

"Two weeks ago," she said. "Man and a woman."

"Why were they here? Tell us what happened?"

Again Maria looked like she was afraid she was in trouble.

She said, "Maria watching *Young and Restless* when cable go out. *Young and Restless* Maria favorite show. I call Cable Company. Tell them problem. They fix. Lady say crew already in the neighborhood. They be right over to fix Speed Gonzales quick."

I looked at Kelly. "Check it out."

"Mrs. Barrington," Kelly said, "Do you happen to have the number for the Cable Company."

"Sure. It's in my office. Come with me."

They left the room.

I looked at Maria. She seemed calmer now that Mrs. Barrington was gone. I said, "So tell me what happened when they arrived."

"Not much. No take very long to fix."

"Nothing unusual happened?"

"No."

"And you were with them the entire time?"

She thought for a second and then said, "No. Woman thirsty. I take to kitchen. Give woman bottle of water. We chat about soaps. Her favorite *All My Children*."

"How long were they here?"

"Twenty minutes, I think."

"Do you think you can describe them?"

"The woman, sure. Not so certain about man. Just know him very tall, thick. Woman a mouse compared to him. Maria wonder why Cable Company send two of them. Most times, just one man, not two."

I flipped open my cell. "Jack, Phoenix. I'm at the Barrington mansion. Send one of our artists over. The maid has a description of at least one of our suspects."

"The maid?" He said. "I didn't even know they had a maid. When I asked about the housekeepers, Mrs. Barrington told me they didn't have any." He paused for a couple of seconds. "Is she illegal or what?"

I looked at Maria and smiled. "Probably."

"But we're not calling immigration, are we, Agent Perry?"

"Not if you want to retire with full benefits, *Agent Ryan*."

He kind of laughed. "I see why the brass wanted you running the show. You've got one of the richest, most famous attorneys in the country using illegal help and his wife is the district attorney. But I can't use my own people, my best people in fact, to stakeout a material witness's residence?! In the meantime, we're covering up for rich people who can clearly afford to hired legal domestics!"

"And they have a lot of powerful friends. One of them is former president Palmer Davidson. Now do you understand?"

"Loud and clear, Agent Perry."

"Good. Now get the artist over here ASAP."

"Will do, General Patton! I'm at attention and I'm saluting the flag!"

Chapter 26

I hit the end button just as Kelly and Mrs. Barrington were returning. "The Cable Company hasn't sent anyone here in six months," Kelly began, "and they haven't received a call from this address complaining about an outage."

"Do you need Maria for anything else, Mrs. Barrington?" Maria said, suddenly nervous again.

"No, Maria," Mrs. Barrington said. "Thank you. You can return to your duties now." She looked at me like she was expecting me to ask her if Maria was illegal now that she was no longer in the room. "Palmer assured us that we could depend on your discretion where our maid is concerned, too, Agent Perry."

That was her way of confessing without confessing. I played along. My career was on the line too. "Indeed you can, Mrs. Barrington. Just don't say anything that would give me reason to call certain agencies. I'm sworn to uphold the law. Do you understand?"

"I do," she said.

Frowning, Kelly said, "Uh . . . what's going on here?"

I said, "I'll tell you later. Now . . . Mrs. Barrington, you told us yesterday that your husband doesn't give his daughter the kind of money it would take to buy the theatre and all that stuff in Portia's closet."

"Yes, go on."

"Reilly Vanderpool told us that she, Portia, and five other teenage girls were prostituting themselves at $10,000 an hour. $50,000 for an entire evening."

Mrs. Barrington took a deep breath and exhaled. She didn't seem a bit surprised. "Well, if that's true, that explains the alligator boots and the other items in her closet. I thought it was drugs. I really don't know whether to be happy it wasn't drugs or to be outraged that she's a teenage prostitute. I suppose I shouldn't be surprised though. Who knows what happened to Portia when she was at that orphanage?"

I looked at Kelly and then back at Mrs. Barrington. "Portia was adopted?"

"Yes."

"Why didn't you tell us this from the beginning?" Kelly demanded.

I could tell Mrs. Barrington was trying to control her anger, but she couldn't hide her eyes. The fire in them was like a pair of lasers when she looked at Kelly. I understood why Maria was so nervous in her presence. The stress of the kidnapping had clearly gotten to her and her husband, which was understandable. "I don't see what possible difference that information could have made, Agent McPherson."

"You don't?" I questioned. "Your stepdaughter is sleeping around with older men, has porn everywhere, and you don't think she may have been abused at the orphanage?"

"I didn't say that it wasn't possible she was abused at Saint Joseph's. I'm only wondering what relevance it has on the kidnapping."

I looked at her for a few seconds, trying to figure out if she was stupid or naïve or just so shaken by her stepdaughter's abduction that she wasn't thinking clearly. "Is this a Catholic orphanage?"

"Yes. Why?"

I raised my voice several octaves. "The Catholic Church has been thoroughly infiltrated by imposters . . . perverts who prey on altar boys and little girls. How can you ignore that?"

"I'm a Catholic!" She screamed. "I resent you even thinking such a thing. Yes, there have been lots of men raping boys, but you make it sound like everywhere you look, there's perversion going on within my faith. For every so-called priest that rapes an altar boy, there are hundreds, if not thousands who would never ever do such a thing." She took a deep breath and calmed down a bit and continued. "Please try not to put all the apples into a single barrel."

"Mrs. Barrington," I said softly, knowing I was about to deliberately mislead her. I wasn't ready for her to know that we believed her stepdaughter was either dead or soon would be. I was hoping that what I was about to say would trip her up a bit; maybe trick her into saying something she hadn't planned on saying. It was clear that she obviously knew more than she was letting on. "This case is about blackmail. That's why there were three ransom demands."

"Blackmail? We're not being blackmailed."

"According to Reilly Vanderpool, Portia was blackmailing her and other girls at school. Your stepdaughter is a skilled manipulator. I've listen to numerous conversations she was having with her chauffeur. How else would you explain three ransom demands?"

"I have no idea, Agent Perry."

"Did Portia know your husband kept large sums of money in the house?"

"I'm not sure. Again, you should ask Myles about his money and who knows about it other than him and me."

"Do you happen to have the address of Saint Joseph's Orphanage?"

"No, but I'm sure I can find it online for you."

"That would help. Thanks," I said. "By the way, how old was Portia when she was adopted?"

"She was eight."

Brooke Ursula Davis, Norman Green, and their respective girlfriends, Melina Sanchez, and Kristen Greely, were about to have a bite to eat at the Pennsylvania Avenue Friday's Restaurant in Washington. While Brooke and Norm hated each other's live-in, their occasional get together became foreplay and covered up their sizzling affair. As far as Brooke was concerned, Kristen was a spoiled brat. Whenever they went out as a group, no matter where the majority wanted to eat, they ended up going wherever Kristen wanted to go or she'd ruin everybody's evening because she'd pout. Today, Brooke, Norm, and Melina wanted to go to Hooters, but Kristen shut that down immediately. If they went to Hooters, Kristen would've been the only person at their table who wasn't clocking the waitresses. She had told them that she didn't mind Brooke and Melina looking at the scantily clad girls on roller skates, but she didn't want to compete for Norm's attention.

Norm was in love with Kristen, but the hot sex he was having with Brooke was as incredible as it was addicting. Brooke was a lesbian and for Norm, the idea of being with a woman who was only supposed to be with women made the allure too irresistible to stop.

Shortly after their first encounter, his desire to bed Brooke became a fire that could not be doused. At some point during the affair, he started resenting Melina because she was his rival, not that he wanted Brooke full-time. He also didn't like the way Melina acted in public, like she was so head over heels in love with Brooke. Melina was more devoted to Brooke then a dog to its master, worshiping her like she was an amalgamation of the Greek goddesses Athena, Artemis, Aphrodite, and Persephone all rolled into one and it ate at him.

Norm loved sitting across the table from Melina. He enjoyed looking into her eyes and smiling in her face, knowing that she had no idea he was having sex with Brooke two or three times a week. He loved the idea of Melina thinking he and Brooke were just friends, that Brooke was a lover of women only, and that she would never sleep with a man, least of all, Norm. And so he watched Melina and laughed at her stupid jokes more than anyone else. Melina had no idea Norm was laughing at her, not with her, because he knew that he was going to bed Brooke later on that night when they were supposed to be working. Secretly though, he fantasized about sleeping with Brooke and Melina at the same time, but Norm knew Melina would never agree to it because she only had eyes for Brooke.

They were about to dig into their Jack Daniel's ribs, chicken, shrimp, and steaks when Brooke's phone vibrated. She answered without looking at the caller ID, thinking it was Erika, her daughter. It was difficult to hear because the restaurant was jammed pack with patrons. There was a perpetual buzz of loud conversation in the air. The employees were going from table to table loudly singing happy birthday to several of their guests. She screamed, "Hold on a minute! I need to find a quiet spot so I can hear you!" She excused herself. On her way to the ladies room, she looked at the ID. It was Robert Tarantino. She checked the stalls to make sure she was alone.

"Yeah, Bobby, what is it?"

"Having a good time with that beautiful Latin dyke of yours, I see," he crooned.

"Trying to," she said and swung the door open, looking around the restaurant, wondering where he was sitting. "Are you here? In Friday's?"

"My people are. I know every move you two make. Don't ever forget that."

She saw numerous people talking on cell phones. "What do you want, Bobby?"

"Cancel the Jaguar Club."

"What? Why?"

"They're talking to the FBI about our operation."

"All of them?"

"Start with Reilly Vanderpool. Tonight! No excuses."

"So basically you *think* Reilly is talking."

"I don't have to think. I have people inside the Arlington Police Department who tell me things that would affect my operations."

"Did she mention me and Norm?"

"She wants immunity. To get it, she'll have to sooner or later. She'll have to tell everything she knows. And if the boss finds out that I was running a teenage prostitution operation out of his building, I'm fucked too. He'll send his crazy ass wife, Pin, over here to cut my head off—yours too. I can't let that happen. We've all made good money. Time to shut it down."

"If all our asses are in jeopardy, why can't your people take care of the heavy lifting this time?"

"My people didn't steal a million dollars from me! You and your simpleminded partner did!"

"I'm not going to do a bunch of teenage girls, *Robert*. That's bad Karma, man."

"I like you, Brooke. So I'm gonna make you a onetime offer. You two do all of them, and that will square us."

"Doing seven teenagers will more than square us. Don't forget all the work we've already put in."

"I haven't forgotten anything. You have. Besides, it's only six. Portia is mine! Nobody blackmails me! No fuckin' body!"

Flippantly she said, "Technically she's not blackmailing you. She's blackmailing your friend."

"So you think this is a muthafuckin' joke, huh bitch? Listen you dumb ho! Blackmailing him *is* blackmailing me! Blackmailing him is blackmailing you too, but you're too damned stupid to figure that shit out! We're in this thing together! None of us can afford to have our mutual friend in a position to be blackmailed. He knows too much and he's too fuckin' valuable to kill. Besides, he's valuable to the bosses' operation too. Believe me you don't want any of this shit getting back to Jericho. Not a fuckin' word of it. If he finds out . . . if he even suspects . . . prison'll be the least of your worries. Do you understand?"

"Yeah, I think I get the gist of it."

"You still think this is a joke, huh?"

"Only a little," she said laughing. "What's funny is to hear how worried you are about Jericho Wise. That's funny as hell to me."

"You won't be laughing when he puts two holes in your head the size of golf balls."

"A few minutes ago you said I forgot something," she said, no longer laughing. "What did I forget?"

"You forgot the accruing interest and the late penalties on the million dollars you and your partner sole from me. The way I figure it, you can never pay that off. Besides, it's a very good deal. You, your partner, Erika, the dyke, Kristen, your parents, everybody you know will be safe the moment you take care of those bitches. And . . . I'm willing to drop two hundred grand in your purse. Kill the banker and I'll make it three hundred—cash on delivery. All I need is a yes or a no."

"Let me check with Norm. He's here with me."

"I know he's there, bitch! I know everything! And no, you can't ask him shit! You made the decision when you stole my loot. Make the decision to cancel the girls. You . . . not him!"

"Okay, we're in."

"Take out all of them tonight! Handle that bitch Reilly Vanderpool first!"

"Fine, but I want that money tonight."

"I'll give you two hundred tonight and the other hundred when you do the banker, deal?"

"Deal. Now, I really have to go. They're gonna think something's wrong with Erika if I don't get back soon."

"Wait," Tarantino said. "I want you to hear something."

Brooke listened. She heard a girl screaming in the background, crying, begging for her life.

Tarantino said, "You thought you could blackmail me and Chris, huh, bitch?!"

"I'm sorry, Bobby. I'm sorry."

"You gon' be sorry, ho!" Tarantino shouted. "I want you to speak to someone on the phone."

"Is it my father?"

"Hell naw! Now say something."

"Hello," the girl said.

"Who is this?" Brooke asked.

"This is Portia Barrington. Tell my father . . ."

"Tell yo' father what?" Tarantino said. "You ready to die?"

"No! Please don't kill me! I'll suck your dick!"

Tarantino laughed. "Again?"

Blam! Blam! A weapon discharged.

The shots were so loud that Brooke jerked suddenly and pulled the phone away from her ear.

"You still there, Brooke baby?" Tarantino asked, calmly.

"I'm still here."

"I've handled my business—Clint Eastwood style. .44 magnum! Two right in her muthafuckin' grille. Too bad too. Fine bitch. Fine as hell. Not so fine now though. They gon' have to do a closed casket on this one. You renege on this deal, and Erika is next. Then Melina. Then your mother . . . your father . . . your whole goddamned family. Norm's too." He paused for affect. "Now you handle yours. To-night!"

The line went dead.

Chapter 27

I was uncomfortable when Kelly and I left the mansion. The Barringtons were hiding income from the IRS and they had a housekeeper that was an illegal alien. I wondered what else they hadn't told us. It's so much easier for me to trust people when they tell me the hard truth from the beginning. When I have to dig for a precious nugget of truth or it inadvertently comes to the surface, the level of trust erodes and eventually crumbles. If I continue to find the truth on my own, depending on how terrible the truth is, I can't say I would never trust the person again, but it would be so difficult to regain trust that I don't think it would be worth the effort.

I looked at Kelly as we got into my Mustang Cobra. She was thinking the same thing; it was worth the time to checkout Saint Joseph's Orphanage. The orphanage was just outside Manassas, Virginia, about fourteen miles from Fairfax where we currently were. I was convinced that someone at the orphanage had abused Portia Barrington despite her stepmother's objections. If the abuse didn't happen at the orphanage, it happened somewhere which meant that a pervert was probably still walking around free, molesting other young girls.

Even if we never found Portia, we could at least find out who had done such a terrible thing to a defenseless eight-year-old. If nothing else, it would give us some insight into who she was and why she was doing the things she was doing. That's what Kelly and I thought anyway. Call it prejudice, call it jumping to conclusions, but it made sense to me that a priest committed this horrible crime and ruined this kid's life. My cell rang. It was Jack Ryan again.

I put the phone on speaker so Kelly could hear. "Yeah, Jack."

"Two things, Phoenix. First, we tracked the numbers that the doorman called from his security station after we arrived. He called all the penthouses first. All but one call only lasted about ten seconds. The last one went on for a couple minutes."

"Only one tenant answered her door," I said. "Francesca Ferrari, right?"

"Right."

"So he was warning the penthouse tenants that we were there as we suspected," Kelly said.

"Gotta wonder why only the penthouse tenants needed a warning? Why not the other regular folk . . . know what I'm saying?"

"I follow you, Jack. Go on."

"I checked with the phone company and verified the names of the penthouse tenants. Then I ran their names. They're all clean."

"Even Francesca?"

"Even Francesca. Why?"

"She a working girl, Jack. I find it hard to believe a working girl doesn't have a record."

"Maybe that's not her real name, Phoenix," Kelly said. "Maybe it's the name she uses."

"Well, that's the name on record at the phone company," Ryan said.

"Something's going on in those penthouses, Jack. We don't have enough to get warrants, see if we can get one anyway. Also, until we hear from the powers that be, can we put a couple people in the lobby? The penthouse tenants have to come home sooner or later."

"We don't have the manpower for that, Phoenix."

"Put Campbell and Boyd on it."

"I just let them go home. They need to rest. I'll put them on it in the morning, okay?"

"Not okay. Put them on it now. They can sleep later."

After a long silence, Ryan said, "The next call went to a woman named Raquel Mendes. I ran her name and came up with nothing, but I gotta believe she or someone else she knows is in on whatever's going on in that building. The doorman was on the phone with her for about seven minutes before he made his next call."

"What's the number? We'll cross check it against Portia's numbers."

After Ryan read off the numbers, he said, "Now get this . . . the third number was an overseas number. He called the Renegade Hotel and Casino in the Caymans. That call lasted for eighteen minutes."

Kelly and I looked at each other.

"I realize that sometimes employees take advantage of their bosses and make long distance calls," Ryan continued, "but making an eighteen minute international call on the boss's dime? That's going to show up on the bill. The doorman had to realize that. So I'm thinking this Jericho Wise character, the guy who owns the building, must be vacationing there or something. The doorman obviously thought that a murder in his building was important enough to make the call. But . . . why would a guy who is wealthy enough to own a building like that, leave his vacation number with a doorman? I could see him leaving it with his administrative assistant or the building manager even, but the doorman? It makes no sense."

"Good work, Jack," I said. "If you get anything else, give me a call immediately."

"Will do."

I hit the end button and looked at Kelly. "At some point we're going to have to tell Jack that you're dating the owner's brother. You know that, don't you?"

Kelly sighed. "Yep."

"Also, we're going to have to start dealing with the real possibility that Sterling knows what's going on in that building."

"C'mon, Phoenix, we've got a double murder and one working girl. That's it."

"We got a double murder and a working girl that used to bang Portia Barrington's bodyguard at no charge. Williams had a key to her place. We got a working girl that gets a call from the doorman allegedly to let her know we were coming. This same doorman calls the Caymans shortly after he calls the working girl. The working girl then gets on a plane to the Caymans after the call. How much do you wanna bet that Francesca made her flight reservation after she got the call from the doorman?" I thought for another second or two. "Kelly . . . what if Francesca got a call from the Caymans and it's the same international number that the doorman called?"

"I don't even wanna think about it, Phoenix."

I called Jack back.

"Ryan," he answered.

"Jack, find out if Francesca Ferrari got a call from the Caymans. If so, see if it was the same number that the doorman called."

"No problem," Jack said. "What are you thinkin'? The owner is letting her live there rent free and bangin' her or what?"

"I'm trying not to jump to any conclusions at this point, Jack. I just think it's too much of a coincidence that Francesca went to the Caymans and the doorman called someone there, don't you?"

"I see where you're going with this," Ryan said. "I'll call you back when I have something solid."

When I hit the end button, I noticed that Kelly was going back through Portia's phone records—Raquel Mendes."

"Yeah?"

"Portia was calling and receiving calls from her number regularly."

I called Jack back.

"Ryan," he answered.

"Raquel Mendes is a friend of Portia Barrington's. The number you gave us is in Portia's records. Evidently they've had numerous conversations." My phone beeped. I looked at the ID. The call was coming from Matthew Henson Academy. "Jack I gotta run. Get her address and see what you find out."

When I saw Matthew Henson Academy in my ID, I immediately started worrying about Savannah. I was afraid that something terrible had happened. Lots of scenarios ran through my mind. I figured that whatever it was, it happened at gym, a broken arm, leg, ankle, or something like that. Nothing like what I was about to find out.

Normally, if there's a problem at school, one of the women in the administration office called my husband. I can't remember the last time I heard from the school which made me even more concerned. I hesitated before hitting the talk button on my cell, dreading what horrible news I was about to receive. My heart was pounding so hard I thought that if I didn't calm down, I was going to go into cardiac arrest. I took a deep breath and said, "Hello."

"Mrs. Perry?"

"Yes?"

"Anthony George here . . . the principal over at Matthew Henson Academy."

"Yes?" I said. My heart was still racing. I was afraid of what he was about to say.

"Do you remember me, Mrs. Perry?"

"Yes. I spoke with you in your office about four years ago when Savannah had gotten into a fight with a couple of her classmates."

"You have an excellent memory, Mrs. Perry."

"What can I do for you, Mr. George," I said, on the verge of losing patience. Something had happened to one of my children and he was getting reacquainted like this was a social call, like he was trying to get up the courage to ask me out on a date. "Has something happened to one of my children?" Deep down, I knew this call was about Savannah, but I wanted to believe that it could have been Sydney this time. I was just starting to rebuild something with my daughter. If she was in trouble, that meant I had to do something about it and I really didn't like that part about being a parent.

"I'm afraid I have some rather unsettling news," Mr. George said. "Unfortunately, we've had another incident. It's happened again."

"What's happened again, Mr. George? Savannah was fighting with one of her classmates again?"

"She was fighting again, yes. But it wasn't with a student, Mrs. Perry. She was in an all-out brawl with several teachers."

I didn't say a word. I closed my eyes for a quick second as the shocked of it washed over me.

"Mrs. Perry? Are you there?"

"I'm here, Mr. George. I'm just trying to process what you said. Is she okay? Was she hurt during the altercation?"

"Savannah's fine. She looks like she didn't receive *any* blows."

While I would never admit it, I felt a measure of pride that my daughter was able to handle herself. "Will the teachers be okay?"

"Let's hope so."

He paused for a few seconds.

I said, "Are you there Mr. George?"

"Yes, I'm here, Mrs. Perry. Uh, I don't mean to pry, but I need to ask a rather personal question."

"Okay," I said, knowing or at least believing I already knew the question.

"Is everything okay at home," he asked delicately, like he was afraid of how I might respond to such an invasion.

"I take it you mean between me and my husband?"

"Yes. I've seen this sort of thing before. When mother and father are at odds, it affects the children."

"My husband and I are doing just fine, Mr. George."

"Well then I'm at a loss as to why Savannah is behaving the way she's behaving as of late. Except for the one incident, Savannah had been a model student. She's a perennial honor student and she's involved in all sort of extracurricular activities. I've spoken with a number of teachers and they're all saying she's been in a foul mood for several weeks, perhaps a month."

"She's on her cycle, Mr. George," I said, feeling the need to defend my daughter.

"No offense, Mrs. Perry, but that doesn't explain her shift in mood nor does it explain her attitude toward other students and her teachers. I'm being told by a variety of sources I trust that she's been picking fights with other students, but no one would fight her because of what she did to those two girls four years ago."

While he was busy trying not to offend me, my mind had gone back to last night when I was in her room talking to her. I was hoping none of the teachers had the name Savannah had mentioned. With reservation, I said, "Was one of the teachers, Ms. Tobias?"

"Yes, as a matter of fact. Why?

I said, "Savannah recently quit the tennis team, do you think that has anything to do with it?"

"I don't know, Mrs. Perry."

"Well what is Ms. Tobias saying?"

"Right now she's not saying anything. She's unconscious. Savannah did a real number on her. The paramedics took her to the hospital in that state. They put one of those neck braces around her neck. I think she has a concussion. From the way I hear it, Ms. Tobias is lucky to be alive after the pummeling she took. Several teachers were hurt while they were trying to stop the thrashing Savannah was giving her. She struck several of them in the process. Witnesses say it was like she was possessed, throwing people around like they were pillows, kicking others so hard they left their feet and slammed into lockers. It's a real mess here. It'll be awhile before this passes, I'm sure."

"What's Savannah saying?"

"Nothing at all."

"Put her on the phone."

"She's visiting with our resident child psychologist, Dr. Bianca Dewitt. She's also Savannah's academic advisor so she's familiar with her. I'm confident we can get down to the bottom of this mess."

I raised my voice almost to the point of screaming when I said, "I never gave you permission to have my daughter psychoanalyzed, Mr. George."

"I spoke with your husband, Keyth before I called you. His name is listed for contact. He gave me permission to let Dr. Dewitt counsel her. Then he told me to call you and tell you what I told him. Naturally, I wondered if you two were getting along these days."

"I see." I thought for a split second and said, "Is there any possibility that Ms. Tobias is at fault in this? Could she have hit Savannah first?"

"It's entirely possible, but I sincerely doubt it."

"Why is that, Mr. George? Since Ms. Tobias is unconscious, you only have one side of the story. Let's not rush to judgment on this thing."

"Let me assure you we won't rush to judgment, but just as you defend your daughter, I feel compelled to defend my teachers. Ms. Tobias is the most liked, most respected teacher in this school. All the students and faculty love her. To be fair, until recently, Savannah was equally adored here by all too. As you can imagine, this has been a real shock to the Matthew Henson family."

I said, "Then we can conclude that there is a problem between teacher and student."

"That's a fair statement, but I'm afraid I'm going to have to take action."

"Fine, you have my permission to paddle her again."

"Mrs. Perry, we're beyond a few licks on her bottom with a paddle. I'm in a real pickle here. If it were not for Savannah's previous reputation and my relationship with your husband, I would have called the police and had her arrested for assault. As of yet, I have not called the authorities."

"Thank you, Mr. George."

"I'm afraid it's not that simple, Mrs. Perry. Savannah is going to have to continue getting counseling with Dr. Dewitt."

"Is that really necessary?"

"Yes. If she blows up again, she could kill someone next time. You've trained her well. She's a very dangerous girl. We cannot have our faculty afraid of any student. And we certainly don't want any of our students to be afraid to sit in the same classroom with her. I have a responsibility to my staff, my students, and their parents."

"For how long?"

"Until we feel this issue, whatever it is, is resolved to *our* satisfaction. In the meantime, I have to suspend Savannah indefinitely."

"So you're expelling her, permanently?"

"I said *suspend*, Mrs. Perry. Again, if it were any other student, I would have expelled her immediately. You or Keyth or his parents will have to come here and get her work until this matter is resolved."

"Thank you for not expelling my daughter, Mr. George."

"You're quite welcome, Mrs. Perry. We're not in the business of derailing academic scholars. Matthew Henson is here to guide them and to make sure they stay on the road to success. Have a good day."

"You too," I said, and hit the end button.

I turned off the ignition, closed my eyes, and laid my head on the headrest. I took a deep breath and blew it out. I sat there for a few moments, thinking about what Mr. George had said. My daughter was out of control, I realized. Even if Ms. Tobias did something to start this, Savannah should have never let this happen I was thinking. Immediately, I started blaming myself. I had been a terrible mother. I hadn't spent any significant time with my daughter and now the effects of my neglect was revealing itself in her unacceptable behavior. Before I knew it, tears were sliding down my cheeks.

"What's going on, Phoenix?" Kelly said.

I sniffed and wiped the tears from my eyes. "Savannah's in trouble, Kelly. My baby's in trouble."

"Well, what happened?"

"Other than she got into a fight with Ms. Tobias, no one knows what happened or how it started. The principle wanted to expel her, but thanks to Keyth's involvement at the school, they're only suspending her for now."

"I heard," Kelly said. "Do you think it's possible that Ms. Tobias molested Savannah?"

Stunned by what I heard, I stopped crying and looked at Kelly. "No," I said. "This is on Savannah plan and simple."

"Not necessarily, Phoenix. I never told you this before, but my college tennis coach tried to turn me out. She had slept with all the girls on the team. She had told us that the only way for a woman to be truly liberated was to sleep with another woman. All I can say is that it must be liberating because all the girls on the team were having relations. When it was my turn to join the "fun", my room-mate would always talk about how men were dogs and you couldn't trust them and how they only wanted one thing and so on. What girls and the coach didn't understand was that the one thing they wanted, I was more than willing to give. Anyway, the next thing I know, this bitch is crawling into my bed at lights out, tugging at my panties, trying to finger me. And when I refused to do what she wanted, she told the team I wasn't going along. The next thing I know, no one would talk to me. And since we all had classes together, ate together, and traveled together, I was all alone."

"And you didn't tell anybody?"

"It would have been their word against mine. Besides, no one wanted to hear that from a freshman who had joined a team that had won the National Championship three years in row before I joined the team. I would have been seen as a troublemaker. It went on like that for four years and the coach is still coaching there now."

"Why didn't you quit?"

"I was on scholarship. My parents were broke. That's how they get you. Most of the girls came from underprivileged areas. Some of the girls had come from better circumstances, but the pressure to conform was off the hook! Once I made it through that first year, I knew I could make it through four. I learned to adapt. Each year, when we got a couple new recruits, I told them what was going on, but the pressure was so strong, most of them went along to get along. Out of the nine girls or so that came in during my four years, every last one of them was straight before they came there."

"How do you know they were straight when they came there?"

"They all had boyfriends they were having sex with when they got there.

"Uh-huh."

"One of the girls found out she was pregnant a couple months after the first semester started. All the freshmen talked about guys they'd seen when they visited the campus. Within a month or two, they were breaking up with their boyfriends and no longer talking about men the way they once did. All of the sudden men were subhuman or something. What bothered me was that because I was on the team, the men thought I was a lesbian too. I had to get aggressive to get a date. I knew some of them wanted to date me because they told me that one night with them would straighten me back out. I let them think I was a lesbian.

"After awhile, I'd use it when a good-looking guy was interested but ignored me because I was on the tennis team. I'd tell him that sex with another woman was the greatest thing ever, knowing it would trigger something in his ego. Eventually he'd say something like, 'I bet I could straighten you out.' I'd play hard for a few days and then acted like I was curious which made him pursue me. And if I liked him enough, I let him think he straightened me out."

"I'm sorry that happened to you Kelly, but I don't think that's what's going on here. Something's bothering Savannah and I have to find out what it is."

"Well, let me talk to her and see. I'll know if it is."

"No, Kelly."

"But—"

"I said, no and that's final. Her father and I will handle this by ourselves."

Chapter 28

Robert Tarantino was sitting on the glass terrace of his forty-five hundred square feet Arlington penthouse, finishing his meal with his girlfriend, Raquel Mendes, and their two daughters, Sofia and Tatiana. The lavish dwelling offered five bedrooms, five and a half baths and a host of goodies at a cost of just under three million dollars. Nearly every morning, they had their meals on the terrace where they could see the Potomac River and scenic views of Alexandria, Washington, and Arlington. But today was special. It was Sofia's tenth birthday. They were all wearing tall homemade paper party hats. Tarantino had told Raquel he wanted blackened tuna steaks with mango salsa for dinner, but she quickly reminded him that it wasn't his birthday and that Sofia wanted cheeseburgers and fries.

Raquel met Tarantino when he was staying at a hotel in Fortaleza, Brazil. She was seventeen. He was relaxing by the pool, sipping a steady supply of margaritas, when he saw her trimming bushes with her father. Her beauty arrested him immediately; his mouth fell open, his throat dried. Had she entered the Ms. Brazil contest, she could have easily taken first place. Everywhere she went, his eyes followed her. Even though he was already married, he struck up a conversation with Paulo, her father, a poor Portuguese landscaper. Shortly after the conversation began, Paulo explained that he was in such desperate need for money that he was willing to sell one of his kidneys to the wealthy tycoon who owned the hotel Tarantino was staying in.

The tycoon owned five star hotels along the eastern Brazilian seaboard from Rio de Janeiro to as far north as Fortaleza, yet he was only willing to pay two thousand American dollars for his kidney. His initial offer was a thousand. Even though it was hardly a fair trade for a vital organ, Paulo needed the money to payoff his debts or he would lose his business. Besides, he couldn't afford to lose the hotel as a client. He had to either sell Raquel or sell his kidney. He didn't want to part with either. Two thousand American dollars would not only get him out of debt, but there would be plenty left for a rainy day.

Paulo wanted American dollars because they were more valuable than the Real. Two thousand American dollars was equal to $3,525.00 Brazilian Reals. That sum amounted to more than ten times as much as Paulo made in a single year, which was why the tycoon thought he'd take it. But when he realized that Tarantino was taken with his daughter, he told him she was a virgin and that he would sell her for the right price. He told Tarantino that he had six other daughters, but he had only one business. Tarantino realized that Paulo was getting a raw deal, even at Brazilian prices. He offered him ten thousand American dollars for his Portuguese daughter.

Paulo was so grateful that he told Tarantino if he really had that much cash, he could have Raquel immediately if he promised to treat her well and let her return to Brazil at least once a year to see her family. That's when Tarantino realized that Paulo loved his daughter tremendously and that he too was taking advantage of a poor man who had his back against the wall. He immediately raised the price from ten thousand to twenty thousand.

Tarantino gave her father his suite number and told him he would give him the money as soon as he brought her there. Less than an hour later, Raquel's father had delivered her to the suite. When he looked upon her beauty, he knew even twenty thousand wasn't enough. Instead, he gave her father one hundred thousand, which meant he would have to have more money wired in to complete the drug deal he was there for. He then promised her father that if she wasn't pure, he would find and kill him and his other six daughters. He plundered Raquel that very hour and authenticated her virginity.

Unlike her children who were American citizens, being born in the United States, Raquel was an illegal alien and could be deported if immigration ever learned of her whereabouts. Tarantino was free to marry her because he had divorced his American wife twelve years earlier. He knew that if he married Raquel, he would lose a certain amount of power because in the event of a divorce, he had a lot to lose. While he loved her more than he loved himself, he had already taken a bath on the first divorce settlement. His first wife knew about his underworld dealings and told him she and their two daughters needed to be well taken care of if he expected her to sign a divorce agreement and be quiet about his criminal activities. He would have put a hole or two in her head for demanding outlandish alimony payments, but she was the mother of his beautiful daughters, Sheba and Nefertiti.

As far as Raquel knew, he was still married, but she didn't complain because she was very happy with him. She didn't know anything about the underworld part of his life. Tarantino had skillfully hidden it from her. She thought he was a real estate developer, which he was, but that was such a small portion of his business—the legitimate portion. She had everything she would ever need. Her children were happy too and well educated. They had the very best that life had to offer, unlike her when she was a child. While she loved Robert and would be always grateful to him for taking her away from a lifetime of hardship, she made sure her daughters would never be on an auction block, by demanding he establish seven figure trust funds for them just in case she got old and her beauty faded and he no longer wanted a woman he had no legal obligation to.

Tarantino looked into the faces of Raquel, Sofia, and Tatiana when his cell rang. They were staring at him, waiting for him to turn it off because he had promised them he wouldn't do any business that day. They knew he was busy, but for one day, they wanted all of his time. It was supposed to be Sofia's day, all day. Except for going to get the birthday cake, which was when he killed Portia, he had kept his word until his cell rang. He had spent the night with them and had made them breakfast. He wanted to keep his word, but in his line of work, self-preservation took precedence over birthdays. Birthday parties were only viable as long as he wasn't in jail. Reilly Vanderpool had been talking to the FBI about his business associate. She and her friends had to be dealt with immediately.

He looked at the ID. The call was coming from the men who had been holding Portia. He looked at the love of his life and the little girls she had given him. In Portuguese, he said, "Eu só alguns minutos, prometo. A few minutes. That's all."

"Não fique muito tempo, Roberto," Raquel said. Then she looked at Sofia and said, "Time, Daddy com o seu relógio novo."

"I'm timing you with my new watch, Daddy," Sofia said, repeating her mother's wishes in English.

"Just a few minutes, Sofia," Tarantino said. He kissed her fore-head. "I wouldn't miss your tenth birthday for the world."

He slid the glass door to the left, stepped into the family room, slid the door until he heard it click, and then went into the kitchen so he could keep an eye on his family while he conducted business.

"Is it done?" Tarantino asked in a commanding tone.

"Yeah."

"Good." He closed the phone and took out Portia's cell and called Myles Barrington. "We've released Portia. She's waiting for you to pick her up about a block from your home. He hit the end button. Then he removed the battery and the SIM card. He walked into the kitchen and dropped the SIM card down the garbage dispos-al. He turned it on and listened to it grind for a few seconds. Then he returned to the terrace and cut his daughter a slice of her Lemon Crunch cake. Later that night, after he tucked his daughters in for the night, he was planning to toss Portia's phone into the Potomac River.

Chapter 29

We got out of my car and started making our way up the long path to the gray Gothic building that for some strange reason reminded me of Castle Dracula. All we needed was darkness, a little bit of rain, thunder, lightning and we'd have the makings of a Boris Karloff film. Even though the blaring heat of the sun was beating us into submission, I was glad we were going there during daylight hours. I couldn't imagine having to visit Saint Joseph's at night. I wondered what kind of dreams the children were having when the lights were turned off.

In some ways though, the orphanage reminded me of a small college campus. There was lots of grass, trees galore, and lots of open space for the orphans to roam. Children were everywhere we looked. They looked happy as they ran around playing tag, swinging, using the sliding board, or climbing the monkey bars. Next I saw a few nuns. They were still wearing the habit, the black uniform with the white shawl collar that reminded me of penguins when I was a little girl. I thought I'd read somewhere that the nuns stopped wearing those. I guess I was wrong or perhaps these nuns still wore them and others didn't.

I saw a man who was also wearing the traditional priest robe. I assumed he was in charge since the men still dominated the Catholic Church. Mainly though, I assumed he was in charge because every time I saw a movie, and the Catholic Church was depicted, the men were in charge. *The Thorn Birds* specifically came to mind. To my knowledge, all the Cardinals were men and so were the Bishops. I'm not sure about the priests. Perhaps the church had progressed enough to let a woman run the show at the local level.

My anger flared the instant I saw the man of God. I figured he was the guilty party. He was the one who had done such evil to Portia Barrington. Never mind that Portia lived at Saint Joseph's eight years ago and this particular priest may not have even been here at the time. The funny thing about my rush to judgment was that, as a black woman, if a white person did to me what I just did to a priest I had never laid eyes on before I'd be ready to kick some ass—seriously. How jacked up is that?

When he saw us, he started walking in our direction. "Hello, I'm Father Grissom." His soft soothing voice reminded me of Ying Ming Lo, my kung fu master. Master Lo was always in control, always calm, serene even whenever I saw him. "Welcome to Saint Joseph's Orphanage," he continued. "What can I do for you?"

We flipped open our credentials. I said, "Federal agents. I'm Phoenix Perry and this is my partner, Kelly McPherson. I'm wondering if we could speak to you about an adoption that took place about seven years ago."

Father Grissom smiled before saying, "I see. I'm not the person you want to talk to. You want to speak with Dr. Molly Lester. Come with me. I'll show you the way."

Father Grissom looked like he was in his late fifties or early sixties. He was clean-shaven. His full head of hair was graying near the temples. I supposed I had expected Richard Chamberlain of *The Thorn Birds*. I think deep down, I only think of Richard Chamberlain when I think of priests, much like I only think of Louis Gossett Jr., when I think of drill sergeants. We walked with the priest and entered through an arched doorway. I saw Jesus and his disciples having the last supper at the peak of the arch on colorful stained glass as we entered "Castle Dracula".

"May I ask why you're here?" Father Grissom said. He was looking at me, I suppose, because I had made the introduction.

The priest didn't know it, but he had opened himself up for a quick examination. I wanted to see how he would respond. So I said, "Portia Barrington." I left the words hanging in the air while I searched his eyes, expecting to see a measure of guilt careening through his perverted brain. But I saw nothing. No guilt. No shame. No nothing. Not even bewilderment. His eyes offered me cool nonchalance.

"Portia Barrington?" He repeated.

"Yes," I said.

I foolishly hoped that upon hearing her name, he would fill in the gaps. I hoped he would breakdown upon hearing her name and confess all, but instead, he said, "Is she in trouble, Agent Perry?"

"Yes. She's been kidnapped."

I watched him closely. Again, not the response I had hoped for.

"I see. Can I assume she used to be a resident here?"

"Yes. She was adopted seven years ago."

"I see. Well . . . I'm sure Dr. Lester will be able to answer all your questions. She's now the head of our adoption department. It's a one woman operation for the most part."

Kelly said, "What did she do before?"

"Excuse me?" Father Grissom said.

"You said she's *now* the head of the adoption department. I'm asking what she did before she was the head of adoptions."

"Oh. Dr. Lester used to be one of our residents," Father Grissom said. "She was the protégé of the Mother Superior, who is no longer with us. Dr. Lester went on to Harvard and earned her doctorate. We had hoped she would join the sisterhood, but she fell in love with one of her professors and married him. They have three lovely daughters together. She's such a precious woman. Our own Mother Theresa. While she can be difficult sometimes, we're lucky to have her." He laughed a little and continued. "The children call her Dr. Lector of Hannibal fame. She's a bit of a stickler for the rules, but I'm certain you'll find her as pleasant as I do."

We stopped at a stained wood framed door at the end of a long hallway. I looked through the glass and saw a woman I presumed was Dr. Lester. She was on the phone. What struck me was the scowl that covered her face. I was intimately familiar with it. Indeed all married women are familiar with it. It was the kind of scowl that married women exhibit when their husbands have behaved foolishly or had forgotten an important date, such as a birthday, an anniversary, to pick up the children from school, or just about anything that pisses us off. I continued to observe Dr. Lester as she talked. She was unaware of our presence and Father Grissom obviously had been sufficiently trained not to enter her lair while she was on the phone.

As the conversation seemed to get more involved and she seemed to get even angrier, more animated, Father Grissom lightly tapped on the door to get her attention. She looked through the door's glass and saw us. She must have told her husband she had to go. I figured she'd continue ripping him a new one when we left. "Come in," Dr. Lester called out.

Father Grissom opened the door. "I'm so sorry to interrupt you, but you have a couple of visitors. They're police officers."

"Federal agents," I corrected. I extended my hand, "Phoenix Perry. This is Kelly McPherson, my partner."

He looked at me and said, "You're quite right. I stand corrected. Do forgive me." He then looked at Dr. Lester. "They're concerned about the kidnapping of a former resident seven years removed— Portia Barrington. I told them you could answer their questions. I hope you don't mind the intrusion, but I'm sure they won't be long. Routine questions and all of that, I suppose, right, Agent Perry?"

"Right."

"Well . . . I shall leave you all alone," Father Grissom said. "I have other duties to attend to."

Dr. Lester waited for the door to close before saying, "What can I do for you?"

I looked at Kelly, signaling her to begin the interview. I would observe while I walked around her office, looking at her awards, citations, and photographs.

"May I sit down," I heard Kelly say as I took in Dr. Lester's office.

"I'm sorry," I heard her say. "Please . . . have a seat. You too, Agent Perry."

"I'm fine, Doctor," I said. "If you don't mind, I'd like to look at your pictures and accomplishments. My daughter has lots of awards and ribbons. She's very active in her school. And incidentally, so did Portia Barrington. She had lots of awards too—more in fact."

"And what school is that?"

"Matthew Henson Academy," I said without looking at her. I sensed that she was watching my every move as if she were a security guard in a department store.

"Yes, I've heard of Matthew Henson. Great school."

"Now," I heard Kelly interrupt. "We're here about Portia Barrington."

"Portia Barrington?" Dr. Lester repeated. "I remember her well. She was an excellent student. We all loved her here. Do you have any leads as to who may have abducted her?"

"Yes. That's why we're here. I'm wondering if you can shed some light on a few things."

"Sure, if I can."

"What kind of person was Portia?"

"As I said, she was very bright and well liked by all. She enjoyed horseback riding, swimming, and other athletic endeavors. I'm having a terrible time imagining something like this happening to her or any of our residents, former or present."

"And how long was she here before she was adopted by the Barringtons?"

"I'd say about six months or so?"

"And did anything unusual happen to her while she was in your charge?"

"Anything like what?"

"Anything like molestation," I said recklessly.

I wanted to get her reaction. There's no such thing as the perfect crime. People always slip up. And usually, somebody knew something or saw something. I was betting that one or more of the sisters knew something. If Portia was molested here, other kids were molested too."

I could tell Dr. Lester was insulted when she said, "Agent Perry, let me fill you in on what we do here at Saint Joseph's. First, our sisters still wear the habit because we still believe in the old ways as they have stood the test of time. Second, we take in the children of unwed mothers and occasionally, we take in older children, such as Portia, because they were orphaned. We give our girls plenty of love in addition to a top-notch education to ensure they are competent to compete in a world that's lost its way."

"It's the plenty of love thing that we're here about, Doctor," Kelly said as only she could. I turned around just in time to see Dr. Lester's mouth fall open. I turned back around so she wouldn't see me laughing. Kelly continued, "Now . . . as for Father Grissom, is it possible that he touched Portia in inappropriate ways?"

At that precise moment, I saw a curious thing. Sitting on the fireplace mantel was a white bust of a Roman Emperor. The golden name plate beneath the head read: Caligula. I was blown away. I spun around quickly to address this as the Emperor was known for his decadence which helped in no small way signal the end of the Roman Empire. What was it doing in an orphanage run by nuns?

As if she was reading my mind, Dr. Lester said, "I see you've found the Emperor."

She said it like it was no big deal. I found that incredibly strange too. I would think that she wouldn't have a bust like that in religious surroundings. I was about to say something when she said, "Agent Perry, I keep the bust of Caligula on the mantel to remind me of why I'm here at Saint Joseph's. We are charged with the daunting task of training girls to not only become outstanding American citizens, we are instructing, by way of example, on the virtues of womanhood. It is our hope that when the girls leave Saint Joseph's, whether adopted or not, that they will have been instructed well enough so that they would become excellent mothers. In short, we're trying to break cycles here, not start them, Agent Perry." Having silenced me to her satisfaction, she looked at Kelly. "As to your question concerning Father Grissom, he has been an exemplary example for all of us."

"That's all well and good, but something happened to Portia Barrington and turned her into a scheming blackmail artist, and a teenage madam," I retorted, making my way over to her desk. I guess I wanted her to see the white of my eyes while I got my verbal gun off. "From what you say, perhaps you ought to reexamine your teaching methods. I gotta believe that whatever happened to Portia started right here in these hallowed halls—this righteous institution. It happened right under your watchful eyes. Now . . . is it possible that the good father did something inappropriate to Portia?"

Angry now, Dr. Lester said, "A father molested Portia! But it wasn't Father Grissom!"

"Which one of them did it?" I huffed like I was a living breathing dragon. "Just give us his name and we'll pick him up. If you're worried about repercussions, we'll keep your name out of it."

"It's too late, Agent Perry. He's dead already."

"How long ago did this happen?" I asked.

"It happened about seven years ago, prior to Portia coming here. The man who molested her was her own father."

Prior to leaving her office, Dr. Molly Lester blew us away with an incredible story of incest and murder that she had gotten from Portia with the aid of hypnosis.

Marine Corps Base Quantico
Base Housing Area
2900 Fuller Road
Quantico, Virginia

Portia was only eight years old when her father, a Gunnery Sergeant who trained officer candidates for the Marine Corps, entered her room while she was in the deepest sleep, having the sweetest dream of being in Disneyland, meeting Mickey and Minnie Mouse for the very first time. While she skipped along hand in hand with Mr. and Mrs. Mouse, her world of dreams disappeared and was replaced by a reality so frightening that she never ever dreamed of Disneyland or Mickey and Minnie Mouse again. She heard someone enter her bedroom. She opened her eyes and seeing her father, smiled, stretched forth her arms beckoning him to embrace her.

And he did.

After a rigorous day of training the recruits, he and his army buddies, all of them Sergeants, all of them drill instructors, stopped by their regular watering hole that doubled as a strip joint to throw back a few shots of Jack Daniel's and a few ice cold bottles of Coors. Still in uniform, they laughed heartily and talked about the failings of their officer candidates and how they were going to ream them the next morning. They watched the scantily clad women on stage take it all off and flaunt their God-given sex toys. They let their imaginations run wild as they put brand new crisp one dollar bills in their G-strings and attempted to steal a free feel. By the time he left the joint, he had a nice buzz and sex on the brain. He couldn't wait to get home to satisfy his need to get seriously laid.

"Did you bring me any candy, Daddy?" his little girl asked.

"I sure did," the Gunnery Sergeant said. "I brought you your favorite kind."

"Tootsie roll pops?" She questioned excitedly.

Her father handed her two suckers. One was grape flavored. The other was strawberry. He smiled and said, "You're the smartest little girl in the world kiddo."

"Can I have one now, Daddy?" she said, completely ignoring her father's compliment.

"You mean, may I have one now," he said correcting her.

"May I have one now, Daddy?" she said smiling. "Pleeeease!"

Although he knew he shouldn't let her have one, Portia had his heart. He couldn't refuse her. "Only if you promise not to tell Mommy," he said. "Only if you promise to keep our secret."

"I promise, Daddy."

"That's my little girl," her father said.

He watched her pulled back the purple paper protecting the grape lollipop and hungrily slid it in her mouth. As he listened to her lick the sucker, he stiffened. Imagining what he would have her do next, he touched his engorged tool. Then he took off all of his clothes, got in bed with her, and listened to her slurp the lollipop while he handled himself.

A few minutes later, Portia said, "No, Daddy, no!"

That terrible, unforgettable night was the beginning of a new, but tragic life that would shape the matrix of Portia's mind and establish a future she would have never foreseen. The drunken Gunnery Sergeant's touch awakened her to a secret life they would share nearly every night for six years; a life they both basked in behind her mother's back. When her father first visited her room and snatched away her virginity long before she had a chance to recognize its value, even then she hated him for ripping into her private flesh. The following morning she told her mother, who saw herself as the paragon of Orthodox Catholicism. She waited until she heard the front door open and close before she left her bedroom and went to the kitchen where her mother was washing dishes.

"Mommy?"

"Yes sweetie," her mother said without turning around. "You must be hungry, huh?"

"Daddy hurt me last night."

"Daddy hurt you?" her mother asked, still washing dishes. "Daddy wouldn't hurt you, honey. Daddy loves his little girl."

"But Mommy, he did hurt me," Portia insisted. "He hurt me down there where you said I wasn't supposed to let anybody touch me."

Instead of believing her innocent daughter, instead of checking her bed for blood stains, instead of checking her panties for the same, her mother spun around and in the same motion slapped Portia so hard she fell on her backside. She yelled, "You have a lying demon!"

Portia wailed silently for a few moments as blood streamed out of both nostrils before the sound of the pain she felt worked its way up from the pit of her stomach and out of her open mouth.

"Get up!" her mother screamed, snatching her to her feet.

Although Portia tried to persuade her mother through unrelenting tears that she was telling the truth, her mother rejected what she knew was reality because she herself, had been raped by her father. Unfortunately, when Portia's mother told her own mother what her father had done, her father was jailed and she never saw him again. As a result, they lost their home in the suburbs, and had to move from apartment to apartment because a woman alone couldn't afford to take care of six children on a waitress's salary. Eventually, Portia's grandmother, who she never met, ended up in an insane asylum until the day of her death. Portia's mother vowed she'd never allow that to happen to her family. So when Portia told her mother what happened the previous night, denial became the order of the day. It was so much easier than doing what was right, which could quite possibly cause history to repeat itself.

"Daddy never touched you there," her mother screamed. "Say it."

If it were possible, Portia cried even harder, unable to believe her mother's reaction to the truth she told. "But he did, Mommy! He did!"

She slapped her again and she fell on her bottom again. "Daddy never touched you there! Say it!"

Trying to breathe and crying at the same time, Portia choked out, "Daddy never touched me."

"Again."

"Daddy never touched me."

"Keep repeating it until I tell you to stop."

When her father came into her room that night and ripped into her private flesh again, not only did Portia hate him, she hated her mother for not believing her and thus allowing the hellish abuse to continue. A few years later, puberty delivered a body that Portia's mother envied. She had helium balloons on her chest, a twenty-three inch waist, and a thick rear end that needed no artificial padding. Grown men couldn't take their eyes off of her. Sexual bondage and rehearsed denials caused the relationship with her mother to disintegrate more and more with each passing day until finally, they began to disagree and then argue loudly about everything, no matter how small the issue. They even disagreed on what time the digital stove clock read. Bitterness controlled them to the point where they hated each other.

Although Portia didn't know precisely when, a strange thing happened when her father came to her room for one of his nightly "visits". Not only did she enjoy the debauchery, but she now saw absolutely nothing wrong with it. Nothing father and daughter did together was forbidden. And they did everything their wicked hearts imagined. As a matter of fact, she took special pleasure in knowing she had supplanted her mother and there was nothing she could do about it. She hated her mother so much that one night after a particular pleasurable session, she persuaded her father to slap her mother, his *wife*, around to keep her in line.

The following morning Portia hugged her mother and tearfully told her that she loved her. It had been a while since she had said those magical words. Her mother melted immediately and embraced Portia, holding her tight, apologizing as her own tears flowed. But it was all a charade. Portia couldn't wait for her father to come home so she could see the fireworks. She continued the shameless farce by pretending to be contrite when she got home from school. She apologized for her behavior and they talked for the first time since the sexual abuse began.

Her father entered the premises through the backdoor. He was wearing tightly creased camouflaged fatigues, and black spit-shined boots. He glared at his wife, pretending to expect his dinner to be ready, but knowing it wouldn't be. As if he were talking to an officer's training candidate, he yelled, "What have you been doing all day? You've got one job, Sally. One! And you can't even do that right!"

His wife stood up, bubbling with joy, tried to explain why dinner wasn't ready. Before she could finish her sentence, he backhanded her and she fell backward to the floor, landing hard on her wide rump.

Seeing her plan unfold like a well orchestrated stage play, she felt herself moisten considerably as the realization that she now had more power than her mother and her father materialized. As her mother looked on, she took her father by the hand and led him up the stairs to her parents' bedroom and made it her own. Knowing that her mother knew and could hear their savage lovemaking made it all the more delectable and offered her the ultimate and the sweetest revenge. When the session was over, when the sick act of incest was completed, the Marine Corps Gunnery Sergeant and his daughter talked loudly about how they planned the kitchen episode and laughed uproariously, knowing full well she not only heard the sex they'd had, but their loud conversation as well.

Portia then threw all of her mother's belongings into the hallway.

Calling her by her first name, she yelled out, "Sally, your stuff is in the hall. You sleep in my old room from now on!"

Then she slammed the door and laughed loudly.

Chapter 30

K elly and I were in my Mustang and heading back to Fairfax. Hearing Dr. Lester parcel out the vivid details of Portia's incestuous rape was riveting and it unnerved me. In my line of work, I see lots of blood and gore. Just when I think I've heard it all, I learn of yet another tale depicting human depravity so despicable it seems surreal. In the next instant, I realized just how blessed I had been to have the kind of father I'd had. I thought about my husband and my daughter's relationship and how wonderful it was. I knew Savannah had no idea what girls her age and younger were going through. Dr. Lester explained that lots of little girls were being raped by their own fathers, grandfathers, uncles, and stepfathers. In some cases, the girls are being forced to participate in sexual activity with their own brothers. While learning what happened to Portia didn't justify her behavior, I did understand how she could make the choices she made. The little girl I'd seen yesterday morning on the rectangle flyer came to mind and I wondered what horrors she had to endure because some pervert had to fulfill his sick bent.

My cell rang. Ryan was calling again. I put my cell on speaker. "Yeah, Jack."

"It's a no go on the warrants for the penthouses. Justice says we need more than phone calls from the doorman to go in."

"Figures. Anything else?"

"Yeah, the maid was able to construct a composite of the cable woman, but I don't think it's going to do us any good. It's too generic, if you know what I mean."

"Yeah, what she described could be just about anybody."

"Exactly. I also talked to the doorman who made the calls. He said he called them as a courtesy. He says he knows nothing about Ms. Ferrari being a pro. He also claims that if a call was made to the Cayman Islands, he didn't make it. He says that whoever stole the video tape must have made the call when he was in the bathroom."

"Convenient. That means you were probably right, Jack. He was letting his boss know what was going on in his absence."

"Exactly. I had our researcher dig deeper into Jericho Wise. He's got a record. But guess what else?"

"What, Jack?"

"It's classified."

"What do you mean, it's *classified*."

"I mean whoever this guy is, he's got big-time connections. His records are sealed."

"CIA? NSA? What do you think?"

"Probably. I think we've stumbled onto a CIA front of some sort."

"C'mon, Jack. The CIA wouldn't kidnap Portia Barrington."

"Agreed. What if what's going on in the apartment building and what happened to Portia have nothing to do with each other? What if Williams was involved in whatever Jericho Wise is involved in and Mrs. Spivey happen to be there when it was time to settle with Williams. So they popped her too. We don't know where they snatched Portia. It could have been anywhere. There's no evidence to suggest that she was in the building let alone the apartment."

"What if it's exactly as it seems—a kidnapping. And Jericho Wise's records are seal for something else. I've listened to enough of Williams' tapes to know that he and Portia were involved. Her phone records verify this. If you wanna go with the two separate events angle, why not go with Mason Spivey hiring a couple guys to kill his wife and Williams while he was with the team in Utah."

"I suppose it's possible."

"Jack, how 'bout we just stick to the facts of this case. Jericho Wise . . . Mason Spivey . . . Joel Williams . . . whatever else they were and are into, they're not suspects at this point, okay?"

"Fine."

"Anything else?"

"I've tracked down the address for Raquel Mendes. I'm about to pay Ms. Mendes a visit. She's got a penthouse in DuPont Circle inside the trendy Palomar hotel."

"Fancy. Fancy," I said.

"I was thinking the same thing. Then I'm gonna head on home to the wife, have a good, home cooked meal, and get some shut eye. If I learn anything from Ms. Mendes, I'll give you a call on my way home. If not, I'll check in tomorrow. I'm beat."

"Okay, Jack. Great. I look forward to hearing what she has to say. And Jack?"

"Yeah?"

"I'd feel a whole lot better if you take someone with you. You never know."

"Will do."

I was thinking about the CIA angle that Jack mentioned. I didn't think there was anything to it, but anything's possible. Maybe something was going on in that building other than teenage prostitution and the activities of its resident courtesan, Francesca Ferrari. McAlister Sage came to mind. I had just met him a few days ago when we solved my cousin's murder. It turned out that McAlister was conducting a CIA operation on American soil. That's a huge no-no. So now he owes me big-time for my silence. If we ever needed to go that route, I'd have to call in a favor or two to resolve whatever issues we had.

When I realized that Kelly had been quiet since I hung up with Jack, I looked at her and said, "Give it up. What's on your mind?"

"I'm wondering if Sterling's brother is somehow involved. It is his building. He doesn't live in the States anymore. At this point, I have to wonder, why?"

I said, "You're thinking it's because he's avoiding having to deal with local, state, and federal law enforcement, right?"

Kelly looked at me and said, "Why would he need to avoid law enforcement on any level, Phoenix?"

"Drugs?" I said, helping her come to terms with what she believed but had denied because she was in love with Sterling.

"What else could there be? If it was something legit, wouldn't Sterling have proudly said so?"

"You would think," I said, agreeing with her, listening as the process of revelation continued.

"I mean the Kennedy's amassed their fortune selling an illegal substance. It's well known today, but at the time, Joe Kennedy could get away with it. Now his family is noted for its indefatigable commitment to public service. But, could Joe have gotten away with it now? I seriously doubted. The only way to do it and get away with it now is to mimic the South American Cartels or to get a lot of help from people in high places within the police agencies."

"Uh-huh," I said.

"Joe Kennedy couldn't flaunt his wealth today and continue doing business in the mafia underworld. We'd shut him down. But, he could do it from the Caymans and we wouldn't be all that interested in him because he wouldn't be living here like say, John Gotti. If he ran his business from the Caymans, we couldn't track his money and dog his every step. We couldn't watch all of his people and get legal wiretaps in the Caymans without the help of the locals. And the locals wouldn't be eager to help because people with illegal money fuel their economy. They're not interested in killing the goose that lays the golden eggs. If Jericho Wise is involved in the drug underworld, he picked the perfect place to live and he's near his money."

"The mafia was involved in gambling and prostitution too," I added. "If Portia and her friends were securing big money from wealthy clients, couldn't Jericho have a prostitution ring in the same building in the penthouses?"

"All the penthouses?" Kelly asked.

"Yes, all of them. Why not? I mean, obviously the doorman is in on it. What about the rest of the staff? If I were inclined to have prostitution going on in a building I owned, I would have everybody in on it so that I control all the players. The trick would be to make sure everybody kept their mouths shut. To do that, I'd have to be ruthless so that everybody knows that if they talk, they're finished—them and their families."

Silence filled the car suddenly. I looked at Kelly. She was looking at me like she was surprised that I would think like a drug dealer. I said, "Uh, well, I love *The Godfather* movies. My daughter was playing one of the themes on her violin this morning."

She rolled her eyes and said, "It would make sense to own the building and the people who work in it."

"Assuming we've figured it out, what does Jericho Wise have to do with Portia's kidnapping?"

My cell rang. It was Kortney Malone calling. I answered, "Agent, Perry."

"Portia Barrington is dead," she said.

I paused for a couple seconds, letting her death sink in a bit. Then I said, "Where'd they find her."

"They waited until they were sure we were gone and then they dumped her body at the gate. Then they called Barrington and told him he could pick his daughter up at the end of the block, if he hurried. He almost ran over her corpse on the way out the gate. They didn't tell him she was already dead. They wanted him to run her over."

I was thinking, ruthless.

"I can't tell you how unhappy everybody is with this result, Phoenix. There's blood in the water and the sharks are circling."

"I understand," I said. "Where's the body?"

"They've taken her to the Medical Examiner's office in Fairfax. The chauffeur and the woman are there too. It's on Braddock Road. Do you need directions?"

"I know where it is. We're on our way."

"Do you have anything to report?"

"Yes, but not much. We've got a bunch of bits and pieces. Nothing solid."

"Let's hear it."

I filled Kortney in on everything we had on our way over to the morgue. She was disappointed. She didn't have much to tell Palmer Davidson and Myles Barrington. I was glad I wasn't the one who had to brief them with next to no information. She said that everybody was unhappy with the results. That meant that they were thinking of getting rid of people and ending careers on the upward swing. I knew I had to find out what happened and fast. The original forty-eight hours that Palmer Davidson had given us to find the kidnappers was no longer in effect for obvious reasons, but I still felt the pressure of being blamed because we didn't bring Portia home unharmed. Instead, her father had to see her the way I now see her, dead and alone.

Although I've seen lots of dead bodies, I don't think I'll ever get used to seeing them lying on cold metal slabs, naked, with their eyes closed, strangers starring at them, examining them. Portia was indeed a beautiful girl, I thought as I looked down at her. Then I saw two gunshot wounds in her head. The bullets went in one side of her head and exited on the other. She had been shot at close range with a large caliber weapon. Her brains had been blown clean out. Someone was sending a message, I knew, but was it to Myles Barrington? Or was it to the members of the Jaguar Club?

I knew what the girls in the club were into, but what was Barrington into? If he would have undeclared money and an illegal alien working for him, he just might be into lots of other stuff. Then I thought what if Palmer Davidson has something at stake too. What if he needed the kidnappers caught or killed too? Maybe that was why they both threw the rule book out the window on this one. Maybe they couldn't afford to have something come out and I was suppose to cover it all up.

All of Portia's effects were neatly tucked away in plastic zip lock bags. There were hoop earrings, gold bracelets, iPod with earphones, makeup kit, tampons, and keys. I assumed most of the keys opened doors at the mansion, but two keys got my attention. One was a door key. The other looked like a safety deposit key. The door key looked like Joel Williams' apartment key. It had the word Schlage engraved on it just like his. I grabbed Williams' personal effects, found his apartment key and compared them. They matched perfectly.

Kelly said, "So now we know, she could have been at his apartment when they snatched her."

"Uh-huh. And this other one looks like a safety deposit key."

"Sure does," Kelly said.

"Could we be lucky enough to find something in her deposit box?" I said.

"We might if we knew where she banked."

I decided to call the Barrington mansion. I was hoping Mrs. Barrington answered the phone. Although I'm sure she loved Portia, she was only her stepmother and they'd had some personal conflicts. I guess I would rather talk to her because I just didn't want to hear the anguish in Mr. Barrington's voice and then ask him questions while he was in mourning.

Chapter 31

When we got back into my car, I picked up the manila envelope. The numbers to the Barrington mansion and their cells were written on it. I called the house. Thankfully, Mrs. Barrington answered. "Hello Mrs. Barrington," I said. "I'm sorry for your loss."

"Thank you, Agent Perry. It's a very sad time for me and my husband right now. Tell me you still have some viable leads?"

"Yes, ma'am, we do. We're still working the case. We haven't given up."

"Thank you so much. Is there anything I can do to help?"

"I was wondering if you knew whether or not Portia had a safety deposit box."

"No, she didn't."

"She didn't, huh? Well, ma'am we found what appears to be a safety deposit key. Do you have a box?"

"Yes, I have a box."

"You do, huh?" I said. "I was hoping you didn't."

"I keep important papers there. Some jewelry Myles gave me, that kind of thing."

"Okay, well can you check and see if you're still in possession of your key?"

"Give me a minute. I'll check with Myles, too."

A minute or so later, she returned.

"Yes, we both have our keys."

"You do. Okay, well, where do you bank?"

"Wachovia in Crystal City."

"Okay and does Portia bank there too?"

"Yes, she does."

"Thanks Mrs. Barrington. You've been a big help. Someone will let you know what we find."

"Any chance of hearing from you today?"

I looked at my watch. "No, we can't do it today. The bank is closed now. We'll have to go in the morning."

Chapter 32

I dropped Kelly off at the InterContinental and then I headed over to the Virginia Hospital Center in Arlington. I decided to stop by and see how Ms. Tobias was doing. I wanted to get her version of what happened with Savannah. I couldn't help thinking of the story Kelly had told me about her college tennis coach. I wanted to believe that Matthew Henson Academy didn't have child molesters in school.

Just then, I thought about Saint Joseph's orphanage and my rush to judgment concerning Father Grissom. I guess I had seen and heard so many reports of perverted priests that I misjudged him. Master Lo once said, "If you hear a thing long enough and the thing you heard is never contradicted, it becomes fact in the mind of the hearer." It's a subtle form of brainwashing, but it is very effective.

On the way over to the hospital, I thought I should listen to more of the tapes of Portia and Williams. I thought there might be something there. But when I pulled out the CDs, I found the bootlegged copy of *The Grasshopper*. I was planning to watch it after I talked to Savannah. I remembered that Portia had a rack of DVDs set aside. The rack was full of films about love triangles. I wondered what that was about. While I couldn't remember all the titles, I did remember *Titanic* and *Dangerous Liaisons*. Did Portia know about Joel and Marsha Spivey? Did she think she was in love with him? Did she see herself as Michelle Pfeiffer in *Dangerous Liaisons*? Perhaps she saw herself as Kate Winslet in *Titanic*. Did she see herself as a good girl who had done some very bad things?

As I walked up to the hospital information station, it occurred to me that I didn't know Ms. Tobias' first name. Sometimes hospitals had a rule against visiting patients if you were not a member of the family. I didn't know if Arlington Hospital Center had a rule like that or not. I wasn't about to take any chances though. I walked up to the receptionist and said, "Hi, I'm Phoenix Perry, FBI." I showed her my credentials. "I'm wondering if you can tell me which room Ms. Tobias is in?"

"First name?"

"I don't have a first name, but I know she was brought in today. She's a schoolteacher. I'm told she has a concussion if that helps."

"It does," she said, and gave me the floor and room number.

As I was approaching her room, I heard a man's voice. I listened and learned that he was her husband. I peeked in. He had three children with him—all girls. I realized then that I had really lost touch with Savannah. I didn't even know Ms. Tobias was Mrs. Mary Alice Tobias. I was about to leave when I heard her husband tell his daughters to say bye to mommy.

I went down to the family waiting room and bought a bottle of water. I opened it and drank about half of it in one swallow. The family room had CNN on. They were talking about Portia's murder. Lots of reporters were at or near the mansion gate, giving updates, talking about Joel Williams and Marsha Spivey. They were blaming Joel for Portia's death. They were saying that if he had of been doing his job instead of banging Mrs. Spivey, Portia would be alive. Of course they didn't use that kind of language but that was my interpretation. They were right, I thought. I wondered what Keyth was thinking at that moment.

I flipped open my cell and called him. "Are you watching the news?"

"I see it," he said.

"What are you going to do?"

"Well, I figure they're coming after me next. Just in case they come here, I took the kids over to my parent's house. Mom and dad won't let them see the news."

"Good thinking."

"Where are you?"

"I'm here in Arlington. I'm at the hospital."

"Why? What happened? Are you okay?"

I smiled. It felt good to hear my husband concerned about my well being. I said, "I'm here to see Ms. Tobias. Did you know she was married and has three daughters?"

"Yes."

I was hoping he didn't know. That way I wouldn't feel so bad.

"What are you planning to say to her, Phoenix?"

"I'm not sure. I just want to get her version of what happened before I talk to Savannah."

"Tread lightly," he said.

"I will. Have you spoken to Savannah about this?"

"Yes."

"What did she say?"

"Other than she was defending herself, nothing."

"That's all you could get out of her?" I asked, hoping that he handled the matter so I wouldn't have to.

"She dug in her heels and told me that she would be willing to take whatever punishment I thought was right and fair. Then she gave me my belt and told me she would wait for me upstairs in her room whenever I was ready to spank her."

"So she'd rather take an ass whipping than talk about what happened, Keyth?"

"Hey . . . that's your daughter," he said, laughing.

"So did you beat her ass," I said, hoping he had, that way I wouldn't have to do it.

"Nope."

"Why not?"

"She's too old for a man to touch her like that."

"Not even her father, Keyth?"

"Not even. She might start thinking that it's okay for her boyfriend or her husband to put his hands on her when she gets older. I don't want my daughter's mind twisted like that. So, guess what?"

"I'm gonna have to do it?"

"See . . . that's why I married you. I don't have to spell everything out for you."

"Thanks a lot, Keyth."

"You're quite welcome, Phoenix."

"Just so you know, I also got rid of the kids because I expect to get seriously laid tonight."

"Oh, really? And why should I?"

"Well, for one reason, you don't have to talk to Savannah tonight. I know how you hate being the heavy. The other reason is I know you want it just as badly as I do. I got the whip cream and everything."

I laughed. "You're so bad. I love it. See in a few."

I hit the end button, sat down and watch more of the news.

I took another swallow of my water. A smile emerged when I thought about what my husband and I were going to do when I got home. It's hard to let loose when the kids are home. We have to try to get it quietly so they can't hear us. I can't really enjoy it the way I want because I like to get my moan on. And when Keyth is talking in my ear and giving me all he has to give, I often get a little loud. I felt myself starting to moisten as I thought about it. I felt naked all of a sudden, like people could read my lust filled mind. I looked around the family waiting room to see if anybody was watch me. No one was. Relieved, I smiled, took the last swallow of my water, tossed the empty bottle in the trash, and headed back down the hall to Mrs. Tobias' room.

I knocked on the door. "Mrs. Tobias?"

She looked at me. "Yes."

"I'm Mrs. Perry, Savannah's mother. May I come in?"

"I'm very tired, Mrs. Perry. Perhaps you can come back another time."

"I understand, but I'll only stay a few minutes."

She stared at me for a few seconds and said, "Five minutes."

"Thank you," I said and walked into the room. I cringed when I saw just how battered and bruised she was. Her jaw was the size of a grapefruit, both eyes were black, and her nose was full of gauze. I think it was broken. "May I sit down?"

"Please."

I sat in the leather chair next to her bed. "As you've probably guessed, I got a call from the principal, Mr. George. He told me there was an altercation between you and my daughter. I'm wondering if you can tell me what happened. What started it?"

"I really don't remember how it started, Mrs. Perry. The doctors say I have a concussion. Memory loss was to be expected."

"I understand. Can you tell me what problems you were experiencing with her before the altercation?"

"Before the altercation?"

"Yes. Savannah told me she quit the tennis team. You're the coach, right?"

"Yes, I'm the coach."

"Why did she quit?" I asked.

"I have no idea, Mrs. Perry. She didn't even come to me with it. Another student did. Savannah was a valued member of the team, but she's been awfully moody lately. All the teachers are talking about it. Forgive me for saying, but we all thought you and Keyth . . . you and Mr. Perry were having trouble at home and it was affecting Savannah. She had been a doll until recently."

"How recently? When did you notice the change?"

"I don't know . . . maybe a month or so ago. Is everything all right at home, Mrs. Perry?"

"Yes."

"Well I'm at a loss as to why all of this has happened."

I looked at my watch. The five minutes she had given me had expired. I knew something was amiss, but deep down I didn't really want to know. She wasn't talking and neither was Savannah. And this business about memory loss wasn't true either. She could remember Savannah being moody about a month ago, but she can't remember how the altercation started earlier that day.

I said, "My husband and I are very sorry about all of this. We understand if you want to pursue legal satisfaction."

"Mrs. Perry, I'm sorry all this happened too. Savannah is a good student and she's very talented. The last thing I want to do is have her record marred by a single incident. She has a wonderful future waiting for her. All she has to do is reach out and take it. Perhaps she needs some professional help. In any event, let's move on and put all of this behind us."

"Well at least let me and my husband pay for your medical bills."

"No need. I'm one hundred percent covered. I'll be going home in the morning. I could have left with my family, but the doctors wanted to keep me for observation. My husband insisted I stay the night. You know how doctors are, I'm sure."

"Yes, I know," I said. "Well, I'm gonna go. Thanks for your time and please try to rest."

Jack Ryan entered the chic Palomar hotel. The lobby was packed with guests checking in and out. For some strange reason, there was only one desk clerk who had to service a long line of angry people. He thought about flashing his badge and telling the clerk it was a federal matter, but he didn't want to take any chances. The desk clerk might call Raquel Mendes' penthouse and alert her to his presence. He wanted to surprise her and maybe she might tell him why the doorman from Joel Williams' building called the day Portia Barrington was kidnapped. To rattle her, he was planning to implicate her in the kidnapping by making sure she understood that if Portia didn't survive the ordeal, he would arrest her for accessory to murder.

But to pull it off, he needed to know the desk clerk's name. He figured that Raquel Mendes, being a permanent resident of the hotel, knew the entire staff by name. He pushed his way through the throng of angry people to see the name of the desk clerk. His name plate read: Alvin.

The clerk was frustrated. Sweat was dripping off his forehead. He could hear the resentment in the voices of guests and the pressure had gotten to him.

Ryan walked over to the Concierge station and asked her where he might find a courtesy phone. She smiled and told him he could use hers. He returned her smile, but he said he needed a little privacy. She told him where the nearest phone was. When he found it, he called the penthouse.

"Hello," Sofia said.

"Hello. This is the UPS man," Ryan said. "What's your name, sweetie?"

"Sofia. Today is my birthday. Do you have a present for me?"

"I might. Is your mommy home?" Jack said, thinking, your birthday, huh? I can use that too.

"Mommy," Sofia called out. "The UPS man wants you."

"Hello."

"Is this Raquel Mendes?"

"Yes."

Jack thought she had the sexiest accent he had ever heard. He was so smitten by her voice that his throat went dry. Right away he began to wonder what she looked like. He assumed she was Spanish. As the memory of her accent echoed in his mind, images of two smoking hot Latina actresses came to mind —Raquel Welch and Eva Mendes. He had always been a fan of Raquel Welch ever since he was a boy. He'd had posters of her on his wall and tried to dream about her every night.

"Yes, this is Raquel Mendes. Are you still there?"

Jack composed himself, tried to clear his dry throat, and said, "United Parcel Service." His voice sounded scratchy so he cleared it again. "I have a package for Sofia Mendes."

"Can you leave it at the front desk? I'll be down to pick it up later."

"I'm afraid I can't ma'am. I need a signature. I'd be happy to bring it up, but they won't let me up unless you say so."

"I'll call the desk and tell them to let you come up."

"Forgive me for saying so ma'am, but the clerk is a guy named Alvin and he was a royal pain in the ass. The lobby is full of people and he's the only one working the desk. I doubt that he'll even answer the phone. If he does, I think the people trying to checkout to catch their flights will riot. When I asked him to call you and let you know I was down here, he told me to fuck off. I'm very busy ma'am, but I cannot leave the package without a signature."

"That doesn't sound like Alvin at all. He's usually a very pleasant young man. I'll be right down," she said.

Jack smiled and waited for her at the elevators. While he had no idea what she looked like, he was sure he'd be able to spot her immediately. Visions of Raquel Welch and Eva Mendes wearing teeny, tiny bikinis kept coming to mind. He had lots of ideas about how a rich man's woman would look. He thought she'd be beautiful, with dark shoulder length hair. Women that lived in multimillion dollar penthouses were generally well kept queens who were also well groomed, he believed. They wore the latest fashions and shoes. He imagined that Ms. Mendes' nails would be manicured and professionally painted, probably the same color as her lipstick. Her makeup, if she wore any, would be flawless and nearly undetectable. And she would smell so good that he wouldn't be able to stand it.

For all Jack knew, Raquel Mendes was a courtesan too, like Francesca Ferrari, who he hadn't met yet. To him, there were two kinds of prostitutes. They were both good-looking and stunning, usually. But the difference between the two was like night and day. One wore clothing that revealed lots of cleavage, skirts that barely covered her backside, fishnet stockings, and spiked high heeled shoes. Johns didn't want to talk to her. Johns did what they had to with her in the car, paid her, got rid of her, and then hoped to God she didn't give them an incurable disease. Johns never asked her name because they didn't give a damn what it was. Once she had served her purpose, it was time to move on.

The other is elegant, sophisticated, well read, and conversant on a variety of subjects including politics, philosophy, history, and sports. She is thoroughly magnificent—as is her price. The really expensive courtesans could speak several languages as well; whatever the clientele needed. She doesn't wear revealing clothes. Instead, she wore clothing that added to her splendor; clothes that didn't reveal much of anything. She understands that sex starts in the mind and therefore seduction starts there as well. She didn't have to lure Johns in with her sexual goodies. If a John was going to be with her, she knew him and he had to be able to afford her services.

A night with that kind of prostitute was more like going on a very expensive date, but no matter what, he was going to get lucky that night. Her job was to make sure the John enjoyed her conversation and her company, in general. They would have dinner, talk about whatever subject interested him, and then they would have sex together. And unlike the first prostitute, the second was so good at seduction, the John not only wanted to know her name, he usually wanted to marry her. Many of her clients often tell her they would gladly leave their wives for her.

Jack also considered the possibility that Raquel Mendes wasn't a courtesan. He thought that perhaps she was Jericho Wise's woman and that's why the doorman called her home. Maybe the doorman was trying to contact Jericho and she gave him the number to the hotel in the Caymans. There were a number of scenarios that played out in his mind while he waited.

He looked at the floor lights above the elevator doors. It was on the 30th floor now, but descending rapidly. He hoped it was the kind of elevator that gave penthouse guests the privilege of by passing all the other floors and took them straight to the lobby. It was.

Seconds later, the doors opened. A woman stepped out.

"Raquel Mendes?" Ryan asked. She looked just like the vision he had of her—only better—so much better.

"Yes."

He flashed his credentials. "My name is Jack Ryan and I'm a federal agent." Then he walked into the elevator. "I need to speak to you about a very important matter."

R aquel's mouth fell open and her eyes bulged when she heard the man standing in front of the elevator doors say he was some sort of government agent. She thought he was there because she was an illegal. She had heard his name, but she felt so guilty for being what she heard the newsmen on television say about her status as someone who did not rightfully belong in the United States. In an instant, she remembered what life was like back in Fortaleza, Brazil, how she had to work from sun up to sun down, how she had to share a room with all six of her sisters, and how she didn't have much privacy at all.

She remembered how it felt when she learned that her mother was pregnant again and she might even have twins or triplets. She had told God that if he would shut up her womb, she would be a perfect girl for the reminder of life. Then Robert Tarantino came along and rescued her from it all. The idea of being deported and having to go back to a life of squalor terrified her. She had been in the United States for twelve years now, in the lap of luxury, wanting for nothing, but in the back of her mind, she had always wondered when the immigration people would catch up with her.

Attempting to outwit the government man she believed was there to send her back to a life she had come to hate, she said, "But I have to pick up a package for my daughter. The UPS man is waiting for me."

"It's Sofia's birthday. I know. There is no package, ma'am. It was me. Now let's go up to your home. I need to ask you some questions."

"I've been meaning to get my Visa, Mr. Ryan. I'll make sure I get it right away, okay? No need to send me back to Fortaleza."

Jack smiled inwardly. He knew he could use that against her. The fact that she thought he was from immigration might help her cooperate. It never ceased to amaze him how often scared criminals told on themselves on the way to being booked. Guilt often does that to a person. Sometimes he didn't even have to ask a question. It was usually some hard-luck story about mom and dad, how dad used to beat mom or whatever excuse they had for breaking the law. For whatever reasons, criminals thought that if they told him the truth, he'd cut them some slack. They hoped he would feel sorry for them and let them go.

As the elevator ascended, Jack noticed that Raquel was trembling. He thought she was so scared that she might even offer him a freebee. And he might even accept, if he didn't love his wife so much. Nevertheless, he couldn't ignore her beauty, her spectacular curves, those luscious lips, those beautiful light brown innocent eyes that were looking into his, begging him for clemency. He smelled her perfume and inhaled deeply, like it would be his very last time. She smelled more wonderful than he could have ever imagined. And she was more beautiful then Raquel Welch and Eva Mendes. He stiffened, even though he didn't mean to. His body wanted to forge ahead and take whatever pleasure she was about to offer him, but his mind thought of his wife and Portia Barrington.

"Are you Spanish?" Ryan asked.

"Portuguese."

"Well, I gotta tell you, you are absolutely beautiful."

Raquel didn't smile and she didn't thank him for the compliment. "Does that mean you're not going to send me back to Fortaleza?"

"No, ma'am. You still might have to leave. Depends on what you tell me."

The elevator doors opened. They walked to her penthouse. She was about to open the door, but instead she turned to him and said, "My two daughters are American. They were born here. You can't send them back to Fortaleza. You can send me back, but they can stay, right?" Her eyes were pleading.

"Like I said, it depends on what you tell me, Ms. Mendes."

Raquel frowned. She was wondering what he meant by that. "Is it possible that you have made a mistake? Perhaps you have confused me with someone else."

"Open the door, Ms. Mendes. Let's talk inside."

"Promise me you won't send my children back to Brazil. Promise me that you'll only send me back."

He locked eyes with her for a few seconds and then said, "You tell me what I want to know and you can all stay here, but I suggest you get that Visa as soon as possible. Now . . . open the door and let's go inside."

R obert Tarantino was playing backgammon with Tatiana and chess with Sofia on the terrace. He was deliberately losing both games. He loved putting a smile on his daughters' faces. He loved them so much, almost as much as their mother, but not quite. They were finishing their slices of homemade lemon cake with delicious lemon icing, topped with golden vanilla ice cream. Sofia was about to make a move that would leave her queen and king vulnerable to his knight.

"You don't wanna make that move, sweetie," he said.

"Why not, Daddy?"

"Because if you do, I'll have to take your queen, birthday girl. You don't want Daddy to take your queen, do you?"

Sofia studied the board for a couple minutes, trying to figure out what her father was talking about. She didn't see it yet.

"I'll tell you what honey, keep looking while I get us another slice of cake."

Tatiana said, "Mommy said we can only have one slice, Daddy."

"I know, Tatiana, but I don't think mommy meant that you can only have one slice on a birthday, do you?"

"No."

"So who wants more cake?"

Both his beautiful daughters sang, "Meeeeeeeee!"

"Okay. Daddy'll be right back. Don't cheat, okay?"

"We won't," they said.

Tarantino slid the glass door to the left and walked into the kitchen. He picked up a butter knife and lifted the glass bubble that covered the cake and sliced three wedges. Then he opened the freezer and took out the ice cream, put some on top of the cake, and put the rest away. He was about to take Sofia and Tatiana their desert when he thought he heard voices from somewhere inside his home. He listened closer. Someone was talking. It was Raquel and a man. It sounded like they were in the library. At first he thought it was the UPS man and that whatever she had purchased for Sofia was too big for her to carry. But, as he got closer to the library, he could hear their conversation. There was a cop in his home, his palace, his sanctuary, asking Raquel questions about the doorman calling the house the day of the kidnapping. He slipped back down the hall and took the cake and ice cream out to his daughters.

"Put your iPods on for a few minutes. Daddy'll be right back. But no matter what, don't come into the house. Mommy has another surprise for you Sofia, but if either of you take off your iPods or come into the house, I won't give it to you and you won't be able to have any more cake and ice cream. Understand?"

"Yes, Daddy."

"Just watch the ducks in the river and listen to music for a few minutes, okay? Will you do that for Daddy?"

"We will," they said in unison.

As quietly as he could, Tarantino slipped back into the kitchen and through the foyer and to the den, where he kept a nine millimeter and a sound suppressor. He pulled out a set of keys. He kept the den locked. He wouldn't be able to live with himself if either Sofia or Tatiana found the weapon and killed themselves. Or worse, if one sister killed the other and had to live with the knowledge of that. He took the case off the shelf and opened it. The sound suppressor was already attached to the muzzle. Then he quietly crept over to the library and listened at the double doors.

"Ms. Mendes," Ryan was saying, "We have phone records proving that the doorman called and spoke with you."

"I've told you, Mr. Ryan, I don't know what you're talking about," Raquel said. "I don't want to go back to Brazil."

"Do you live alone?" Ryan asked. "Who pays for this place? Do you have a husband or a boyfriend? Is his name Jericho Wise?"

"No, she doesn't live alone," Tarantino said. "And yes, she does have a boyfriend. It isn't Jericho. I work for him. Now who are you and what do you want?"

"Take it easy, Pal," Ryan said after turning to the man who had spoken. When he saw that he was holding a weapon with a sound suppressor, he knew he was in trouble. "I'm a federal agent. I'm going for my ID, okay, Pal?"

"Don't bother, Agent Ryan. I believe you." He looked at Raquel. "Come to me, my love."

Raquel was so happy that Tarantino had rescued her, she ran to him, but in the process of running to the man who had rescued her from a harsh life in Fortaleza, she stepped into his line of fire which gave Ryan, who thought he was about to be killed, an opportunity to go for his weapon.

Tarantino stepped to the side and fired three times. All three bullets found their way into Ryan's chest. But Ryan got off one shot before Tarantino's bullets hit him and took him down. He dropped his gun and it slid a few feet from him, but the bullet he fired slammed into Raquel's back and burrowed into her heart.

The force of the bullet carried her into Tarantino's arms. He held her up. She looked into Tarantino's eyes and said, "Robert?"

"Yes," Tarantino said, desperately. He knew she was about to die and there was nothing he could do about it. "I'm here. I'm here."

"I don't think I ever thanked you for bringing me here," Raquel said. "Promise me you'll never forget me."

"I won't, my love," Tarantino said. "I swear I'll never forget you."

Then her eyes vacated the premises while Tarantino looked into them. With tears dripping off his chin, he walked over to Jack Ryan. His shirt was soaked with blood. He was desperately trying to reach his gun, but he couldn't reach it in time.

As Ryan looked into the eyes of his killer, he remembered what Phoenix Perry had said. He could actually hear her words ringing in his ears: "Take someone with you. You never know."

"You killed the woman of my dreams," Tarantino said. Tears were free falling. "You're done too."

He pointed the gun at Ryan's forehead.

Ryan closed his eyes, accepting his fate.

Hiss! Hiss! Hiss! Hiss! Hiss! Hiss! Hiss! Hiss! Hiss!

When Tarantino turned around, he saw his daughters standing there. They had seen it all.

Chapter 33

On my way home, I thought about what Kelly had said about her college tennis coach coming on to her. I was wondering if she could be right about Mrs. Tobias. But it didn't make any sense that a married woman with three daughters of her own would molest my daughter. So I rejected it. If it had been a man, I would be all over the situation, as men are well known for doing that kind of thing with little girls. But a woman? A married woman? A married woman with children? No way.

I had jumped to conclusions about the priest and I didn't want to blame Mrs. Tobias for the altercation between her and Savannah. I started telling myself that it was just a misunderstanding. That way I didn't have to make a bunch of further inquiries that might lead to a truth I wasn't ready to deal with yet. I found much comfort in the fact that if Mrs. Tobias had tried to molest Savannah, she wouldn't dare try it again, considering the wounds and bruises she sustained after the first attempt. And with that, I left the thing alone.

It was dark by the time I got home and I was horny as hell. I had thought about the whip cream all the way home and I was more than ready for my husband to deliver on his promises. I walked into the bedroom. Keyth was lying across the bed watching ESPN. I saw the whip cream on the nightstand. I laughed. "You ready for what I'm about to put on you?" That's when I heard Keyth snoring. I was about to wake his ass up. He had business he needed to handle. He had gotten me ready and I expected to get seriously doused, whip cream and all. Then I thought, "That's okay". I'll let him sleep for now. When he wakes up, I'll get him then.

I went into my office and turned on my desktop. I thought now would be a good time to watch *The Grasshopper*. I laughed a little when the television series, *Kung Fu*, came to mind. David Carradine's character was called grasshopper by his blind master. I must have seen the reruns a million times when I was in Beijing. I absolutely loved that show. I read somewhere that Bruce Lee had came up with the project, but Warner Brothers was afraid that an American audience wouldn't accept a Chinese actor in the lead role. If that story's true, Warner Brothers must have realized what a big mistake they made and got in on the greatest martial arts picture ever made, *Enter the Dragon*, starring none other than the man they didn't think would be accepted in the first place, Bruce Lee.

I went to the Google website and put in *The Grasshopper*. I wanted to see what the movie was about so that I'd have some idea of what Portia Barrington may have been thinking and why she put it in the stack with her love triangle pictures. Google offered over a hundred and ten thousand references on the title. The second one was the Turner Classic Movies site. They were selling the DVD for $17.99. I noticed that Amazon was selling it for $19.99. I click on Turner site. I'm not exactly sure why. Even though I wasn't going to purchase the DVD, I went for the cheaper price.

"Hmpf," I said after reading that Jacqueline Bisset's character leaves home at nineteen after leading a boring life in Canada and eventually became a prostitute on the Las Vegas strip. I slid the DVD into the disc drive and started watching the film. I suppose it was okay. For a movie filmed in the seventies, it was probably provocative at the time. I closed my eyes so I could concentrate on the film and what it meant to Portia, if it meant anything at all.

I wondered if that's what drew Portia to the film and eventually to Joel Williams. Did she see herself as Christine Adams? Did she see Joel Williams as Tommy Marcott, a washed up former professional football player? If she did see herself as Christine Adams, is that why she was taking advantage of people, blackmailing them. Was she afraid she'd end up like Christine Adams, used up, broke and alone with no one to love her or care for her?

Before I knew it, I was drifting off, but I didn't fight it. I was so comfortable. I just let myself drift as if I were on a magic carpet, floating on the clouds with the sounds of Motown in the background. The next thing I knew, my husband was carrying me to our bed. My head was in a fog.

"What time is it?" I asked him.

"Time for you to get some sleep," he said.

"I saw the whip cream. You still wanna do it?"

"Tomorrow, sweetie. I want you to be alive for this."

I smiled and nodded right back out.

Chapter 34

Julie Campbell and Steven Boyd were sitting in a fully loaded burgundy 2003 Infinity a couple houses down from Reilly Vanderpool's house. The car belonged to Steven, which was why he was sitting behind the wheel. They had been watching the house for three hours and there hadn't been any movement near the house or even in the neighborhood that they could see. While the temperature had dropped from ninety-one to seventy-five, it was still muggy. They knew it was going to be a long, hot night so they packed a cooler with plenty of ice and water. Julie had made sandwiches for lunch when they got hungry. Julie drove her car too, that way, when they needed a bathroom break one could leave while the other watched the house. They were getting married in two weeks and they planned to honeymoon aboard a Holland American cruise line during a fourteen day Alaskan cruise.

First, they would fly out to Seattle early in the morning. According to the itinerary, they had eight ports of call that included Anchorage, Kodiak, and Homer. They had been saving for a couple years. They could have gotten an interior cabin for $499.00 each, which was the cheapest available, but they wanted to travel in style. They choose the penthouse verandah suite, that offered 1,159 square feet, a king bed, whirlpool bath and shower, a large sitting area, and a host of goodies that would make the honeymoon memorable that cost nearly six thousand each. The regular price was upwards of nine thousand, but they got a discount because Julie's sister was a travel agent. Two weeks earlier, they had closed on their dream house and were set to take possession next week.

"You almost packed," Julie said.

"Yeah. You?"

"I'm almost there."

"My passport came today."

"Good. I was afraid it wouldn't get here on time."

"I wasn't going to say anything, Steven, but I'm like totally pissed right now."

"About?"

"Phoenix fuckin' Perry. Are you going to sit there and tell me she doesn't get on your very last nerve?"

"I roll with team's consensus, you know that. But hey, it's not like she pushed her way in. The order came from the top. She followed it."

"I'm not talking about that, Steven. I'm talking about what she told Jack. She has a lot of nerve telling Jack she didn't want us on this job. This is a piece of cake."

"Yeah now that's a problem. I totally agree with you on that."

"And then telling Jack she was worried about us having sex on duty."

"Well, she didn't actually say that, Julie."

"That's what she was insinuating, Steven and you know it. I've got half a mind to blow you right here, right now." She looked around to see if anybody was watching them from their homes. She turned around and looked out the back window. She didn't see anybody. "Pull your pants down."

"What?"

"You heard me."

"Are you ordering me to pull down my pants, ma'am?"

"I am. Now pull them down now!"

"I loved it when you give me orders," Steven said and did exactly as he was told. He scanned the area with the night vision goggles, checked all his mirrors. Seeing nothing, he said, "We're clear. Go for it."

"Let the seat back as far as it'll go," Julie ordered.

He followed her instructions and then pulled down his trousers and underwear. For the first three or four minutes, Steven continued to look around the neighborhood. He checked his mirrors a dozen times before relaxing his head on the headrest and enjoyed the incredible pleasure Julie gave him.

Julie stopped and looked up at him. "Hey, you're supposed to be watching."

"I am," he said, and pushed her head back down. "You probably better hurry though. Just in case someone does come out or take a walk or something."

"Okay," Julie said and sped up.

Steven rested his head on the headrest again and closed his eyes. He was almost there, almost there. A split second later, he heard a hissing sound at the same time he arrived. He felt moisture on his face, like it had suddenly rained inside the car. He opened his eyes. Julie's head had been blown to bits, but he was still in her mouth. He looked up. He heard another hiss. He had taken a bullet in the eye.

Brooke Ursula Davis said, "You were supposed to be watching Reilly Vanderpool. Thanks to you, she's gonna die too—her and her family. Hiss. She shot him in the other eye. Then she and Norm started walking toward the Vanderpool house.

I was dreaming that Kelly and I were in some restaurant and for whatever reasons, all the waiters and waitresses just kept walking by us like we were ghosts or something. Don't ask me why we didn't just get up and leave. I was dreaming and things in dreams often don't make sense. But on the red and white checker table cloth was a large cowbell. No utensils. No napkins. No water. No glasses. Just this enormous silver cowbell. When another waiter walked passed our table, I picked it up and shook it like there was a fire in the joint. The next thing I knew everybody in the restaurant were in an all out brawl. It was crazy. When a woman hit me over the head with a whiskey bottle, and don't ask me where she got it, I woke up and my phone was ringing.

I opened my eyes. Keyth was gone. I grabbed the phone. "Hello."

"Turn on the TV and put it on Fox News," Kelly said.

"What's going on?"

"Some kids found Campbell and Boyd this morning."

"What? They're dead?"

"Uh-huh." I grabbed the remote and turned the TV on. Then I switched the channel to Fox News.

"You'll never guess where they were?"

My screen was on now and I could see the same things Kelly was seeing. "They were at the Vanderpool house?"

"And you gave Ryan orders to send someone else."

"Hold on, let me call him and put us on three-way."

"Don't bother. I already called, but he didn't answer."

"What?"

"Did you call his wife?"

"I did."

"Let me guess," I began, "He didn't come home last night. He didn't call either. And she's been up all night waiting for him, blowing up his cell, leaving messages, and text messages, right?"

"Yep."

"And you're thinking that if he sent Campbell and Boyd to the Vanderpool house against orders, he went to Raquel Mendes' place alone even though I specifically told him to take back up."

"That's exactly what I'm thinking. Let's hope we're wrong. Let's hope he ended up sleeping with Ms. Mendes and he's afraid to come out and play."

I looked at the clock. 6:17. "Hold on. I'm going to call Kortney so we can brief her." A few seconds later, the phone was ringing. I clicked Kelly on.

"Hello, Phoenix," Kortney said. "I was just about to call you."

"I have Agent McPherson on too."

"Agent McPherson."

"Director Malone."

I didn't say anything. I could feel the tension between them. That's how those two dealt with each other. Only when necessary. And begrudgingly. We remained silent for a few seconds.

I said, "Agents Campbell and Boyd are dead. Have you heard?"

"I have," Kortney said without emotion. "I'm afraid a lot of other people are dead too. The entire Vanderpool family for starters. The killers tied their hands behind their waists, and tied a plastic bag over their heads. They suffocated. Are you watching Fox News?"

Kelly and I said, "Yeah."

"Good. They're about to read off a list of names."

I looked at the blond anchorwoman that sat in the middle on Fox & Friends. I can never remember her name. I turned up the TV. Then I heard five very familiar names being read. Skylar Harris. Keira Everhart. Sabrina Mathias. Kai Romero. Caprice Gunnar. All dead. The killers kicked their doors in and shot all five girls in front of their families. According to the anchorwoman, the killers told the families that if they said anything to the police, they'd be back to kill the rest of them.

"Kortney, we're on our way over there right now."

"You most certainly are not."

"But we have agents down. It's all hands on deck now. You know that."

"Not you two. The last thing we need is for your name to get out. Before you know it, they'll have your husband's name. They already know that Campbell and Boyd were seeing one another."

"How do they know that?"

"Hmm, let me think. It was probably the fact that Campbell had Boyd's cock in her mouth when she took a hollow point in the back of her head."

Kelly laughed.

"You think this is funny, Agent McPherson?"

"No. It's never funny when agents go down. It's how you put things, Director Malone.

Kortney was about to respond, but I thought I better jump in there before we lose sight of what we're supposed to be doing. I said, "It's not my fault they were there. I gave strict orders to put someone else on the Vanderpool house just in case something like this happened. Ryan obviously didn't think I had the authority to give his team orders."

"Speaking of Ryan," Kortney said, "Have you heard from him?"

"No," I said. "We think he's done too. And again . . . I specifically told him to take back up and I bet he didn't."

"Where was he going?"

"To see a woman named Raquel Mendes. She lives in the penthouse of the Palomar Hotel in DuPont Circle."

"We'll get over there right away."

"Agent Perry, I want to be very clear on this. Do not . . . I repeat . . . do not go anywhere near the Palomar. If Ryan is dead, it ends with him. I know that sounds ruthless, but all of our asses are showing on this one. Besides, you ordered him not to send those two. And you told him to take back up to the Palomar. It's on him now. He screwed up, not you. As far as you're concerned, he was in charge of everything. This thing started out as a kidnapping, and now it's turned into mass murder. Now . . . acknowledge my orders."

Angrily, I said, "What are we supposed to do, sit on our hands while other agents clean up this mess?"

"Turquoise Barrington told me you've found a safety deposit key. Follow that lead and see where it goes. I want you at that bank the moment they open. And for the last time, don't go near the Palomar and don't go over to the Vanderpool house for any reason."

"We'll need warrants to get her box if it's there."

"I've already faxed the warrant to your home office. If you need more, use the Patriot Act and throw your weight around until they cooperate."

W e entered the Crystal City Wachovia Bank at 9:00 sharp. We walked straight over to a woman sitting behind a desk. I assumed she would know how to check Portia's savings and checking accounts. I made the obligatory introductions and then showed her the legal documentation she needed to see in order to cooperate with the wheels of justice. She told us her name was Penelope and that she was a loan officer. Her fingers moved swiftly on the keyboard as she punched up Portia's accounts. There was only about three thousand between the two accounts. I wasn't surprised given all the money she spends.

With only three thousand dollars, I assumed she was spending the money almost as soon as she gets it. I had the woman print out her account for the last year, and it looked normal for a fourteen year old. Deposits were no more than two hundred dollars. Two things struck me immediately. She never made any withdrawals and she never wrote any checks. I thought that perhaps she was using a debit card, but she didn't have one, which explained why she never spent any money from either account. I was wondering how she was able to purchase that theatre if she only had a few thousand dollars. Then I remembered that Reilly Vanderpool had said there were wire transfers. According to Portia's bank statements, she never had any money wired into either of her accounts.

I pulled out the safety deposit key and said, "Does Portia have a box with Wachovia?"

"I'll check," Penelope said and clicked the keys again. "Yes, she does."

"We need to get into it."

"I just need to grab the key. Follow me."

We entered the vault and went through the procedure of turning the keys. Penelope slid out the box, which was rather large, handed it to me, and gave us some privacy. I opened the box and instantly knew we had hit the mother lode. The box contained a ton of cash in new hundred dollar bills, a bank book that documented her money transfers, and a diary. I looked at Kelly. We both smiled. Instinctively we knew this was what we needed to break the case wide open.

I said, "If Jack had just followed orders, he and his team might be alive."

"True," Kelly said, "But in all likelihood, other agents would be dead instead of them. The team that killed Reilly Vanderpool and her family were professionals. They were probably the same people that killed the other girls in front of their families. You might have saved Jack, Julie, and Steven, but whoever watched the Vanderpool house probably wouldn't have made it either."

I nodded then I opened the diary. There were hardly any entries, like she had either just bought it, or had bought it some time ago, but just started using it. The first entry mentioned Saint Joseph's Orphanage and what really went down there while she was a resident. Kelly and I couldn't believe how wrong we had been. We were going back out there, but Saint Joseph's would have to wait. Right now, we wanted the people who kidnapped and killed Portia Barrington. Saint Joseph's wasn't going anywhere. It would be the easiest bust of our careers.

Next, the diary talked about Joel Williams. Apparently, Portia thought she was in love with him. She compared him to Tommy Marcott from *The Grasshopper*, just as I suspected. According to the diary, Williams was telling her all the right things, like how she should stay in school, get the best education she could get, find a good man and settle down when she was old enough, but what got me was, after having said all of that, he was still having sex with her on the regular. Another entry told of how jealous Portia was of Marsha Spivey and how she was collecting information on both of them. She was planning on sending the evidence to Mason Spivey. Then she wrote, "Maybe he'll kill her and get her out of my way. Joel is mine. When I have enough money, we'll run far, far away together—maybe Australia. Street Weight knows Mason. I'll tell him and maybe he'll get rid of her."

The next set of entries blew me away.

Apparently, Williams and Portia had made some sort of financial pact. He told Portia when he was going out of town with Marsha Spivey. It was usually on the weekends when he was off-duty and Mason Spivey was on the road. Williams had also given her a duplicate of Francesca Ferrari's penthouse so she could use it if she needed to. Francesca was often gone, just as she had told me. Williams got fifty percent of the twenty percent Portia was getting, which he split with Ms. Ferrari. So it was in Williams and Ferrari's best interests to be gone when the clients came to his apartment and Ms. Ferrari's penthouse as well as the other penthouses, which were occupied by other prostitutes of the male and female variety.

Under the heading: Jaguar Club was a username, a password, and a list of coded titles. No names, just titles and phone numbers.

1) Capital Administrator
2) Legal Assistance
3) Street Weight
4) Chief Justice—recently deceased
5) Connoisseur

Reilly Vanderpool came to mind all of a sudden. I remembered our conversation in the interview room yesterday before her attorney showed up. Obviously, that's Legal Assistance. I figured the others to be: Capital Administrator, a Stockbroker; Street Weight was probably the person who handled disgruntled Johns, collected debts, and if necessary killed people. The Connoisseur was probably Jericho Wise. I had no idea who the Chief Justice was, but if it was a real Chief Justice, we could easily find out. I knew it wasn't a member of the Supreme Court. That would make the national news if one of them died, but I hadn't heard a thing. I figured that the judge would have to be someone fairly close to the District of Columbia because with the exception of Jericho Wise, all the other players were right here too. Even Saint Joseph's was within driving distance. What unnerved me was that a Chief Justice could even be involved with any of this mess.

"Kelly, have you heard of any recently deceased Chief Justices in the area?"

"No."

"Theodore Twist," Penelope called out. She was obviously eavesdropping. I can't say I blame her. Two FBI types come in to the bank asking questions broke the monotony.

"When did this happen?" I said.

"A couple weeks ago, I think. They found him in Russian Hill Park, San Francisco. People think he was killed somewhere else and dropped there—shades of Vince Foster and the Clinton Administration. I thought they'd talk about it for awhile, but then a celebrity did something news worthy, and the judge story went away rather quickly. I never heard another thing about it."

"Thanks, Penelope," I said. "And please, say nothing about this. If the people who killed the judge are the same people who killed Portia Barrington, they might flee and we may never catch them. We don't even know who they are."

"So are you going to deputize me?" Penelope said smiling.

"Consider yourself deputized," I said, playing along.

We looked at the next set of entries. We saw what looked like nine account numbers.

I said, "The first three are in brackets. They probably belong to Portia."

"And the other six belong to the Jaguar Club," Kelly said.

I looked at Penelope. "Do you have any idea what these three numbers mean?"

She came back into the vault, put on the glasses that hung around her neck, and looked at the diary. "The first one looks like one our account numbers. I think the second one is an international number. And the third is a SWIFT code. Whenever you see a bunch of capital letters and a number or two, it's probably a SWIFT code."

I said, "What's a SWIFT code?"

"It's the bank identifier code," Penelope said. "SWIFT stands for Society for Worldwide Interbank Financial Telecommunication. Each bank has a unique identification code. That one's ours."

I said, "Why would Portia have a SWIFT code? What's it for?"

"It's a way to wire money from an overseas account," Penelope said.

"Can we take a look at these accounts?" Kelly asked.

"Sure. Are you finished with the box," Penelope asked.

"Yes," I said.

We secured the box and then went back to Penelope's desk. She put in the first number. The name Pussy Galore came up. There was over $600,000 in the account.

Kelly laughed, "Holy Goldfinger, Batman!"

I said, "Is that a real account?"

"Yes," Penelope said. "Apparently that's someone's real name."

"Try the others," Kelly said.

The names on the other six accounts were, Fatima Blush, Solitaire, Holly Goodhead, Lupe Lamora, Vesper Lynd, and my all time favorite Bond girl, Xenia Onatopp. She reminded me of Coco Nimburu. All the accounts were loaded with cash.

I said, "Who set up these accounts?"

"The bank president, Martin Sanchez, set them up."

"Is he here? We'd like to speak with him."

Penelope picked up the phone to dial. I said, "Put the call on speaker. Don't tell him we're listening. I wanna hear his reaction."

"Agent Perry, I don't think I should do that," Penelope said. "I mean he is my boss. He might fire me."

"I fully understand, but we're talking about a murder. In fact were talking about multiple murders. Six teenage girls were killed last night."

Shocked, Penelope said, "I saw that on the news this morning. Does that have anything to do with this?"

"It has everything to do with this, Penelope," I said. "We interviewed Reilly Vanderpool about this yesterday. Now she and her entire family are dead. You tell us that a District of Columbia Chief Justice was killed in San Francisco and Portia Barrington has "Chief Justice – deceased" written in a diary that's in a safety deposit box? And to top that off, your boss set up six accounts under salacious Bond girl names? Put it together, Penelope. Six girls were killed last night. Six Bond girl names. If Mr. Sanchez did set these accounts up, he is probably the key to breaking the case wide open."

She pushed the speaker button and hits three numbers. "Sorry to bother you Mr. Sanchez, but two FBI agents would like to have a word with you about the seven accounts you personally opened."

His voice broke when he said, "Uh . . . what names are on the accounts?"

Penelope looked at the screen. The first account number read: Pussy Galore. She looked at me and said, "How about I read you the account numbers, sir?"

We could hear Sanchez typing in the first account number. He stopped typing. I assumed Ms. Galore's name and account information appeared on his screen. He stammered a bit before saying, "Uh, and the other six accounts?" He typed them in one at a time and then said, "Wait ten minutes and then send them up."

"Yes, sir," Penelope said, and clicked the speaker off.

"We're not waiting ten minutes," I said. "We're not waiting ten seconds. Where's his office?"

K elly and I walked quickly over to the elevator and hit the up button. The doors opened immediately. When we got off the elevator, we saw a woman sitting at a circular desk. She was looking at a computer screen. His executive assistant, I guessed, as we zoomed by her with our credentials in the air. "FBI," I said, not bothering to stop. When I opened Martin Sanchez's door, he was sitting at his desk, talking on a cell phone. "I'll have to call you back, Bobby," Sanchez said and slowly pulled the cell away from his ear. I could tell he knew who we were and why we were there. His eyes bulged. If his hair could stand up, I'm certain it would have.

"What can I do for you?" Sanchez said after clearing his throat.

"Agents Perry and McPherson," I said. "Talk to us about the personal accounts you set up."

Sanchez offered the woman sitting at the desk an unblinking stare. She closed the door.

"What accounts are you referring to?" Sanchez asked.

"The one you set up for Portia Barrington," Kelly said.

"I did no such thing."

I said, "So you know who Portia is then?"

"I most certainly do. I met her at the Barrington mansion several times during social events. Her father has a rather sizeable account with us. When I heard the news about her death, I was stunned. She was a very charming girl."

I said, "So you didn't open an account for her under the name Pussy Galore."

"I most certain did not."

"But you did open the account?" Kelly asked.

"Yes, but not for Portia."

"Who then?" I demanded.

"I'm afraid that's confidential, Agent Perry," Sanchez said. "Now, I'm quite busy. If there's nothing else, I have a tight schedule."

"Doesn't it bother you that six innocent girls were killed last night?" I asked.

"I'm sure it would, if I knew them," Sanchez said, growing more confident with each of his responses. "But since I have no idea who died or what you're talking about, I cannot be bothered, can I?"

I watched him closely before saying, "So you're saying you're not in any way involved with Portia Barrington and teenage prostitution?"

"I categorically deny having anything whatsoever to do with Myles Barrington's daughter. And I know absolutely nothing about teenage prostitution, other than that it exists."

I looked at Kelly and then back at Sanchez. "So you're not transferring money into seven accounts from the Cayman Islands?"

"No, I'm not."

"Why would Jericho Wise say you were?" I asked, goading him, trying to get an honest reaction."

"Jericho Wise? I don't know the man and I have never heard of him before now. You've been given some very bad information, Agent Perry. I suggest you look elsewhere for the answers you seek. Perhaps you should speak with this Jericho Wise person again. Now please leave. Or do I have to call Myles and tell him you two are here harassing me."

I flipped open my cell and searched the last numbers dialed until I found the number to the Barrington mansion. I hit the call button and looked at Sanchez while the phone rang. Turquoise Barrington answered.

"Mrs. Barrington," I said, still looking at Sanchez, "I'm in Martin Sanchez's office. He seems to think you and your husband would have a problem with some of the questions I've asked."

"Why would he think that, Agent Perry?"

"I'm not sure, ma'am, but I'm under orders to question every-body on this. That's probably going to include more people you and Mr. Barrington know and associate with."

"I understand. What do you have on Martin?"

"I told you yesterday that Portia had a safety deposit key. When we opened her box, we found a diary with numerous account numbers in it. Seven of them to be exact. Just so happens we have seven dead girls too. I don't think it's a coincidence."

"I don't either, Agent Perry. Do what you have to do."

"Thank you, Mrs. Barrington. Is Mr. Barrington available?"

"No, he isn't. He went to the office. His ex-wife refuses to come here. We don't get along. They should be there for awhile making the funeral arrangements for Portia. His office is right there in Crystal City if you want to stop by and talk to him in person. You can catch him there or you could call. The number's on the manila envelope. Do you still have it?"

"Yes," I said. "Thanks."

I hit the end button.

Still looking at Sanchez, I said, "Now that we got that cleared up . . . I'll give you one more opportunity to come clean on this thing. We know you're deeply involved. And sooner or later, it's going to all come out. It always does. Help yourself out now while you still can."

Sanchez shifted in his chair like he was uncomfortable. "If you're finished, I'd like you to leave my office."

We turned to leave, and then I turned back, tossed my card on his desk, and said, "When you change your mind, and you will, give me a call. These guys are tying up all loose ends. And you're a really big loose end they can't leave floating around, going with the flow of the tide. Sooner or later, they're going to realize you're a huge liability. And when they do, you're going to end up like Portia, Reilly Vanderpool, Skylar Harris, Caprice Gunnar, Keira Everhart, Sabrina Mathias, and Kai Romero."

I said all their names, hoping to break him, if only a little. He was involved, I believed, but he wasn't a killer. "They've already killed over a dozen people that we know of. Two of them were FBI agents. A third agent is missing. We think he's dead too. The point

I'm making is this: these people will stop at nothing to avoid some serious jail time. They know that if they go in, they're not coming out alive. So they have all kinds of motivation to kill you too. They'll get another banker. You're just a patsy like Lee Harvey Oswald. And you know what happened to him. The way I figure it, you've got less than twenty-four hours to come clean."

Myles Barrington's office was about a mile or so away from the bank. Traffic was heavy. It was going to take about ten minutes to get there. As Kelly drove us over, I said, "Do you think there's any chance that Sanchez is telling the truth?"

"Not a chance in hell he's telling the truth," She said as only Kelly could. "He's knee deep in it. I bet he's been up in all seven of those girls and if we search through enough of the DVDs, we'll find him in them."

"Not if he was smart enough to meet Portia at a hotel," I said. "Listen to this entry in Portia's diary. It's dated, Monday, June 6th. Had a meeting with Legal at the Crystal City Gateway Marriott today. Presidential Suite!!! Agrees to pay me more in two days. Made out! Enjoyable. But kinky. Saw a sign welcoming the college cheerleader competition. Maybe I'll check it out."

Amazed, Kelly said, "So we just missed her a few days before she was snatched. We were about to go up to the Presidential Suite when we saw our suspects."

"I know," I said. "I hope the manager still remembers me." I called information and got the number to the hotel.

"Front Desk."

"Hi. This is FBI agent, Phoenix Perry."

"I remember you, Agent Perry!" a foreign female voice said. "This is Jasmina Dris, remember me!"

"I certainly do," I said. Her face actually came to mind. Jasmina was Moroccan. I think I remembered her because she was probably the nicest of all the helpful employees at the hotel. She was in the country on a Student Visa, studying at Georgetown. "Are you taking any summer courses?"

"Yes, I have about 15 semester hours."

"That's gotta be tough, huh?"

"Yes, but I'm determined. I'm hoping I'll be able to stay if I'm gainfully employed by one of the firms in the area."

"I'm sure you'll be just fine. Listen, the reason I called is because I'm wondering if you can give me the names of the guests that checked into the Presidential Suite for the last month, going back to about the middle of May." I wanted to know if this was a one-time thing or if they had encores.

"Sure. It's usually open so there shouldn't be that many names. Give me a couple of seconds."

I heard the keys clicking rapidly.

"Got another exciting case, huh?" Jasmina said. "Or is this from the same case?"

"This is a different case," I said.

"Well this place is still buzzing about what happened last week when the cheerleaders were here."

I ignored that comment; I wanted her to focus on what I called for. "To narrow the search, just give me the names of men who live in the Arlington, Alexandria, and DC area, okay?"

"No problem. Ah, here we go. There were only two men from this area. Their names are Martin Sanchez and Christopher Choice."

"And how did they pay? Cash I'll bet."

The keys were clicking rapidly again.

"Yes. Both men settled their bill in cash."

"Do you still have their credit card information?"

"No. They must have used American Express or perhaps a Chase Manhattan card. American Express drops off the reservation within 24 hours of settling the bill and Chase is nearly as fast. Most banks can take a week or so before it drops off. Why is that important?"

"It means that the addresses you have for them are fakes. They used their real names because they held the room with their credit card. But they didn't want a permanent record so they paid in cash when they left."

"Hmpf, okay, sorry I couldn't be more help, Agent Perry. Is there anything else I can do for you?"

"Which one of them was in the suite on the 6th? Martin Sanchez, right?"

"Nope, it was Christopher Choice. Hmm, that's interesting."

"You have something else?" I asked.

"Well, Mr. Sanchez was here on the 8th. He had a late checkout too."

"Thanks, Jasmina. You've been a big help." I hit the end button. "She was there with somebody named Christopher Choice. He's Legal. That's probably who Reilly Vanderpool called too. I'm guessing all the girls had his number just in case they were busted."

Kelly said, "I'm also betting that since the 6th was a Monday, that's why they didn't go to Joel Williams' building. The penthouses are probably available on the weekends."

"According to the hotel records, Martin Sanchez was there on Wednesday, the day of the kidnapping. I bet Portia was there with him. And Joel Williams' apartment is only about a block away from the hotel."

Kelly said, "Yeah, she probably went to the hotel to take care of some sexual and financial business. Then she walked over to Joel's apartment so he could take her home. And that's where they snatched her. The limo was still in the garage."

"Makes sense to me." I started reading the entries again and said, "Listen to this. On New Year's Eve, she was suspicious of some kind of alliance with Legal. On Martin Luther King Day, she writes: Alliance confirmed. Will they pay? On February 12, she writes JW delivered pictures. JW could be Jericho Wise, but I'm thinking its Joel Williams."

"Pictures of what?" Kelly asked. "Does it say who?"

"No, but it says that on Valentine's Day, collections would begin. A few weeks after that, she's expecting her home theatre to arrive. She writes, 'My new Home Theater is being delivered today! The Jaguars are going to just die with envy! Gotta have the girls over and watch some slut flicks from the UK.'"

"Phoenix, don't trip on this, but, do you think there's a chance that Portia was intimate with her father? Is he Legal? Couldn't Christopher Choice be a fake name? I mean, doesn't the name sound cheesy as hell? It could be code like the other entries. And why is she using code in the first place?"

"I'm not sure. Maybe she didn't always keep the diary in the safety deposit box. I don't know."

"Maybe Barrington made all of this up to hide an incestuous affair with the beautiful girl he adopted. Isn't it possible that Portia's mind was so twisted from what happened to her that she went as far as getting involved with the man who adopted her? And being a prominent attorney known throughout the country, this thing would have been covered nationally and that's why he drummed all this up? I'm sure he has some unsavory clients that would help him in a situation like that, don't you? Make threatening phone calls and whatnot."

"That would mean that Mrs. Barrington is in on it too. She said the voice was Portia's too. Why would she do that? What's her motivation?"

"Did you see that house? C'mon, Phoenix. She's not giving that up. And let's face it. She didn't get along all that well with Portia to begin with. Besides, what if he promised to leave her a bundle? Or better yet, what if he gave her a bundle already to keep her mouth shut? She admitted Barrington kept large amounts of cash on the premises, but we're supposed to look the other way on that, remember? That's probably money he hasn't reported to the IRS. If he's cheating the IRS, he could be doing other things too."

"I suppose it's possible, but what's all of this stuff in the diary? I just don't see Barrington being that ruthless. I don't, Kelly. You saw the wounds in her head. They were fresh. That means Barrington would've had to be acting this whole time, knowing he was going to have her killed. Besides, how does Joel Williams, Marsha Spivey, Francesca Ferrari, and the Jaguar Club figure into his thinking?"

"I don't know, but he had to come up with some sort of story. And paying five hundred grand? Why not call the police from the very beginning? By not calling us, we have no way of verifying he paid one nickel. With no money trail, we have to take his word for it, don't we?"

"I like Christopher Choice as Legal and her lover. That's who she met at the Marriott. I don't think the father's in on it."

"What if Christopher Choice is Barrington?"

"They had kinky sex, Kelly. I refuse to believe Myles Barrington had kinky sex with his daughter, but I do believe Martin Sanchez did and so did Christopher Choice. If Sanchez knows nothing about teenage prostitution as he claims, why was he stammering when Penelope gave him the account numbers he set up? Also, who was

Sanchez talking to when we walked in? He knew we were coming and he made a personal call on his cell."

"Or a personal call came in when we had Penelope call him. It could have been anybody."

"No. It was someone named Bobby. I heard him."

Kelly was quiet for a few seconds. Then she said, "Let's call some of those numbers."

I started at the top and dialed Capital Administrator's number. I put the call on speaker so Kelly could hear. "You've reached Martin Sanchez, president of Wachovia Banks. Please leave your name, number, and the time of your call, and I'll return your call as soon as possible."

I looked at Kelly and said, "You still think her father is in on it?"

"Let's call the other numbers and then I'll decide."

I called Legal Assistance. We listened. "You've reached Christopher Choice. Please leave a message." The next number belonged to someone Portia dubbed as Street Weight. I dialed the number. A man answered. "Yeah? Who is this?" He sounded sad, like he had a lot on his mind.

"This is Phoenix. Who is this?"

He kind of laughed, like he thought I had the wrong number or something. He said, "You mean like the bird and shit?"

I faked a laughed and said, "Yeah, like the bird and shit. Who is this?"

"This is Bobby Tarantino, sweetie and you obviously have the wrong number."

"Sorry," I said, and hit the end button. I looked at Kelly. "That's probably the same Bobby that Sanchez was talking to."

Kelly said, "I know who Bobby Tarantino is.

Chapter 35

W e got out of the car and entered the building where Barrington kept his law offices. Kelly had told me on the way in that Bobby Tarantino was a street hood from San Francisco. He was the drug kingpin of Baltimore and Washington. A couple years ago, he had been busted for cocaine trafficking. He was looking at eighty years in prison, but had gotten off on a technicality because two cops stole a million dollars of the drug money. Officers Brooke Davis and Norman Green left the force in disgrace. Kelly hadn't heard anything about them since. We were in the elevator alone on the way up to Barrington's floor, so I dialed the judge's number and we listened.

"This is Judge Theodore Twist. I'll be unavailable until Monday, June 6th. Please leave a message."

Kelly looked at me and said, "Portia knows the cell numbers of a judge, a bank president, and Bobby Tarantino? What the hell was this kid into?"

"Sanchez knows Barrington. The judge probably does too. But it doesn't explain why she had the numbers in her diary, safely tucked away."

"What about Tarantino?"

"One of Barrington's clients? If he is one of his clients, he might be the source of all the cash in the first place."

"Which would support my theory, wouldn't it?"

"Or they had a falling out." I dialed a number with an 866 exchange. We heard, "Welcome to First Caribbean International Bank. You have reached our Customer Service Center." I hit the end button as we left the elevator. I looked at Kelly and said, "San Francisco is coming up way too often, Kelly."

"I know."

"Do you think Sterling knows anything?"

"If he does, he's not saying."

"How may I help you?" the receptionist said.

"Agents Perry and McPherson," I said. "We're here to see Myles Barrington."

"I see," she said. "I feel so sorry for Mr. Barrington. He loved Portia very much. One moment." She hit a button and spoke into her headset. "Sorry to bother you Mr. Barrington. Agents Perry and McPherson are here to see you, sir. I'll let them know, sir." She looked at us and said, "He's meeting with the first Mrs. Barrington. She just arrived from Maine. It'll be just a few minutes, he said. There are fruit and bagels at the refreshment bar. There's water and coffee too if you like."

She told us we could help ourselves at the refreshment stand in the corner, but as we were headed over there, I heard the next call come in. The receptionist said, "Mr. Choice . . . it's Mr. Sanchez again. He's on line one."

I looked at Kelly. She was thinking the same thing. We fast walked back to the receptionist. I said, "That wouldn't happen to be Martin Sanchez, would it?"

"Yes. Do you know Martin? He's a sweetie."

"And he called earlier?" I said.

"Yes, about ten minutes before you got here as a matter of fact."

"You mentioned, Mr. Choice. That wouldn't happen to be Christopher Choice, would it?"

"Yes, Chris has been an associate with the firm for about eight years now."

Needless to say, Kelly and I were stunned to find out that one of Barrington's own associates was involved with Portia. We didn't know how involved he was, but we did know that Portia was in a position to blackmail him. Whatever she had on him must have been a bombshell for him to have given her the money it cost to build that home theatre. I was glad that Christopher Choice turned out to be a real person, but at the same time, I felt bad for Myles Barrington. His friends and associates were not people he could trust.

So far, we had Christopher Choice on statutory rape, but we wanted it all. To get everything and everybody I knew we would have to make a deal. We would have to give him some kind of plea agreement where he did minimal time. If he was involved in the kidnapping, he'd want immunity. About a dozen people were dead, not including our own people. While I wouldn't want to make the deal, we might have to because of all the pressure to bring Portia's killer to justice. Whoever we got for her death would be liable for all the other murders.

We hustled over to Christopher Choice's office. When we entered, he didn't seem the least bit surprised to see us. He greeted us with a smile and told us to have a seat as if we were about to have cocktails before dinner or something. He was sitting in a chair behind his desk. His head was resting on his laced fingers. He looked almost bored, like he had expected us sooner. After we sat down, he leaned back and looked at me. Then he said, "So . . . you must be Phoenix Perry."

I could tell by the way he looked at me that he wanted a piece. That sometimes happened when Kelly was in the same room with me, but not often. Men generally looked at Kelly the way he was looking at me. I usually had to fight to get them to look my way while they were talking to me. Christopher Choice had no such problem. He was leering and didn't care that I knew he was. Perhaps he thought it was a compliment. I took it that way. I wasn't one of those women who thought that a man staring at her was analogous to some sort of evil indigenous to males.

I like it when men look at me. I like it when they tell me I'm beautiful. It lets me know I still have it, that I'm still desirable. Most women want men to notice the work they put into looking good. Christopher Choice noticed. Besides, I found him attractive also, but of course I had to hide that fact from his imposing gaze. To me he looked like a taller version of Matthew McConaughey, who I had a thing for. I recognized Choice from the Barrington mansion. Myles was talking to him when the call came from the kidnappers. That's when I realized he was in on it all.

"Yes, I'm Phoenix Perry."

"I heard Palmer Davidson telling Myles about you a few days ago. You're far more beautiful than Davidson described, I must say." He looked at my wedding ring and then into my eyes. "Unlike most women, over a decade of marriage obviously agrees with you. I so wish it didn't. I would love to sweep you off your feet."

His compliment almost made me smile. I liked him already. Kelly must have sensed it because she did what I normally had to do in these situations. "We got you on statutory rape, Christopher. We can take you in right now if we want to."

Still wantonly looking at me, he said, "Why don't you then, Agent McPherson? Could it be because you think that I have certain information that could lead to the capture of the kidnappers who killed Portia and all those other lovely precocious young girls?"

Kelly stood up and said, "Christopher Choice, you're under arrest for statutory rape. You have the right . . ."

Still looking at me, he said, "Now stop right there, Agent McPherson. The moment you read me my rights, this little meeting becomes official and I'll have to get an attorney and everything. He'll get me out on bail due to lack of evidence and no corroborating witnesses. I believe they've all had an early rendezvous with death. Anything you may have found can't be cross examined and I could get off. You don't want that. You want to arrest the man who hatched this fiendish plot, do you not? In the meantime, you still won't know who killed Portia or why. So sit down and shut up, Agent McPherson. Relax for a few minutes while I take in the essence of the heavenly creature I can't seem to take my eyes off."

Even though I thought he was wrong for sleeping with Portia, he was good-looking. Plus, I like being thought of as a celestial being. I said, "So you want to make a deal?"

"Ah, she speaks," Choice said. His charm was magnetic. "Of course I want a deal. And guess what? You're going to give it to me. I've drawn up an immunity plea just in case it came to this. I believe in contingency plans. It was an excellent arrangement while it lasted, but things change and when they do, you never know what kind of situation you'll find yourself in." He opened a drawer and pulled out the contract. He handed it to Kelly without looking at her and said, "Here you go, Agent McPherson. This ought to keep you busy for a while." Still looking at me, he said, "So how did you find me? Did Martin Sanchez send you here?"

"Actually he didn't. He denied everything, but he was sleeping with Portia too, wasn't he?"

He kind of laughed. "I've always found the term "sleeping with" to be a misnomer when referring to conjugal relations. For example, when a man pays a woman for sex, no one ever says they're sleeping together. They call it what it is."

I said, "What would you prefer I call it, Mr. Choice."

"There is a term called freedom of speech and so I guess you can call it what you like, but me . . . I prefer to call it what it is . . . fucking. When people are fucking, they're not sleeping. Most of the time, after the fucking is done, people are in a hurry to get on with other business."

Suddenly Christopher Choice wasn't all that attractive. He had just blown Matthew McConaughey's chances if I ever met him. Yet, his assessment of sexual activity in relation to sleeping could not be denied.

I said, "So was Martin Sanchez fucking Portia too?"

Choice laughed out loud. "I would love to answer that question, but you see, if I did, I would be giving away my hand. I have a Royal Flush and you have a pair of twos as in two plus two equals four and not much else I'm afraid. This problem is more like a quadratic equation—quite complicated and involved. There are lots of players, lots of variables that you won't be able to figure out on your own. In other words, you need me to put the others away. I'll tell ya what . . . looking at you and allowing my imagination to run absolutely wild has put me in a really good mood. While your friend muddles through the plea agreement, why don't you tell me why I should answer the question?"

I glared at him and said, "You obviously know how to be charming, but you can be rude at the same time. Kelly is my friend. I don't appreciate you talking to her like that."

For the first time since we entered his office, he looked at Kelly. "I apologize for being rude to you just now." He looked at me again. "As you can see, I have become your subject. Now, please . . . tell me why I should answer your question."

I smiled and decided to play along with him. "Because you want to tell us. You think he sold you out and if he didn't, you think he will. You think he's the weak link in the entire operation. And you know that he probably won't live another day because of it. So by confirming what we already know, you won't be saying much of anything, will you Mr. Choice?"

He clapped his hands and said, "Bravo."

The phone beeped. "Mr. Choice?" The receptionist called out.

"Yes, what is it?" Christopher said. "I have guests."

"Mr. Barrington is ready to see Agents Perry and McPherson. He's in the conference room."

"Thank you. Please let him know we'll be right there." He looked at Kelly and said, "Do we have an agreement or not?"

Kelly looked at me and said, "I say no deal. Let's take his arrogant ass in. We'll take our chances in court. We'll get you on RICO. As you know, that carries 20 years and a $250,000 fine per count. We're talking about seven beautiful girls. You corrupted them and the jury won't like that."

"Agent McPherson, I assure you, all those girls were corrupt long before I came along. But if you insist on pursuing me when I'm offering you the ring leader on a platter, you'll be very sorry." He looked at his watch. "You're running out of time."

I said, "We're running out of time?"

"They're all going to try and leave the country."

Kelly stood up again, "Let's go. We're taking you in. You're under arrest. And I hope to God you resist."

"I'm so sorry you said that, Agent McPherson. So sorry for you, indeed." He looked at me and said, "Phoenix, I'm implore you not to let her anger get in the way of a sound business decision. Call someone who can make the deal without emotion. For openers, I can give you the people who killed Judge Twist in San Francisco."

Chapter 36

After Phoenix and Kelly left his office, Martin Sanchez called Bobby Tarantino back and told him everything that happened. Bobby assured him he didn't have anything to worry about, but Sanchez didn't believe him although he pretended that he did. As soon as he hung up the phone with Tarantino, he called Christopher Choice and told him that he and his family were leaving the country. He also told him that he thought Bobby was going to kill him to tie up loose ends and that he feared for Choice's life too. When Choice said nearly word for word what Tarantino had said, he knew he had been right and that Choice knew it. They both had conspired to kill him, thinking he was the weak link. Sanchez thought Choice was only trying to make him relax so that he wouldn't run, but Sanchez called his wife and told her to pack enough clothes for a week and to be ready to leave immediately upon his return. He was on his way home and he would explain when he arrived.

He walked into his home and called out, "Naomi. I told you to be ready! We have to leave right now!"

"Hiya doin', Mr. Sanchez," Bud said. She was pointing a pistol with an attached sound suppressor at his chest.

The blood drained from Sanchez's face. He knew that he had been too late. He knew that he should have run the moment he saw the news the previous night and learned that all those pretty young girls he'd had sex with had been brutally murdered. His heart was racing. He found it difficult to breathe. His voice cracked when he asked, "Where are my wife and daughter?"

"They're safe," Bud said. "For now, they're in your office, waiting for you to rescue them."

Sanchez swallowed hard before saying, "Are you here to kill us?"

Bud pushed him in the small of his back and said, "Just keep walking. We'll talk when we get there."

"I have money," Sanchez said. "If you let us go, I can pay you."

She pushed him into his office, which looked like a James Bond Shrine. Large brass frames of blown up autographed photos of Sean Connery, Pierce Brosnan, Roger Moore, and David Niven lined the walls along with authentic advertising posters of *Goldfinger, Live and Let Die, Goldeneye, Casino Royal* and several other Bond hits. A duel pen holder with a replica of the yellow and black Rolls Royce from *Goldfinger* sat between two pens at the edge of his desk.

He saw Naomi and Mercedes, his daughter, sitting in the two chairs in front of his desk. Their hands were tied behind their backs. He ran to them and kissed them both. "Did they hurt you? Either of you?" he asked.

"Give them whatever they want, Martin," Naomi pleaded. "They promised me they wouldn't kill Mercedes if you cooperate."

"I'm afraid they're going to kill us all, my love," Sanchez said. "It's all my fault."

Bud said, "That kinda talk is dangerous, Mr. Sanchez. It makes me think you're not going to cooperate."

Norm looked at his watch and then at Bud. "We're up against the wall on time. We don't have time for this shit. Lets just pop 'em all and get the hell outta here. We have other business to handle before we head to the docks."

"He's right, Sanchez," Bud said. "We are running out of time. In fact, we're out of time. We were supposed to do you and your family last night, but, I figured we could pick up some severance pay if we threatened your wife and daughter, but I didn't count on Mercedes going over to her boyfriend's house."

"How did you know that?" Naomi asked.

"When we got here, she was just backing out of the driveway," Bud said. "Luck is a variable no one can control. We followed her. It looked like she was going to be there a while. We had other things to do and I didn't want to take the chance of coming back here and have her show up all of a sudden."

Hiss! Norm put a bullet right in the center of Naomi's head. Her blood and brains sprayed the back of her chair. A piercing scream forced its way out of Mercedes. She quickly became hysterical.

Bud slapped her and said, "If you don't shut up, you're next."

Norm yelled, "Let's wrap this shit up! We're up against the clock."

"Put the girl in the van, Norm," Bud said. "And wait for me." She looked at Mercedes and said, "Your mother's dead. She's not coming back. If you want your father to live, I suggest you keep your mouth shut and get in the van with Norm. Do you understand?"

She nodded.

"Get her outta here, Norm." Bud said.

He grabbed the girl by the arm and walked her out of the office.

"Now, Mr. Sanchez," she handed him a slip of paper. "I need you to call your bank in the Caymans and transfer this amount into this account."

Sanchez looked at the paper and then looked at Bud. Confused he said, "You only want $300,000?"

"I know you got a lot more than that, but if I took it all, you'd never cooperate, would you? All I want is the money. The FBI is looking for all of us. I'm looking out for number one now. Fuck Tarantino! We're all on our own now. I left you enough to run if you want, or you can turn state's evidence and get immunity. I don't care, but we're outta here for good. I suggest you do the same. Your three hundred thousand, plus what I've already got, will go a very long way in Brazil."

"What about my daughter?"

"We'll drop her off someplace safe. If I give her back to you now, you might get stupid and call the cops. I'll keep her for a while and let you know in six hours. We'll be long gone by then, no matter what you do. Make the call."

When the transfer was confirmed, Bud called Norm. "Put the girl on the phone. Let her speak to her father so she knows he's alive." She handed Sanchez the phone.

"Hi sweetheart," Sanchez said, his voice was still cracking. "I fixed everything. They're just going to keep you for a little while and then they're going to release you, okay? Do whatever they say and you won't be harmed. I'll see you soon."

He handed the cell back to Bud. She closed it up and put in her pocket. "Before I go, what's in the briefcase?"

"Nothing important. Just papers."

"Let's see," Bud said.

Martin swiveled his chair to the right and reached for the brief-case.

Hiss! Hiss! Bud shot him in the head twice. She went out the front door and got into the van.

"How much did we get?" Norm asked.

"A hundred fifty," Bud said.

"That should cover my month long cruise to Japan rather nicely," Norm said.

"What about me?" Mercedes said.

"You heard your father," Bud said. "I'm going to sedate you, okay? That way you don't know where we take you. And when we release you, you can't tell the police anything you don't know."

"You promise to let me go?"

"In a little while, when we know we're safe. Otherwise, we'll have to go back and you can watch your father die before we kill you. It's your choice. The needle or the pistol. Your choice."

"You promise?"

"Promise."

When she was sure Mercedes was sound asleep, Bud said, "We're almost home, Norm. If we can just keep it together, we're home free. We can retire in style."

Chapter 37

I believed the right move was to make the call and get Christopher Choice immunity. It made sense because we could close several cases by letting one good-looking scumbag off. In other words, Choice agreed to give us three for the price of one, you might say. But, Portia wasn't my daughter so I wasn't completely comfortable with the decision. To be honest, I'm not sure I'd want someone letting anybody off if someone had kidnapped and killed Savannah. I'd want them all. Every last one of them would have to pay for Savannah's death with their own. So I decided to get Barrington's opinion. He loved his daughter very much. I thought he'd make the right decision.

By the time we entered the conference room, the first Mrs. Barrington had already left. Barrington had no idea that Choice was in on what happened to Portia. I knew what his reaction would be so I escorted Choice to the opposite end of the conference table, far away from the victim's father. When I filled Barrington in on what Choice had done and what Portia was into, he went after Choice. We let him bloody him up pretty good before we stopped him. There was nothing in the immunity agreement that said we had to stop Barrington from kicking his ass. Frankly, after what he had done, he needed his ass kicked. I enjoyed watching it, to be honest.

Moments later, Barrington, after having regained a measure of composure, broke down and cried like a baby. I gave him a few moments to grieve, but reminded him that we were running out of time. He called Palmer Davidson and explained what we needed. It's good to have friends in high places, is all I can say. Palmer was able to get the Attorney General on the phone pretty quickly. I wasn't surprised how quickly it happened because Davidson had appointed him. We faxed a copy of the agreement over to Justice. Once the agreement was in place, Choice started talking.

"The people you want for the Judge Twist's murder are, Brooke Davis and Norman Green . . . former police officers that—"

"We know who there are," Kelly said.

"You do, huh? Okay, well they killed the judge in San Francisco. Judge Twist was a family values conservative who had a homosexual bent. He had been seeing a transvestite named, Gloria Dunes. Gloria's real name was Leon James. He was a member of the Chiefs, a street gang in San Francisco. A rival gang raped him in prison and he never recovered, but he was still a Chief until death. Gloria let it slip that Bobby Tarantino was trying to leave the drug business in favor of teenage prostitution.

"Bobby's trying to leave the business for two reasons. He's in love with his long time girlfriend, Raquel Mendes, who was the mother of his two daughters. He wants to settle down with her and be a good father to his children. The other reason he wants out is because the drug business has gotten too dangerous and he is almost forty years old. He thinks it's a young man's game and he's afraid of going to prison for the rest of his life. Besides, he's made a ton of money supplying street dealers. He thinks that if he gets caught doing what amounts to pimping, he wouldn't have to do a long stretch. But what he didn't know was that a conspiracy to commit sex trafficking of a minor could get him a maximum of five years. If he actually gets caught trafficking minors, he'll get a minimum of ten years and up to life imprisonment."

I said, "And you didn't tell him this?"

"No, why should I? I owed the man a ton of money. I was hoping he'd get caught and go away so I could get rid of him. But when he realized that trafficking teenage girls and children in general was a multibillion dollar industry in places like The Netherlands, specific parts of Asia, and Brazil, he wanted in. The big money was in dealing with rich perverts who only wanted children."

I was thinking, "Portia was much older" but kept my mouth shut and let him run his.

Choice continued, "The boys and girls you see on flyers that come in the mail. That's how sick he is. Tarantino knew most people didn't even bother to look at the kids anymore. The only people looking at those flyers are the parents who hadn't given up hope their children would one day be found."

Kelly said, "How did Tarantino get Brooke Davis and Norman Green involved?"

"They ripped Tarantino off during a drug bust. In order to payoff their debt, he made them work for him. And he was smart enough to pay them good money so that the money would silence their consciences and keep them coming back for more and more work. Before long, Davis and Green were snatching kids left and right. They didn't want to do it at first, but Brooke's mother had medical expenses that couldn't be met unless she got really lucky and won the lottery. I don't know what Tarantino was paying them per kid, but it was enough money to keep them both comfortable, but not satisfied. In other words, they couldn't quit working, but they both lived well."

I said, "How did he get you to compromise yourself?"

"I was over my head in gambling debts—money I owed someone else."

"Who?" I asked.

"He doesn't have anything to do with this."

I looked him the eye and said, "It wouldn't happen to be Jericho Wise, would it?"

Choice cut his eyes to the left briefly and said, "If the girls got busted, I was supposed to get them out on bail. It was supposed to be pro bono work, but Tarantino was paying me cash so I could continue gambling and remain indebted to him. I knew my debt would never be paid off as long as Tarantino was alive. Tarantino wanted to keep me happy so he took care of any problems I had and as a perk, he let me have any of the high class prostitutes I wanted, whenever I wanted."

Kelly said, "So there's a prostitution ring in Joel Williams' building?"

Surprise registered when he heard the question.

I said, "Is Jericho Wise involved with high class prostitution?"

"Listen, I agreed to talk about the kidnapping and the murders, not prostitution."

We were getting close to discussing Portia's exploits and how she figured into all of this. Barrington decided he didn't want to hear any more and left the room. I didn't blame him. If I had to sit there and listen to all the things my own daughter was doing, I don't think I could take it either. I mean everyone is familiar with the world's oldest profession, but professionals are always someone else's daughter. I guess knowing that makes us all tolerate prostitution. We tolerate it because it isn't our daughter. It's our neighbor's daughter and we don't give a damn about our neighbor.

In fact, our fathers and brothers and uncles and sons, buy our neighbor's daughters and we don't think twice about it. I guess we tell ourselves that if our neighbors can't keep their daughters from prostituting themselves or becoming strippers, that's their problem. We tell ourselves it's none of our business. I guess that's how we live with ourselves. Perhaps we'll care when everywhere we look, we see the immoral cesspool that we've allowed the United States to become due to our own participation or neglect.

C hristopher Choice waited until Barrington left the conference room. Then he said, "I regret that I let myself get involved with Portia, but sadly, I did. It all started when she was about thirteen."

I immediately thought of Savannah when he mentioned Portia's age. I thought of just how vulnerable she and other young people like her was. I fought off my anger and said, "I find it hard to believe that a thirteen year old teenager, who probably just started her period, initiated a sexual relationship with you. Tell the truth. You saw how beautiful the girl was even being so young and you just couldn't stop yourself, could you?"

"Believe it, Agent Perry. But you're right though, she was very good-looking even at thirteen. Initially, I refused to get involved with her. Frankly, had she been eighteen when she first came on to me, I wouldn't have hesitated."

Kelly laughed and said, "That's an understatement seeing that you were involved with her at fifteen."

He looked at Kelly and rolled his eyes. "About a year and a half later, she came on to me again at one of Barrington's functions at the mansion. I gotta be honest. She was smoking hot by then. I'm talking a five alarm fire hot. She told me she knew I could get into trouble and swore to me that she would never tell a soul. That it would be just between me and her. I told myself that I would try it out one time and one time only, just to see what the attraction to young girls was and then I'd move on. But one time turned into two times and two times turned into three times and after the third time, I was hooked. I'm talking crack cocaine hooked. And the strange thing was that I no longer saw anything wrong with what I was doing with a teenager."

In a way I felt sorry for him. Most men allow themselves to be enslaved by their passions, thinking they can walk away anytime they feel like it. Perhaps it did become some sort of addiction.

"We used to meet at my place," Choice continued, "but one night I'd fallen asleep and Portia went through my desk and found DVDs of older men having sex with underage girls."

I said, "Wait a minute. You were keeping discs of this stuff?"

He closed his eyes and slowly nodded his head as shame finally took hold. He sighed heavily and said, "You know . . . I think that's how I ended up sleeping with Portia in the first damned place. It was those DVDs Tarantino was selling to his clients."

Kelly said, "Hold up. Are you saying the men knew they were being recorded?"

"A couple clients wanted a recording, but then Tarantino got the idea that he could sell DVDs overseas. And he did. He made a ton of money too. But anyway, Portia recognized some of the men were clients of the firm."

I said, "Her father's firm?"

"Yes. She told me she'd seen a DVD that had several different kiddy shows on it and that she had some friends who might be interested in getting in on the action for the right price and that we could probably get more at Saint Joseph's Orphanage. By this point, I was so out of control that I made the deal with the stipulation that I'd have to try them out first. Portia agreed."

Kelly said, "What did Portia have on you? I mean, she was blackmailing you, wasn't she?"

I could tell Choice didn't expect that question. He wasn't going to tell us he was being blackmailed. He exhaled hard. He thought he wouldn't have to tell this part.

"Things were going well with the Jaguar Club for a while, but when Portia found out I was seeing Turquoise and her at the same time, she got really angry and resorted to blackmail to keep her father from finding out that his wife hadn't been faithful to him."

Without thought, I shook my head and said, "Um, um, um."

"Portia had found out about the affair when Turquoise was in a hurry to get to court and recklessly left her cell phone bill on the kitchen counter. The envelope had already been opened. After looking through the catalog of calls, she learned that her stepmother was calling my cell late at night regularly, which was suspicious at the very least, but the duration of the calls seal my doom. At first she was going to tell her father about the affair, but Myles worshipped the ground Turquoise walked on. Instead, she decided to get paid for her silence. In addition to payments, she told me I had to break off the relationship with Turquoise. The thing that bothered me about breaking it off was that I couldn't tell her why. I had to break Turquoise's heart without explanation. Portia told me that if she thought I had told Turquoise anything, she'd tell Myles everything.

"My back was against the wall. I couldn't let some teenage girl have me on the gallows for who knows how long. I told Tarantino what had happened. He knew what I knew, that if it ever got out that he was trafficking teenagers, he'd be out of business. He wanted to kill her immediately, but I convinced him that a more stylish plan of disposing of Portia was the way to go. I then constructed an elaborate kidnapping as misdirection to convince the cops that Portia was killed because Myles didn't pay the ransom. I thought that if she was killed without it being a result of a kidnapping, or some kind of believable accident, Myles wouldn't rest until he found out what happened to her. Myles has enough political pull to have the whole matter thoroughly investigated. That meant the FBI would dig very deeply into Portia's activities. And once that happened, we'd all end up doing time."

I said, "So that's when you decided to write the immunity agreement."

He nodded. "I knew that if it ever got out, you guys would question everybody she knew, but if she was killed because Myles called the cops that would probably be the end of it. No further investigation needed. When Myles paid the ransom, that screwed up everything and we had to improvise, which is why we kept demanding more money. After talking to the Barrington's housekeeper at another Barrington function, I had learned that the best time to have Brooke and Norm plant the bugs was while she was watching *The Young and the Restless*. I knew from talking to her how much she loved the show. I figured she would want the program back on as soon as possible so she wouldn't be suspicious of Brooke and Norm when they came over."

I was thinking that if there was a good morsel of information in the whole sordid affair it was learning that Joel Williams had nothing to do with Portia's kidnapping. His sin was that he slept with her in the first place. That gave her the leverage she needed to get him to go along with her schemes.

I said, "What does Jericho Wise have to do with all of this?"

"Again . . . I agreed to talk about the kidnapping and the murders only."

Kelly said, "So you're saying Jericho Wise had nothing to do with the kidnapping and the murders."

Choice exhaled. "I'm telling you everything relevant to Portia Barrington's kidnapping and subsequent murder. Is that clear enough for you?"

I said, "It's very clear, but you know a lot more than you're letting on."

He tried to hide a burgeoning grin that fought its way to the surface. It was obvious that both he and Martin Sanchez were scared to death of what Jericho Wise was capable of doing if he found out they had mentioned his name. While I was glad Choice was filling in a lot gaps for us, his smugness really bothered me. Then it occurred to me that he had said we were running out of time. I was about to ask him what he meant by that, when his cell rang.

"Yeah," Choice said after looking at the caller ID. "I'm on my way. I'm leaving now. Hold the ship for me." He closed his phone. "That was Brooke. They're at the Baltimore docks. They'll be aboard a cargo ship call Droomvanger. That's Dutch for Dream Catcher. It's in area B. If you hurry, you can still catch them."

I called the Baltimore Port Authority and told them to delay the Droomvanger until we got there. Then I called the Baltimore Field Division and explained the situation. They agreed to send a SWAT team over to area B of the dock. We put on our Kevlar vests, boarded one of the Bureau helicopters, and headed to the Baltimore dock. By the time we got there, the SWAT team was already shooting. Apparently, they had our suspects cornered in one of the buildings. From what I could see from the air, it looked like our guys were taking the worst of it. I counted six of our guys on the ground. I couldn't tell if they were breathing or not. Davis and Green must have been using armor piercing rounds.

As we descended, a round came through the windshield and hit our pilot in the shoulder. The copter was spinning out of control. I could hear more rounds hitting the tail rotor. A bunch of crazy high pitched mechanical sounds filled my ears as we spun. Smoke was filling the cabin. My heart was pounding. Another round shattered the pilot's visor. He was dead. We were about to crash. For some reason the film *Blackhawk Down* came to mind. We were only about twenty five or thirty feet in the air. I was sure we'd survive when we crashed, but I was scared of catching a round before then or soon after we exited. I was certain there was a sniper out there shooting at us and he was pretty good.

I saw a couple more of our guys go down just before our copter hit the ground. I was starting to choke on the smoke. We grabbed our M4A1's and put them on full auto. I had about six clips in my bag. I looked at Kelly. She was ready. Brooke Ursula Davis and Norman Green were about to die. There was no doubt about that. While I would never tell anybody that we summarily decided to be judge, jury, and executioner, that's exactly what we were going to be. Our guys were dead or dying. Brooke and Norman were going to die too. I opened the door and started shooting. I was shooting in the same direction as the Baltimore SWAT team.

"Sniper down! Sniper down!" I heard over the radio.

I took that to mean our sniper had gotten one of them. I saw the other one firing at us from the dock of an old building. The person firing at us was small. I assumed it was Brooke Davis, which meant Norm was probably the sniper. With Norm down, she was in serious trouble. She jumped down on the tracks and ran at us, firing round after round. She obviously wanted to die. We all opened up on her all at once. A hail of bullets ripped into her. A mist of blood shot into the air. We must have fired over two hundred rounds.

One of the reasons for so many rounds was because we were scared she'd kill us if we didn't kill her first. The main reason for so many rounds was because she and Norm had killed eight of our brothers in arms. She went down. We all advanced on her position.

Blood was everywhere. She was trying to breathe, but it sounded like asthmatic wheezing to me. She was trying to say something so I got down on my knees and listened.

"Choice . . . sold . . . us . . . out?"

I nodded.

Her eyes rolled back into her head. Then as if she was willing herself to live a few more seconds, she opened them. "Don't . . . tell . . . Erika . . . how . . . I . . . died."

"Who is Erika?" I asked.

"My . . . my . . . my . . . daughter."

Her eyes lost their light.

I guess I shouldn't have been stunned, but I was. It amazed me that even though she had a daughter of her own, one that she obviously loved, yet she had no compunction about killing other people's children or selling them. What made it so bad was that she was a woman. Being a female, I guess I expect more from us than I do from men. On the other hand, I had a daughter too, and I don't know any of the people who teach her. Mrs. Tobias came to mind. I didn't even know she was married until I visited her at the hospital and overheard her husband talking to her. I realized at that moment, it was time for another conversation with her. It was time to find out exactly what was going on between her and Savannah.

Chapter 38

D
r. Lester was looking out of her office window. She saw a black Corvette a long way off as it was driving up the long path that led to the orphanage. She smiled thinking that the car contained another set of well-to-do parents that she would work hard to get them one of her prized little girls. Moments later, the car parked and Agents Perry and McPherson were getting out of the car. They were talking to each other. She wished she could hear their conversation. She remembered watching them leave a few days ago. Now they were back. Although she was hoping that they only had a few follow up questions, she knew in her heart they knew she had lied to them about Portia being molested by her father. They had somehow found out that she was the one who had been molested by her father and that she had enjoyed it as much if not more than her father.

Her heart sped up and pumped hard as she realize that the reputation she had built over the years was about to shatter and come crashing down right before her very eyes. She had dreamed of this moment many times. They were nightmares actually; nightmares of the publicly humiliation she would suffer on the evening news when her deepest darkest secrets of her lurid lifestyle surfaced. As she watched the agents walk up the path to the building, she could see it all again in her mind's eye.

O
n a particularly cold New Year's Day, early in the morning, exactly one minute after midnight in 1998, thick snowflakes were falling and covering the grounds of the Saint Joseph Orphanage, where unwed teenage mothers abandoned their children. Several hours earlier, Kathleen Wildman and a few of her girlfriends were in the library playing a competitive game of Monopoly. Monopoly was her favorite board game and she was used to winning. She took pleasure in seeing the girls land on properties she owned

that were improved with red plastic hotels, which often sent the players who landed on them into bankruptcy.

There they were, four little girls, eight years old, wearing an assortment of Flintstones pajamas, featuring Wilma, Betty, Pebbles, and Dino. They drank eggnog and laughed like little girls do. Normally they would be in bed long before midnight, but they were allowed to stay up and play, being the top students in the orphanage—at least that's what they were told. The truth, however, was truly appalling. In order to stay up late, Kathleen had made certain promises to the powers that be and procured a carton of eggnog and extra hours of playtime in the library with her friends.

It was Kathleen's turn again. Smiling, she shook the dice, rolled them on the board, and then moved the car three spaces from Boardwalk, past go, and landed on Community Chest. Her face lit up when Portia, her best friend, and resident banker handed her two hundred bucks. She picked up a yellow card and read: "Proceed to Go, collect two hundred dollars." Just as Portia handed her another two hundred, Molly Lester walked into the library and flicked the light switch on and off rapidly to get their attention. Even though she wasn't a nun, she was wearing a loose fitting habit, which always frightened the girls. The uniform was a symbol of power and reminded Molly of her father's fatigues and the fear she felt when she saw him in it.

Molly loved putting the fear of God into them. She loved it when they immediately stopped whatever activity they were involved in, stood up, and snapped to attention whenever she entered a room they were in. She loved the way they stood still, barely breathing, frozen, not even batting their eyelashes as she walked around the room, inspecting everything she saw. Nothing could be out of place. Her father, a Marine Corps Drill Instructor, had done this very thing to her when she was their age—Stockholm Syndrome.

The girls quieted themselves as Molly walked passed them, eying them, inspecting their pajamas as if they were Marine Corp issued fatigues. She looked for eggnog stains, spots of any kind, and when she didn't find any, mimicking her father, she shouted, "Hands . . . out!"

In unison, all four girls snapped out their arms two by two.

"What are the rules?" Molly asked in an even tone.

They shouted, "Everything must be clean, dry, and serviceable!"

"I can't hear you!" Molly shouted.

"Everything must be clean, dry, and serviceable," They screamed as loudly as they could.

Molly snapped to attention like she was a Captain trying to impress the generals during a parade. She pivoted on the balls of her feet, took a step to the right, and stood in front of the first girl. She looked her up and down and then leaned in and smelled her. She snapped to attention again and did the same thing to all of them. She was behind them now, looking for dirt on their pajama bottoms. "Is everything clean, dry, and serviceable?"

"Yes, Ma'am!"

"I sincerely hope so for your sakes," she replied, as she returned to the front of the line.

She stopped in front of each girl again. This time she would be even more scrutinizing. She looked at each girl's hand and then her fingernails, inspecting them closely, hoping to find particles that shouldn't be there. The first two girls passed inspection, but Kathleen Wildman and Portia had a spec or two of red and blue glitter underneath their fingernails.

A triumphant gleeful smile emerged just before Molly said, "What do we have here?"

The girls looked at their hands. When Portia saw the glitter, her face drained of blood as the horror of what was about to happen arrested her.

Molly looked at the two girls who passed inspection and said, "Put the game away and then off to bed with you. And I had better not hear a peep from either of you. You read me?"

"Yes, Ma'am," They said and saluted.

She returned their salute with one of her own, dismissing them from formation.

Relieved, the two girls quickly packed up the game and practically ran off, glad they had been meticulous when they bathed; glad the wicked witch from the west hadn't found anything on them.

"We don't run . . . we what?" Molly called out to them.

"We walk," the girls said and walked quickly out of the library.

Molly Lester had been one of Saint Joseph's most promising orphans. She was incredibly intelligent and had a photographic memory. Her ability to remember everything she saw and heard astounded the nuns who taught her, particularly the Mother Superior. In fact, the Mother Superior was quite taken with young Molly, and lavished praise upon her whenever she saw her. She was sixteen at the time and had been impregnated by her father four times. Four times a "doctor" vacuumed the child out of her. When the Mother Superior learned of Molly's tragic upbringing, she saw in her a proselyte that could be molded into her image. She saw someone who would continue setting the females of the species free.

One night, the Mother Superior came to her bed during lights out and took her up to her private bedroom on the third floor and gave her the kind of education she would never forget, even if she didn't have a photographic memory. Afterwards, they both said twenty Hail Mary's and all was forgiven. Twenty more Hail Mary's were said after every session they shared. Their time together had become a ritual of sorts, but not of the variety that the Pope would approve of. The Mother Superior did not believe in the tenets of the Catholic Church. On the contrary, she wasn't even a believer to begin with. She hated the church and what it stood for.

The Mother Superior wholeheartedly believed that the church sexually repressed women and turned them into mind numbed robots who were bred to be a sophisticated courtesan, which in her opinion, was a state of being a couple of notches above the common streetwalker. She believed it was her duty to infiltrate the Catholic Church and bring it to its knees by violating its core belief system, which would eventually be exposed as gross hypocrisy. She believed that all females were by nature lovers of their own kind and must be liberated from the slavery that tyrannical men of the cloth foisted upon them. She further believed that the rise of the woman to her rightful place as Monarch of the world was inevitable. She and others like her were only cogs in a vast machine committed to that end. The loss of innocence was a small price to pay for paving the way to a brave new world where the female of the species would rule without contradiction.

Molly remained the Mother Superior's faithful lover until the day she died. A few days after her lover's death, Molly, having been thoroughly brainwashed by her mentor, selected two little girls to indoctrinate into her mentor's philosophy—Kathleen Wildman and Portia. She would get them one at a time and then use the first to get the second. Kathleen was first.

M olly Lester waited until the other girls were gone and then she looked at Kathleen Wildman and Portia. "Well . . . what do you two have to say for yourselves?"

Portia wept. "I'm sorry, Molly. I thought I got all the glitter. Honest. I really did. Kat checked them over and everything right, Kat?"

Kathleen nodded.

"Well, you didn't do a very good job, Kat. An inspector you're not." She walked around them, looking at their hind parts, particularly Portia's, wantonly, sickly imagining how good it was going to feel when she opened her preadolescent mind to the pleasures the flesh offered. She smiled devilishly and said, "I suppose I'll have to bathe both of you at the same time. It'll be a baptism of sorts."

"But Molly," Portia began, "we already took a bath. Can't you just wash our hands? I promise it won't happen again. Will it Kat?"

Kathleen remained quiet, but nodded again.

"I suppose I could, but that would take all the fun out of it."

Portia looked at Kat, who quietly stood there listening, making no effort to avoid another bath and the naughty things Molly made all the girls do when they didn't pass inspection. She was surprised by her reaction. Her best friend almost looked as if she was looking forward to what had befallen them.

What Portia didn't know was that Kathleen had promised Molly that she would make sure there would be glitter under their nails so that Portia could join their special club—so that she could explore Portia, too, and know the pleasures her flesh offered. While nearly all the girls had private sessions with Molly, Kathleen was the only one who had fully embraced the debauchery.

Molly held their hands as they walked out of the library, down the hall past the administration office, and up the stairs to her bedroom which had its own bathroom. She turned the knob and opened the door. They went in and headed straight to the bathroom. The light was off, but the room wasn't totally dark. Strawberry scented candles were burning. Scented candles were Molly's incredibly sick idea of setting the "mood" for their "romantic" interlude. The tub was already filled with bubbles.

"You like bubbles, don't you Portia?" Molly asked.

She swallowed hard and nodded reluctantly afraid of what would happen if she said, "No".

Molly tentatively put her hand in the water, unsure of how hot it was. The temperature was absolutely perfect. "Quickly now, girls, get undressed and get in before the water gets cold."

Kathleen undressed and got in, but Portia hesitated when she saw Sister Molly taking off her habit. While this wasn't Portia's first time doing this, it would be the first time that Kathleen would be a part of it. There were never any candles and the lights were always off. She had never seen a naked woman before.

Portia just stood there, watching, stunningly amazed at how she looked in her white panties and brassiere. She watched her reach around and unhooked the harness that housed two mountains of flesh. She was big everywhere she looked. Her breasts were large and stretched down to just above her stomach. Her mouth fell open when Molly stepped out of her panties and she saw how hairy her privates were. It looked like an animal had taken refuge between Molly's legs.

Pleasantly, Molly asked, "Would you like me to help you take off your pajamas?"

Without thinking, Portia said, "This is wrong, Molly. This is a sin—a really big one, too!"

"Not if we say our Hail Mary's, right Molly?" Kathleen offered delightfully. "God won't hold it against us, will he, Molly?"

Than Kathleen started singing "Jesus Loves Me."

After Molly had opened Kathleen's mind, she asked her if she liked what they did together. When she said yes, she told her that if she enjoyed it, she was just as guilty as she was. She also told her that if she told anyone, they would both be in a lot of trouble. To ease Kathleen's guilt, they said twenty Hail Mary's after and that made everything all right just like the Mother Superior had taught her.

"That's right, Kat," Molly said. Then she looked at Portia. "Now . . . let's get those pajamas off."

Two months later, after Kathleen had been adopted, Portia took her place and had played the same trick on her best friend, Scarlett Johnson, the new girl with lovely blond curls and ocean blue eyes. However, the next day, Scarlett went up on the roof of the Orphanage and climbed up onto the ledge. She looked down at the crowd of children and faculty watching her, begging her not to jump. And then, a sudden gasp filled the air as little Scarlett Johnson jumped to her death—and Portia saw it.

Initially, seeing Scarlett Johnson plummet to her death shook Molly to the core, but later, she convinced herself that it wasn't her fault. The Mother Superior had told her that in every war there would be causalities. Scarlett Johnson wasn't strong enough to represent "real" women. It was better that she die young and never know how truly awful the world was with men running things. She then went onto college and majored in Psychology with a concentration in Child Psychology, and earned her PhD at Harvard in three years, as her lover planned.

She was far ahead of the curve, having been personally instructed by the Mother Superior, who was nothing short of brilliant in her own right, having earned a Master's degree at Wellesley. Due to her incredibly high test scores, Molly was able to take senior classes at seventeen. By her twentieth birthday, she had defended her dissertation. Her Harvard doctorate was supposed to be a part of her disguise. It was supposed to help her, in no small way, hide in plain sight through the fog of credentialism. People hear Harvard and PhD in the same sentence and they think expert. No need to investigate her psychological condition. No need to question her authenticity.

But something happened when Molly started graduate school. She met a man named Dr. Simeon Simms, one of her professors. He noticed the conflict that raged within Molly. He counseled her. During the sessions, she finally came to grips with what her father had done to her and her complicity in turning out the girls at Saint Joseph's Orphanage, and the tragic death of Scarlett Johnson. Simms helped her realize that the Mother Superior used her and took away whatever remaining hope she had in people in positions of power.

Full of regret, Molly changed the course of her life. She wanted to make sure what happened to Portia's friend and the other girls at the orphanage, never ever happen to anyone else again. Years later, she was a wife and mother of three girls and the director of adoptions. After she had successfully turned her life around, and had done so much good, the seeds she'd sown years earlier had grown up and were threatening her with public humiliation and jail time.

Still looking out her office window, she saw Phoenix and Kelly stop at the water fountain to get a drink. She decided it was time to make up for what she did to Scarlett Johnson. She wrote a quick note, placed a file on her desk, and hurried out of her office. She took the stairs to the roof, climbed onto the ledge and looked for Phoenix and Kelly. They were still at the water fountain, still drinking, still talking. When she saw them coming toward the building again, she looked toward the heavens, cupped her hands around her mouth, and shouted, "I'm sorry, Scarlett!" Then she closed her eyes and leaned forward. As gravity pulled her downward, as the horror of colliding with the earth loomed, she never even screamed. She hit the cement head first—and Phoenix and Kelly saw it.

Chapter 39

While the Medical Examiner collected the remains of Molly Lester, Kelly and I read the note and the file Molly had left for us. Although rushed, the note and the files she left told of what she had done to the girls at the orphanage and what led to Scarlett Johnson's suicide. As Kelly drove us back to Arlington, I remembered that Portia's diary said something about blackmail and alluded to an alliance. I also remembered her special collection of films depicting love triangles. Choice had said that Portia told him to break off the relationship with Mrs. Barrington without explanation. I was wondering if the helpful Turquoise Barrington was another player in the game that Choice was protecting on the same level that he was protecting Jericho Wise. Turquoise had been so eager to help and had given us Portia's phone records, all of which diverted any suspicion I might have away from her.

I said, "Kelly, what if Choice never broke it off with Mrs. Barrington?"

"Yeah, I was wondering about that too," Kelly said. "Once a relationship goes to the level of intercourse, it's difficult to just cut it off. In fact, I can't think of one person who didn't have trouble stopping that aspect of a relationship. One of the reasons Sterling and I can't seem to leave each other alone is because of sex's pull."

"Uh-huh," I said. "From what I've seen, it's easier for people to start having sex with another person while they're in a relationship than to end a relationship without having someone waiting in the wings."

"Yet Choice wants us to believe he was able to just cut it off with her."

"And let's not forget that he acted as if he didn't want to hurt her feelings, which means it wasn't just a romp for him. He had feelings for her—deep feelings. Feelings I don't think he was able to abandon as easily as he made it sound."

Kelly looked at me. "And if he never broke it off with her, she probably knows everything. If he's protecting her, if he wasn't totally forthright on the kidnapping, he's violated the agreement. Why would he risk going to jail if he didn't love Mrs. Barrington?"

"Who's word do we have other than the handsome Mr. Choice."

Kelly laughed out loud and said, "So he made you wet, huh?"

"I wouldn't say all that."

"But you found his movie star smile distracting, didn't you?"

"Just a little, but now, I'm focused again. He looks like Matthew McConaughey. What can I say? What's your excuse for not picking up on this from the beginning? He obviously wasn't interested in you. You should've had my back like I've yours when you see a good-looking man who makes your panties wet."

Kelly laughed. "So this is my fault, huh?"

I smiled and said, "Of course it's your fault. Head over to the Barringtons. I think Mrs. Barrington may have been involved with the kidnapping as well, which meant Portia may have been black-mailing her too. Let's see if we can shake her and get a confession."

"Yeah, otherwise, she'll lawyer up and we might have to cut a deal with her too. Everything we have on her is circumstantial so far."

"If she talks, we'll pick up Mr. Choice for violating our agreement."

I called Penelope at Wachovia and had her email me Turquoise Barrington's bank and credit card statements going back to March. A few minutes later my phone chimed. I flipped it open. An email had just come in. It was from Penelope. The subject line read: T. Barrington's Statements. I opened the email and learn that Mrs. Barrington had been withdrawing a couple thousand a month. Her credit card statement showed that she purchased a home theatre. And there it was—motive.

My cell rang. I looked at the caller ID. It was my husband. I hit the talk button and said, "What's up, babe?"

"I was thinking that since the case is pretty much over, maybe you'd let me take you to dinner. What do you think?"

"Where?"

"Oh, I was thinking about this nice little place in Washington would be great."

"Where, Keyth?"

"Café du Parc."

"In the Willard InterContinental?"

"Yes. Why not?"

"What time am I supposed to be there?"

"Where are you now?"

"We're on our way over to the Barrington's. Turns out that Mrs. Barrington may have been in on it all. That's what we think anyway."

"Are you serious?"

"That's how it looks."

"Hmm, anyway can you get there by about three?"

"Check in time, huh?"

Keyth was laughing. "You know me so well."

"I do, don't I?"

"Yeah."

"How 'bout I just meet you there. We can pick up Mrs. Barrington tomorrow. She's not going anywhere. She thinks she's gotten away with it. I'll just ride over to the hotel with Kelly. Have you gotten a room yet?"

"I gotta suite."

"Which one?"

"The Oval Suite."

I laughed and said, "Behave yourself, Mr. President."

"Not tonight. You fell asleep on me so I have to make sure you're not distracted this time. I want your complete attention."

"Do you have the whip cream?"

"You know it. I'm going to do some stuff to you tonight, girl."

"I'm looking forward to it."

"What time will you be there, Keyth?"

"I'm thinking, about five."

"Five? Why do I need to be there at three?"

"So you can bathe and do all the sexy things you do to make me wanna get all up in you."

When he said that, a blaze ignited down there. I looked at my watch. "That gives me time to arrest Turquoise Barrington then. I'll see you at about five or so, okay?"

"Okay, but don't bother going home. I packed the stuff I want you to wear."

"What did you pack?"

"Your leopard panties and bra of course."

I laughed. "That's what I figured."

"I think those panties and bra turn you into a real tiger, girl."

"You noticed, huh?"

"Yeah."

"See you at five."

When I hit the end button, Kelly said, "So are we picking up Mrs. Barrington or not?"

"Might as well."

I called Kortney Malone and updated her on everything we had so far. She was very disappointed to learn that we thought Mrs. Barrington was in on the kidnapping and consequently, all the murders. I told her that I had plans with my husband and she said she'd have a couple agents meet us at the mansion. I was going to arrest Turquoise Barrington, but I wasn't taking her in. I'd let the other agents do that. Rank had its privileges. I asked if Jack Ryan had turned up yet. Kortney said he hadn't. She added that when our people went into Raquel Mendes' penthouse, it looked as if she had gone out and would return. But so far she hadn't. We still had our people waiting for her, but I thought she was in the wind. I also thought Bobby Tarantino had killed Jack and he had left the country just like Christopher Choice had said and Raquel Mendes had left with him. Unlike Brooke and Norman, he was smart enough to leave on his own while his two flunkies were left holding the bag.

Barrington's housekeeper, Maria, led us to the living room where she served me tea and Kelly had coffee, while we waited for our prey to enter the trap. I was stirring sugar into my tea when the Barringtons walked in. Mr. Barrington was still obviously wounded by his daughter's death, but I also got the feeling he was more wounded by the fact that Christopher Choice had been doing nasty things to her. It bothered me that I was about to pour more salt into his exposed wounds in an attempt to get a confession from his wife.

Mr. Barrington sat down in a big comfortable looking chair and propped his feet up on the ottoman. Mrs. Barrington sat beside him, wrapped her arms around him, and laid her head on his shoulder. If I didn't know what I knew, I'd think she was trying to be there for him, to comfort him in his time of bereavement—playing the dutiful wife role to the hilt. But now the little scene looked like a staged play for me and Kelly to keep us thinking she had nothing to do with Portia's death.

Mrs. Barrington said, "Would either of you like something to eat?"

We declined.

"It's no trouble," Mr. Barrington said. "Are you sure? Maria can whip something up for you in no time."

"We're sure," I said.

I looked at Kelly, telling her to start the unscripted farce. I wanted to watch Mrs. Barrington's reaction as Kelly briefed Myles on our findings. We also wanted to find out if Mr. Barrington had abused his daughter too. If so, we were taking him in as well. We decided the charade would be more effective if we went after him and didn't mention blackmail until Mrs. Barrington was confident that we weren't there to arrest her.

Kelly sipped her coffee and said, "As you know, Mr. Barrington, Portia was into pornography and prostitution."

Barrington's eyes welled. I could tell he didn't want to hear any more about her. I understood how he felt because I understood the male sexual psyche. Nearly all males have no understanding when it comes to women. The exceptions to the rule would be the pimp and the preacher—two sides of the same coin. The only other entity alive that understood women was God himself. The average male conjured up images of the ideal woman and put his faith in the images he himself created, which was why he was always surprised by a woman's behavior.

"Do we have to talk about this now?" Mrs. Barrington asked.

"Unfortunately, we do," Kelly said. "Now, Mr. Barrington, it's clear that Portia was sexually abused long before she got into pornography and prostitution. When a girl is sexually abused, it's usually someone close to her."

I kept a close eye on Mrs. Barrington, watching her as she watched Kelly. I got the feeling that a sense of relief had washed over her, making her relax, which is right where we wanted her.

"So . . . you think it was someone we know?" Barrington said. "Someone other than Christopher Choice and the men who paid her?"

I saw Mrs. Barrington flinch. Not much, but enough to let me know her heart was now racing. I sipped my tea and continued to observe.

Kelly said, "Mr. Barrington, how well did you get along with your daughter?"

Barrington frowned. "How well did I get along with my daughter? What the hell are you asking me, Agent McPherson? Are you asking me if I abused my daughter? Is that what you're asking me?"

Kelly sipped her coffee again and let his questions linger for a few seconds.

"Answer me!" Barrington shouted.

"I think it's time for you two to leave," Mrs. Barrington said. She was standing now. I guess she was going to show us the way out.

Kelly sipped more of her coffee, unmoved by their reactions. "Sit down, Mrs. Barrington." She looked at Myles again. "Tell me . . . why you were giving her so much money, Mr. Barrington. Was she blackmailing you?"

Mrs. Barrington flinched again.

"What the hell are you talking about? I only gave her a couple hundred dollars or so a week for lunch and other things, like movies and clothes, and girl stuff. That can hardly be considered blackmail money!"

Maria came into the living room. "Excuse Mr. and Mrs. Barrington, but more FBI agents are here."

I said, "Maria could you have them wait for us in the foyer. We'll be making the arrest in a few minutes."

"What?" Barrington screamed. "You're arresting me? Me? This is an outrage!" He looked at me and said, "Palmer is not going to like this, Agent Perry. Your career is on the line."

"Palmer knows all about this," I lied. "We have his approval." The look on Barrington's face was priceless. He relaxed and leaned back. "After all, Portia is his goddaughter and he loved her too." Calmly, I said, "Mrs. Barrington, I'm wondering if you could let me use your computer to download the evidence we have to prove our charges."

"Proof?" Myles shouted. "I want to see this proof you say you have. There can be no proof because I'm innocent. You two are going to lose your jobs for this."

I looked at Mrs. Barrington. "May I use one of your computers, please? Then we can stop all this right here and right now."

"Sure," she said. "Follow me."

"Come right back, dear," Myles said. "I want a witness of everything they say."

"I promise I'll be right back. I'll just show her where the computer is and I'll be right back."

Myles said, "I'm not answering another question until my wife returns."

Mrs. Barrington led me down the hall past the agents. I said, "We'll be with you in about ten minutes."

They nodded.

"I think there's been some sort of mistake, Agent Perry," Mrs. Barrington said when we reached her office. "Myles loved his daughter. He would never do anything to harm her."

I said, "When you've been in this business as long as I've been in this business, you learn that anybody is capable of anything."

Mrs. Barrington sighed and offered a demure, "I'm afraid I have to agree. Well, I have to get back. My husband needs me."

Chapter 40

I watched Mrs. Barrington hurry back to the living room and then I entered her office. I was fairly certain she had no idea we were here to arrest her, not her husband. The computer was already on. The screensaver was of a beautiful snowcapped mountain against an azure blue sky that I presumed was somewhere on the Alaskan frontier. Using the mouse, I clicked on Internet Explorer and then went to my AOL account. I opened the email Penelope sent me and printed out Mrs. Barrington bank and credit card statements. I saw another email with an attachment and then another came in from the San Francisco office.

I opened it and watched a video of Brooke Davis and Norman Green going into the San Francisco apartment building that Christophe Choice had told us about. They came out about fifteen minutes later. And then a slew of people wearing white overalls entered the building shortly after they left. They were carrying buckets of paint, carpeting; all the things carpenters would need to make a murder scene look like a normal apartment where nothing unusual happened. I fast forwarded the video and less than an hour later the carpenters came out with two rolls of carpet that I presumed concealed Judge Twist and his transvestite lover, Gloria Dunes. The other email showed the apartment that Dunes lived in.

That's when I knew we had to get over to Raquel Mendes' penthouse. If she was Bobby Tarantino's love interest as Ryan had presumed, Tarantino may have lived there also. Drug dealers often put houses and cars in other people's names to keep us law enforcement types off their backs. There could be something in the penthouse that our guys missed because everything looked normal. If you don't know exactly what you're looking for, you could easily see it and not recognize it as a clue or even evidence. I rifled through a few drawers looking for a highlighter. I found one and started marking off Mrs. Barrington's withdrawals and purchases. Then I left the office and told our two guys to follow me. Having two tough looking federal agents would be good for intimidation. We wanted the confession. We didn't want Mrs. Barrington to lawyer up.

I walked back into the living room. Kelly was standing by the French doors that led to the terrace. I figured she was talking to Sterling when I heard her say, "We should be done here in a few minutes." Then she closed her phone and looked at her watch.

I had the evidence, so I took over the interrogation at that point. I walked over to Barrington. He was sitting on the ottoman now.

"What's that?" Barrington asked. "Is that the so-called evidence? I hope you have me cold on this, Agent Perry because if you don't, you're through at the Bureau."

"They're bank statements," I said.

"Let me see them," he said and reached out. "I can explain everything you think you have on me."

"The kidnapping was a farce, wasn't it Mr. Barrington?" I said, beginning the charade. "You were having sex with the beautiful little girl you adopted, weren't you? And there was never a ransom demand, was there? Portia was threatening to expose you for who you were and you knew your career would be over, didn't you?"

"No, I never—"

I cut him off. All of this was a show for Mrs. Barrington. I wasn't asking real questions expecting real answers. I wanted her to be as relaxed as possible so when I pounced on her she would be caught completely off guard and confess to everything. I shook the statements in Mr. Barrington's face and shouted, "So you're saying you didn't buy Portia all those expensive clothes and shoes?"

Barrington frowned and yelled, "What expensive clothes and shoes are you talking about, Agent Perry?"

I looked at the statements and pretended I was reading facts when I said, "So you're saying you didn't buy Portia a pair of $14,000 alligator boots?"

"$14,000?" Barrington questioned. "For a pair of boots?" He reached for the papers I was holding again. "Let me see that."

"Answer the question," I yelled.

"I have no idea what you're talking about, Agent Perry." He started crying again. "She must of have gotten the money from selling herself. She must have sold herself a lot of times to get that much money."

"I suppose you didn't buy the theatre she had built either?"

He looked at me and frowned. "What theatre? I have no idea what you're talking about."

"You didn't buy Portia a $150,000 state-of-the-art Egyptian themed theatre?"

"No!" he said as tears slid down his face.

"All right! That's enough!" Mrs. Barrington screamed. "I want all you out of my house this instant!"

"You're right," I said, looking at Mrs. Barrington. "It is enough. It was you, Mrs. Barrington. You bought the theatre and the clothes and the boots because Portia was blackmailing you, wasn't she?"

Mrs. Barrington recoiled and said, "What?"

I handed her bank and credit card statements to Mr. Barrington.

"Ah, c'mon now," I continued. "You're caught. We know all about you and the affair you were having with Christopher Choice. He told us everything this afternoon. He made a plea agreement. You're all done. End of story."

Mr. Barrington looked at the bank and credit card statements. But he obviously couldn't believe it even though I had highlighted everything for him. He must have loved her very much to see the evidence we had and still find it difficult to accept the truth.

"Is this true, Turquoise?"

She looked at the floor.

"Is this true?" he repeated. His voice quivered as the truth slowly penetrated his heart. "Answer me, damn you?"

Still looking at the floor, she said, "Yes, it's true. I didn't mean to hurt you, Myles. I swear I didn't."

Without thought he slapped her hard. She fell off the ottoman. Then he dived on top of her. Kelly and I watched him beat the hell out of her before we stopped it. As he punched her, he screamed, "I loved you! I loved you! I loved you!"

When our guys got him off her and took him out of the room, I said, "Turquoise Barrington, you're under arrest for the kidnapping and murder of Portia Barrington. You have the right to remain silent."

"I know my rights," She screamed. "Just tell me one thing."

"What's that?" I said.

"Did Chris give me up?"

"No, actually he protected you," I said. "He clearly violated his agreement by doing so. You won't be going down alone. He must love you very much."

"And I love him too," she said, like she was suddenly proud of what they had done together.

"I answered your question, Mrs. Barrington. Please answer mine. Whose idea was it to kidnap Portia and kill her?"

"It was mine. The greedy little bitch had to die."

"So you knew Christopher and Bobby Tarantino were running a teenage prostitution ring out of Joel Williams' building?"

"Yes. We were trying to get Bobby off my back."

I frowned. "What do you mean? Bobby had Chris for gambling debts, right?"

"No. Bobby had me because Chris told him that Portia was blackmailing us. My career was on the line."

"Because you were having an affair?" Kelly said. "That doesn't make any sense."

"The whole thing began long before Portia started blackmailing us. It all started two years ago when Davis and Green stole a million dollars from Tarantino. I was seeing Chris and he was representing Tarantino. Judge Twist was presiding. I was prosecuting. Twist wasn't going to go along with dropping the charges. He felt he had an obligation to try Tarantino regardless of the theft. He told us that the money was stolen after the bust and we could prosecute Davis and Green for that if we wanted, but the Tarantino case was still moving forward. Michael Brunner was originally assigned to the case, but he had told me that Twist had come on to him a number of times at the Round Robin Bar where we all tended to go after work. I told Chris and he threatened to expose Twist. Tarantino decided he might need to blackmail Twist in the future so he set him up. Gloria did too good of a job on him. The man had left his wife and was ready to come out of the closet and if that happened, who knows what he would have said once he had nothing left to hide."

"Why didn't you just tell the truth?" I said, incredibly dumbfounded by what she was telling us. "It would have ended your marriage, but you could have at least maintained some level of dignity and character."

"You don't understand, Agent Perry. Once you get in bed with these people, you never get out. I was having an affair with a man who was representing a big-time drug dealer. I loved him enough to help him. Once I did, I was in for life. I had no idea it was going to go to this level. We needed Tarantino to help us get Portia off our backs. The only way to do that was to kill her and neither of us could get our hands dirty and hope to keep our licenses. Twist knew nothing about Tarantino's prostitution ring until Gloria told him.

"She had fallen in love with him and couldn't keep her mouth shut. She thought that since Twist was a conservative, he would look the other way because he couldn't afford to let the world know that a conservative who had preached family values was a flaming homosexual. But when he decided to leave his wife, he told Gloria he was going to go public with it all. Both our careers were on the line. And once Myles found out about the affair, he was going to divorce me and then where would I be with no way to support myself?"

"I hope it was worth it," Kelly said with rancor. "Maybe you two can write each other love letters in the penitentiary."

Then she laughed from her belly.

Mrs. Barrington's face twisted into an ugly scowl. I thought she was going to attack Kelly for laughing at her.

"I hope you do try it, Mrs. Barrington," Kelly said. "Please try it. I'd love to finish the job your husband started, you dumb ho! You had it all and you fucked it up! Do you know how many women would love to be in your position? Do you?! You were living in a fucking mansion. You had a housekeeper and shit! You drive a goddamned Jaguar for Christ sake. You fucked it all up! And for what? Sorry ass Christopher Choice? A man who wasn't loyal to you? You blew it all for a man who was sleeping with prostitutes and with your stepdaughter while he was sleeping with you?" She snatched her by the arm and turned her around and put the cuffs on her. She looked at our guys and said, "Get this dumb bitch outta my sight!"

Chapter 41

I told Kelly about the video I had gotten from the San Francisco office while we were on our way over to the Palomar Hotel where Bobby Tarantino may have lived with Raquel Mendes. Two of our people were still waiting in the lobby, hoping he did live there and would soon return. I told them about the video I'd seen and then Kelly and I retrieved the penthouse and elevator keys and went up to take a look around. Everything seemed normal just like the San Francisco apartment I'd seen, but I had the feeling that Jack Ryan had been killed in that penthouse. I went out on the glass enclosed terrace. It offered a breathtaking view. Not only could I see a picturesque view of the Potomac River, I could also see the Capitol building, the Lincoln and Jefferson Memorials, and the Washington Monument.

Kelly said, "It seems like the criminals always know how to live, doesn't it?"

I said, "Hmpf! If you want to marry Sterling, you should tell him."

"Huh? Where did that come from?"

"You know where it came from, Kelly. That little speech you gave Turquoise Barrington, that's where. You're obviously jealous of what she had. She's not the first woman who had it all and blew it because she decided to have an affair. You went off because you wish you lived in a mansion like that and had your pick of either a Jaguar or a Bentley to drive to work every morning. I'm just saying that if you want that life and you think Sterling can give it to you, let him know. Otherwise, it's going to eat at you until you do."

"I have absolutely no idea what you're talking about."

"Play the dumb role now if you must, but give it some thought."

I left her on the terrace and started walking through the penthouse, unsure of what I was looking for. But whatever it was, I knew it was still there. I believed Bobby Tarantino was in a hurry. Killing Jack Ryan wasn't on the agenda that day, which means he was probably in panic mode. And if I was right, he could not have remembered to take everything that would lead to him. It was probably something easy to forget. If he had a safe, I'm sure he cleaned it out. He'd also take any drugs and weapons he may have had. Those would be the first things he'd pack up before he hit the road.

I looked at the phone and smiled. I realized he probably made a phone call or two before he left. "Kelly," I said. She was still on the terrace. Again she was on the phone. Again I figured it was Sterling. I wondered if she was letting him know how she felt. She saw me looking at her and closed the phone.

"What did you find?" She asked when she came into the room.

"Use your cell to call downstairs. Ask them if there was any work done up here recently."

I looked at the phone again. I assumed there were more throughout the penthouse. I thought that if Tarantino killed Ryan, he didn't erase the numbers on any of his phones. Ryan had told us that Raquel Mendes lived here, but there were pictures of a dark-skinned black man with an exotic looking woman and what I presumed to be their two daughters. If I had to guess, I'd say the woman was of either Spanish or Portuguese descent.

I put on a pair of surgical gloves and picked up the receiver. Then I hit redial. A woman answered, "Concierge. How may I help you today, Ms. Mendes? Taking the children on another tour?"

"Hi this is Phoenix Perry. I'm with the FBI. I was just checking the line."

I hung up and walked through the penthouse, looking for the rest of the phones. There was a chance that he made a call from one of them. I was hoping that he panicked. As I walked through the penthouse looking for the phones, I kept seeing pictures of the woman I presumed to be Raquel Mendes and her children. I went into the kitchen, picked up the phone and hit redial. Room service answered. I hung up.

"Phoenix," Kelly said. "Yes, there were some people here yesterday evening at about four or five. And get this. Mr. Mendes told the desk clerk he was expecting some men to replace the carpeting and paint a few rooms."

I said, "All we have to do is follow our noses."

"I asked him if an FBI agent name Ryan was here. He said the Mendes' didn't have any visitors yesterday other than the carpenters. To get up here you have to be announced or have a special key."

I wondered how Ryan was able to get up here without hotel security knowing about it. "Have one the agents downstairs check their video. Let's make sure Ryan was here and that there's no video of him leaving. I'm going to take a look around and find the room with the new carpeting and a new paint job."

I left the kitchen and entered the foyer. The place had more doors than an ocean liner. I opened several closet doors and a half bath before opening a door that led to the elevators. I went back down the hall and entered the dining room. I sniffed, but I didn't smell paint. I opened door after door and got nothing but more bathrooms, five and a half so far, and five bedrooms, but no smell of fresh paint so far. Except for the closets, all the rooms had phones. I'm sure I had gotten on the staff's nerves with all the calls. The residence was over 4,500 square feet; so big that I think I may have entered several rooms twice. Finally, I entered the library. That's when I smelled the fresh paint and saw the new carpeting.

"In here Kelly," I called out. Kelly came in. "On our way out, we'll have the criminalists go over the place."

I looked at my watch. 3:12. I wanted to look around more, but I also wanted to get over to the hotel. We had a few more rooms to check. If we got lucky, we might get a redialed number that actually led somewhere. Eventually, we got to the den. We went in and looked around. There were more pictures in there, just like all the other rooms, including the bathrooms. I sat in the chair behind the desk and pushed the speaker button. Then I hit redial and listened.

After about three rings a woman picked up and said, "What the hell are you still doing there? You were supposed to be in Sag Harbor yesterday! You should be in the middle of the South Atlantic by now!"

I looked at Kelly. "This is Phoenix Perry of the FBI. Who am I speaking with please?"

The line went dead. When I called back, no one answered. I opened my cell and entered the number. I'd have it checked out later.

"Who do you suppose that was? Ms. Mendes?"

Kelly shrugged her shoulders.

I saw a floor model globe inside a hardwood base. I went over to it and turned it to the United States. I quickly found New York and The Hamptons where Sag Harbor is located. Then I looked south beyond Florida and the islands.

"What are you looking for?" Kelly asked.

"I'm looking for where Ms. Mendes might be from. I get the feeling that's where he's going. Judging by her pictures, it's not the islands. I'm thinking South America. It'll be easy to find out. The staff should know her and where she's from."

I picked up the phone.

"Concierge," the same woman said.

"This is Phoenix Perry again. How long have you worked here?"

"About two and half years. Why? What's going on? Did something happen to the Mendes family?"

"We're not sure at this point. Do you know Ms. Mendes personally?

"Not personally, but I've talked to her a number of times. Why do you ask?"

"I'm wondering if you can tell me where Ms. Mendes is from."

"Fortaleza, Brazil. She's Portuguese."

"And can you tell me what Mr. Mendes looks like?"

"He's African-American, but really, really nice. He's really black but handsome in a rugged kind of way. I could see why a white woman like Ms. Mendes would go for him."

"You wouldn't happen to know his first name, would you?"

"His name is Robert."

"Thanks," I said and hung up.

"So do we have our guy or what?"

"Oh we got 'em all right. She says he's really black, but really, really nice."

"What?"

"Yes, Kelly. Then she said she could see why a white woman would go for him."

"And you let her get away with that?"

"She is who she is, Kelly."

"Well on our way out you should introduce yourself so she can see who she was talking to."

"And that's going to do what, exactly? Turn her into Mary, the mother of Jesus, all of sudden? She doesn't even know she's being offensive. Confronting her isn't going to change her perceptions. Like I said, she is who she is."

"If you won't say anything, I will."

"Why? Because Sterling's black?" I said and laughed.

"I don't see anything funny about this, Phoenix."

"Okay, well, we're on the clock, Agent McPherson," I said, smiling. "Perhaps we should do what the taxpayers pay us to do before you go postal again."

Kelly rolled her eyes and started looking at the map again. "Tarantino could also be going to the Caymans."

"Not if he should be on the South Atlantic by now. There's no way he'd be in the Caymans. He'd be in the Gulf of Mexico if he was, but she specifically said the South Atlantic." I looked at my watch. 3:26. "Let's go back to your hotel. Keyth reserved a room for the night."

"Really?"

"Yes! The Oval Suite. He expects me to be there now so I can bathe and perfume. We have some business to take care of."

Solemnly, Kelly said, "You've got it made, Phoenix. I hope you appreciate what you have."

That was Kelly's way of admitting I had been right earlier when I told her why she went off on Turquoise Barrington. We walked out of the den. I stopped in my tracks and backed up.

Kelly said, "What?"

I looked at the picture on the wall near the door. There it was. The small item I thought Tarantino would miss. "Look at this, Kelly."

"What?"

"Isn't that Mason Spivey in the photo?

"Uh-huh. And that's Tarantino?"

"What if Mason knew about the affair his wife was having with Joel Williams? And he had his friend kill her while he was on a West Coast road trip thinking it would solidify his alibi?"

"It can't be a coincidence," Kelly said, shaking her head. "They're in it together. Let's arrest him. We'll sweat him and see."

Chapter 42

The agents stationed in the lobby told us the hotel video showed Jack Ryan waiting at the elevator. I asked the manager if she would allow me to watch the video. I needed to see what happened myself to get a feel for what occurred. The manager took us into her office and ran the videos for us. We saw Ryan waiting for the elevator just as our agents had said. A few minutes later, the Palomar manager identified the woman who had gotten off as Mrs. Mendes. Then the two of them got back on the elevator together. Less than an hour later, the carpenters showed up just like they had in the San Francisco videos. Next, we saw the carpenters get off the elevator with two rolls of carpet.

If Jack Ryan was in one roll, who was in the other? Then we saw Tarantino and two young girls get off the elevator and hurry to the exit. Another video showed them getting into a limousine. Two things bothered me. First, assuming Jack Ryan was dead, how could Tarantino get a cleanup squad here so soon? What kind of connections did he have? Second, since we didn't see the woman identified as Mrs. Mendes leave the building and she wasn't in her penthouse, was she dead? Is that why there were two rolls of carpeting? Did Ryan kill her? Or did Tarantino?

Kelly made sure we stopped by the concierge station so she could give the woman a piece of her mind. While she didn't go postal a second time, she made sure the woman knew I was the lead agent, that I was reared in Beijing, that I had a Master's degree in Criminology, that I spoke the Mandarin and Cantonese languages, and that I had mastered the art of kung fu and could probably take her apart in a matter of seconds. I actually felt sorry for the woman because she really didn't mean any harm. She was probably raised that way. After Kelly got off her racism soapbox, we left the Palomar and headed over to our hotel.

I didn't realize I had been quiet until Kelly said, "What's on your mind?"

"Huh? Oh, I was just thinking about the cleanup crews."

"And?"

"And I'm wondering how a drug dealer, even one making the kind of money he was obviously making, has access to a cleanup crew reminiscent of the CIA? Even if he had a crew here, would he have one in San Francisco too? And how often does he use them to have them on standby? Exactly how many murders is he responsible for?"

"So you think the Agency's involved?"

"At this point, I don't know what to think. I just know drug dealers are not that sophisticated. Yet in this case, Jericho Wise has an entire staff involved in his underworld dealings at Joel Williams' building. I'm wondering how deep this thing goes."

"We do have a contact within the Agency now," Kelly said tentatively. "But when you get in bed with them, having the orgasm isn't enough for them. They wanna make you their bitch so they can get their rocks off for the rest of your life. They never let you outta bed. They tie you to the bedposts and there you are, spread eagle waiting for them to come back for another twisted round."

"I know, but McAlister owes me," I said. "It couldn't hurt to give him a call. See if he knows anything about a rouge CIA crew operating within the borders again."

Kelly took a deep breath and said, "If you don't mind getting ganged by the Agency I guess it's worth a try."

Chapter 43

E ven though the Willard InterContinental was only five and half miles away, it took us about twenty five minutes to get there. Getting around in Washington can be difficult. And forget about finding a place to park on the streets. While I was only in the heat for a few minutes, I was glad to get in doors so I could feel the cool air that I didn't have to pay for. I made my way over to the front desk, checked in, and went up to the suite right away. I could hear Johnnie Gill's *Quiet Time To Play* wafting throughout the suite. Keyth thought of everything; he knows how much I love that song and what it does to me when I hear Johnnie sing it. To me, that was Johnnie's signature hit.

I was thoroughly impressed by the Oval Suite and all its amenities. I went into the bedroom. My overnight bag was sitting on the bed and next to it were my leopard panties and bra. A basket full of bathroom goodies with my new favorite aroma, Black Currant Vanilla, was next to my undergarments. Keyth had gotten the basket from Bath & Body Works. Seeing his attention to detail put a smile on my face as I thought about what we were going to do when he got to the hotel. I decided to take a hot bath so I'd be ready when he arrived.

I went into the bathroom and was even more impressed when I saw the sunken tub. Keyth had really out done himself. Red roses were everywhere I looked. He had already set up scented three wick Japanese Cherry Blossom candles. The bathroom was glowing from the flames. I smiled again and inhaled deeply. Then I turned on the hot water, poured in some Black Currant Vanilla bubble bath, and then got my overnight bag. I undressed and looked at myself in the mirror. I have always had a complex about my breasts. I'm only a 32B cup, but I always wanted to be a 36c. I had even considered a breast augmentation, but I don't think I could go through with it. I decided I had to make the best of what God gave me. Besides, Keyth didn't mind. He always said more than a hand full is a waste. I've

275 Keith Lee Johnson

often wondered if he told me that to make me feel better. If he did, it worked.

I got in the tub, found a comfortable spot, closed my eyes, and relaxed. The hot water felt so good. I could feel the stress of a very busy day disappearing. Even though I didn't want it to, the Barrington case entered my mind again. I had forgotten to have the number traced Bobby Tarantino had called. I got out of the warmth of the sunken tub and splashed my feet across the marble floor into the bedroom where my purse was. Then I made the call. Then I hurried back into the bathroom and into the heat of the tub. I closed my eyes again and again the Barrington case came to mind.

I wondered how Tarantino knew Mason Spivey. I didn't think the picture of them was a picture of a fan meeting a famous ballplayer. There was no autograph. Besides, that picture had been taken in the living room of the penthouse. That meant Mason Spivey and Bobby Tarantino were friends. Or at the very least, acquaintances. I guess it could also mean Mason Spivey was on drugs and Bobby was his pusher, but why would a pusher kill a woman for someone who was strung out on drugs? I don't think he would. He'd probably kill the addict first, if the woman was innocent or of some value.

For Bobby Tarantino to have made it as big as he had, he couldn't be a fool. I didn't think so anyway. He had to be a smart man. Smart enough to have a crew to clean up his mess, which still bothered me. It bothered me even more when I realized that both cleanup crews were white men, not black. If they were black, I would think that Bobby was a very thorough drug dealer, leaving nothing to chance. A white cleanup crew meant white people were cleaning up murder scenes for black people. That made no sense at all unless they were in on it. But why would white men be involved with a black drug dealing thug who was also pimping white teenage girls? Again, none of it was making any sense.

Chapter 44

I wasn't sure how long I'd been asleep, but when I opened my eyes, the water wasn't nearly as hot as it was when I got in it. I thought I heard sounds in the living room of the suite, but it wasn't Johnnie Gill. I listened intensely. The television was on. That meant my husband was there. He must have come in the bathroom and saw me sleeping, and didn't want to wake me. I flipped the lever that drained the water and stood up. Bubbles hid my assets. I grabbed a towel and absorbed them. Then I sat on the cushioned stool in front of the vanity mirror and put on some cucumber lotion. After that, I slid into my leopard panties and bra. As a final touch, I sprayed on some White Diamonds perfume and left the bathroom.

Keyth was watching a pregame show on ESPN. The Wizards were about to play the Atlanta Hawks. I went over to him and sat in his lap. I kissed him and then said, "Mr. President, are you planning to watch the game or what?"

Keyth was shaking his head like he was disappointed. "The Wizards are through. They're not going to the playoffs this year."

Curious, I said, "That's what's bothering you?"

"Yeah. I guess you haven't heard, huh?"

"Heard what?"

"Mason Spivey was arrested an hour or so ago at the arena. He's been charged with being an accessory to his wife's murder."

"Oh," I said. "I know. I was the one who made the connection. I saw a picture of Mr. Spivey this afternoon in the home of Bobby Tarantino, our lead suspect in the Barrington case. They looked like old buddies."

I doubled over laughing when Keyth said, "Please tell me she's not white."

"Well, I guess she could pass for white," I said. "She's Eurasian. You can't see much Asian in her though."

"Good, because I wouldn't want this to blow up like the O.J. Simpson trial did. And you know it would if she were white and blond. White folks love blacks like him."

I frowned. "What do you mean by that?"

"What do I mean? Come on, Phoenix, you know the deal. Mason's a clean cut guy who never gets in trouble. He's the spokesman for a ton of high profile products. He's so hot right now that he's making more money off the court than on. He's almost as hot as Tiger Woods and you know how beloved he is by the 'mainstream'."

"You think that's why it blew up?"

"Yeah, don't you? If race didn't play a significant role in the Simpson trial, how is it that when Rae Carruth, who played wide receiver for the Carolina Panthers, was charged with being an accessory to killing his black girlfriend, it got virtually no coverage. It was on Court TV, sure, but it wasn't nearly the sensation that the Simpson trial was."

I laughed and said, "Well, he didn't have a dream team like O.J. did."

"Please, girl, you were raised in Beijing so maybe you don't know the deal. Simpson's ex-wife was white and blond and very dead with her head nearly cut off. That's a bad combination if you're black and the only suspect. And it didn't help that he was kicking her ass on the regular—at least that's what was reported."

"So you're saying he didn't do it?"

"No, I'm saying it wouldn't have been as big of a deal if Simpson had killed his first wife who was black period. I bet most folks don't even know who Rae Carruth is, nor do they care about him or the victim in that case. Why do folks care so much about Simpson and his ex-wife still? Because she was white and blond, that's why."

"Okay, well I thought we came here to take care of some business," I said and massaged his crotch. "You up for it."

He smiled and said, "If you keep doing that, I will be."

While I won't go into all the details, twenty minutes later, we were in the king size bed seriously getting our swerve on. I said seriously, okay? An hour or so later, we were at the cutting edge of sleep even though we had ordered room service, which had apparently arrived. When Keyth went to the door to get our food, I heard his phone sample Michael Jackson's *Another Part of Me*. He had gotten a text message. I knew I shouldn't look at it, but curiosity got the better of me. So I picked up the phone and read: "We're here. Give us another hour or two and then come on over. She should be ready to talk by then." The text came from Kelly.

At first I thought it was some sort of mistake. I thought that Kelly had inadvertently sent Keyth the text. But something told me to check his calls. I did. My heart started pumping hard when I saw that they had talked several times that day. When I thought Kelly was talking to Sterling, she was actually talking to Keyth. It wasn't my birthday. So I knew it wasn't a surprise party for me. I wondered who "us" was. And who would be ready to talk by then? Did she mean me? If so, what would I be ready to talk about in two hours?

Keyth wheeled our dinner into the bedroom. "I hope you're hungry."

I tossed him the phone. "What's going on?"

He caught it and read the text. "I'll tell you about it later."

"I wanna know right now, Keyth. Why are you talking to my partner behind my back and don't tell me it's some sort of surprise for me either."

He calmly sat down like he didn't have anything to hide. Then he lifted the lid and started eating as if he didn't hear me. "Keyth! I know you heard me? I hate when you do that!"

He offered me a long menacing stare, like he was trying to intimidate me. Then he started eating again.

"Are you going to answer me?" I yelled.

"Listen," he began, staring into my eyes, "let me tell you something Phoenix Drew Perry. You don't scare me, okay? I'm not afraid of you in the least bit. You might be able to kick my ass . . . but believe me . . . you would feel the wrath too. You need to get that shit through your head, okay? Now . . . I'll tell you about the call when the time is right." He looked at his watch. "Eat your dinner and I'll tell you when you finish. I have some things going on that you can't know right now, but I will tell you in about an hour."

"You promise?" I said.

"I promise I'll tell you everything after we eat."

It always made me wet when my husband put his foot down. I don't know why, but it did. I got out of the bed and went over to where he was sitting. Then I ravaged him again before we ate—once more after.

Ninety minutes later, we were heading over to the Arlington Police Department. It turned out that Keyth and Kelly were co-conspirators. Kelly had gone to Keyth behind my back and told him the story about the tennis coach that tried to turn her out in college. Instead of coming to me with it, Keyth had given Kelly permission ask Captain Downs to have a couple of his uniforms pick Savannah up for assault and battery. They had fingerprinted her, took a mug shot, the whole nine. Apparently Keyth's mom and dad were in on it too.

I was not happy and that's putting a good spin on it. I was the only one who didn't know what was going down and why we were at the Willard. They all knew I would never let the police handcuff my daughter and take her in without kicking some ass. We all would have gone to the hospital before I ever let that happen. So, wisely, my husband decided to get me out the way for a few hours so that Savannah would be isolated. Of course Kelly was there the entire time, supervising the charade, but still, it pissed me off that this was happening to my daughter and there was nothing I could do about it.

On the way over to the station, Keyth had told me we had to find out what was going on with Savannah. He was concerned that her temper had gotten out of control. I told him he knew she gets it from me, but he wasn't buying it. He told me he thought something else was going on. He said Kelly's thoughts on the subject had lots of merit and should be explored. I vehemently disagreed with him. We argued fiercely all the way to the station. Part of what pissed me off was that he had gotten plenty of sex from me and he knew it was going to be a while before he got more.

So when he got in me, he acted like there was some oil up in there. He had me folded in half like an accordion, going deeper than I ever thought he could go. I mean he had me going completely out of my mind, to the point where I was trying to talk but the only thing that came out of my mouth was something incoherent, like a baby's babble. I could have sworn I heard William Shatner doing his opening monologue on the original *Star Trek* series when he said, "Space . . . the final frontier," and "boldly going where no man has gone before." I thought he was showing me how much he still loved me after fourteen years of marriage, but he was just savoring his last piece. What pisses me off even more is that I totally loved it and he knows I did.

We walked into the observation room. Captain Charlie Downs, who I thought would do anything for Kelly, was there along with two uniformed female officers. It was going to be another version of good cop, bad cop. If it were possible, I'm sure steam would have been coming out of my ears. I'm also sure the scowl I was now wearing let all the boys and girls in blue know I how unhappy I was about what was going on.

Kelly said, "Phoenix, I know you're pissed, but I think something's going on with Savannah and Mrs. Tobias. I hope I'm wrong, but honestly, I don't think I am."

I looked her in the eyes and said, "I'm only going to say this one time, Kelly. You better be right. Just so we're clear, if you're wrong, the relationship will survive, but I'ma hav'ta get in your ass."

"Don't worry, Kelly," Keyth said. "She's not going to do anything to you. She loves to sell wolf tickets, but nobody's buying today. Let's get the show on the road."

One of the uniforms left the observation room. A few seconds later she entered the interview room. My daughter was nothing like a lot of young people the cops bring in who acted like they had nothing to live for, like they were ready to die because they had seen so much death. Savannah looked like a frightened little girl who needed her mommy and daddy more than anything. I got the feeling that she was ready to talk. I wanted to go in and be there for her, but deep down, I knew that if I did, she would feel secure again and she wouldn't talk.

The uniform sat down and looked at her clipboard, remaining silent; waiting for Savannah to say something so she could scream at her, which would let her know this was serious business. I've seen it many times, but never with my own flesh and blood. I looked at Keyth. He looked equally concerned, probably more. It was his little girl in there too.

"Did you call my parents?" Savannah asked tentatively.

The officer screamed, "You don't speak unless you're spoken to, you got that? You're mine. I own you. Do you understand? I get so sick of seeing so many young girls like you who think they know everything and they don't know anything. They all end up on crack, and selling themselves to get their next high. Then they end up here.

And most of them never see their mother or father again, because they never leave prison alive. So the bottom line is, you should have thought about your mommy and daddy before you beat up Mrs. Tobias."

"But my mother is Phoenix Perry. She's a great FBI agent and my dad is a great private detective, officer."

"We know who Phoenix and Keyth Perry are. They can't get you outta this. To be honest with you, we cops don't like either one of them so this is pure pleasure for me to have you here as a guest, knowing they can't do anything about it."

Chapter 45

After the officer told Savannah there was nothing her parents could do to help her, she broke down and cried, which signaled Kelly and the two female officers that it was time for act two of the deception. They left the room and seconds later, the officer was telling Kelly she wasn't allowed in the room while an interrogation was going on. All of this of course was for Savannah's benefit. She had to see that Kelly was coming to rescue her. She needed to see a familiar friendly face in a sea of angry strange resentful faces.

Kelly screamed, "I'm a federal agent, officer! I have jurisdiction here! And this is my niece! Now you two get outta here right now!"

"We'll leave for now, but we'll be back in five minutes. She's going away for a long time, Kelly. And there's nothing you or Phoenix can do to stop it."

Then they stormed off and slammed the door. Seconds later, the officers were in the observation room with us. I looked at Savannah. She looked relieved and confused at the same time which was the point of this little farce. "Are you going to take me home, Aunt Kelly?"

"I don't think I can, Sweetie. Assault and battery are serious charges and you have the rank of black sash. You're a lethal weapon. You could have killed that teacher. Do you realize that?"

"Aunt Kelly, I took it easy on Ms. Tobias. I just wanted to teach her a lesson."

"A *lesson*? Why?"

Savannah got quiet again and lowered her head. She was obviously holding something back. The trick for Kelly was to get her to volunteer the information, which meant she had to be silent as long as Savannah was silent. Kelly was patient enough to wait. Nearly three long minutes passed before Savannah said, "I promised not to tell."

My heart almost stopped beating. I was thinking it's true. Kelly was right all along. Mrs. Tobias had molested my child, my daughter, my little girl. I started thinking of ways to seriously jack her up. The beating Savannah put her on was nothing compared to what I wanted to do. The images that flowed through my mind after hearing what my daughter said were enough to get me fried in an electric chair in a state that doesn't have the death penalty.

"Who did you make the promise to?"

I knew Kelly was trying to lead her to the truth one step at a time. If she could get her to tell part of the story, she might tell it all.

"Luther."

"Luther Pleasant?"

"Yeah. He's my friend."

"I know he's your friend, honey. So you were protecting Luther like you did a couple years ago when girls were picking on him? Was Mrs. Tobias picking on Luther?"

Savannah shook her head. "She wasn't picking on him."

"But she was doing something to him?"

Savannah nodded.

Kelly knew she had to figure it out and get Savannah to confirm the truth. That way she could keep her promise to Luther.

"So Mrs. Tobias was touching Luther?"

Savannah nodded.

"Was she touching his privates?"

Savannah nodded.

Two things immediately came to mind when my husband and I looked at each other. First, we'd had an argument about Keyth thinking it was okay for women teachers to have sex with their male students an hour or so before Director Malone called and told me about Portia Barrington's kidnapping. I had argued that it was just as important for boys to be pure as it was for girls. Not only should the males be sexually pure, they ought to be leading the charge. Why? Because it all begins and ends with males. With all the available and willing adult and teenage females, how is it that the sex industry is worth billions every year?

It occurred to me that traditional prostitution cannot long survive without the male's demand for it. Promiscuous females cannot long exist without the male's demand for promiscuity. I now knew that if the men didn't learn to control themselves, not only wouldn't women control themselves, but their lack of control would soon be as aggressive as a malignant cancer. Mrs. Tobias and women like her were living portraits of these phenomena. It further occurred to me that we've subtly been sold an idea that has destroyed every society where it's been practiced. We've bought into the historical debauchery of the Greeks and Romans. If the psyche of American males didn't change soon, our society will fall just as theirs did.

I don't know what stupor I was in, but it was clear to me now that Americans in general had forgotten, or at the very least we have ignored, the elementary facts of sexual intercourse in our unrelenting pursuit of pleasure without consequences; pleasure without responsibility; pleasure without or in spite of the children left in pleasure's disastrous wake. Perhaps the pleasure we receive from sexual intercourse is so addictive that we've forgotten that its primary purpose is reproduction, which is the replication of those who are engaging in it, reproducing essences of both their visible and invisible selves—the good—the bad—the ugly.

If this were not so, males would not shoot millions of sperm cells into a female every single time they climax. The sperm cells have but one goal: to seek out the female egg and penetrate it—reproduction. If males could achieve the same erotic euphoria without shooting their miniature selves into females, they would, but they can't so they resort to prophylactics in an effort to avoid the hazardous path of procreation.

Although I would never admit it to anyone other than my husband, and I'm not sure I'd admit it to him, the second thing that came to mind was that I was glad it was Luther and not my daughter. Don't get me wrong, I wouldn't want any child to suffer through the pangs of molestation. When a child is molested, it screws them up on the inside and they often become predators themselves. It's rare when it doesn't and I would guess the reason they become predators is because they never get the help they need to deal with what happened to them. In fact, because they enjoyed the pleasure, they often think nothing's wrong with it and that it's okay to do it to a child when they're an adult.

"Where was this, at school?" Kelly asked.

Savannah nodded. "In the coatroom. I was waiting for Luther after school. It was his birthday and we were supposed to have ice cream and cake. My grandmother made a lemon cake with lemon icing for Luther and everything. I got tired of waiting so I went in the school to look for him. I went to his last hour class. I thought he might be there doing something for Ms. Tobias. I walked in the classroom. No one was there. I turned around to leave, but then I heard these strange noises. It sounded like my mommy when her and daddy lock their bedroom door. They think we don't know, but me and Sydney always listen to them through the vents."

Keyth and I looked at each other. We thought we were being quiet.

"But don't tell them I told you that, Aunt Kelly. Mommy might get mad if she knew that we listen to them do it. They do it all the time. I think they're trying to make me another sister or brother. They're probably doing it right now. Daddy told me he was taking mommy away for the night. He thinks I don't know what they're going to do."

Kelly laughed. "Those two cops will be back any minute, Savannah. Tell me what happened next. With Ms. Tobias and Luther, okay?"

"Well, like I said, I heard a noise so I went to see what was going on. I walked into the coatroom and I saw Ms. Tobias on her knees. Luther was leaned up against the wall. His eyes were rolled back up into his head. And he kept making those noises like my mother so I know he was liking what she was doing to him. She had his thing in her mouth and she was going real fast."

"So did they see you there?"

"Yeah. When I saw what Ms. Tobias was doing, I guess I kind of screamed or something and Luther eyes rolled down and looked at me. Then I ran outta there. Luther ran after me shouting "wait", but I kept running until I got outta the building. And when he caught up to me, he begged me not to tell. I promised I wouldn't."

"So why did you and Mrs. Tobias get into it?"

"I was looking for Luther and I thought he was back in her classroom again. I knew what they were doing was wrong and I didn't want Luther to get into trouble. My mother told to me to always help the weak because I'm strong. I knew somebody had to help Luther and I was the only one who could. So anyway, when I walked in the class, she told me Luther wasn't there. I went into the coatroom, thinking he was in there hiding, but he wasn't. I was about to leave when Ms. Tobias told me to close the door, but I didn't. I left it open. She told me I didn't see what I thought I saw. I told her I did see it. Then she said Luther would never betray her and that nobody would believe me anyway because she was the most loved teacher in the school and that she had just gotten word that she was selected as Teacher of the Year. I told her I would tell the principal and see who he believed. That's when she grabbed me by the shoulder and told me I wasn't going anywhere to tell anybody anything. That's when I busted her up pretty good. She was trying to fight and when we ended up in the hall, a couple more teachers started grabbing me like it was my fault so I busted them up too. Then I gave Ms. Tobias a little bit more before they stopped me. I thought a few more licks would help her think it through the next time she decided to put her hands on me or her mouth on Luther."

At that point, me, Keyth, and the good cop went in. For the first time in a long time, Savannah ran to me and hugged me. A wave of emotions washed over me when I heard my daughter say, "I love you, Mommy."

The next morning, I called the principal of Matthew Henson and got my daughter immediately reinstated. Later that afternoon when we knew Luther would be in Mrs. Tobias' class, Keyth and I met the same two female officers at the school. I thought it best that Luther see what his future would be if he didn't get counseling immediately. We went to the principal's office, where an older substitute teacher was waiting for us. The principal escorted us up to Mrs. Tobias' class. When we all entered the room, she knew why we were there. She knew it was all over. She looked at the floor and wailed loudly like a paid mourner. She wailed so loudly that teachers from other classrooms came over to see what was going on. The officer who had played the bad cop handled her roughly and then handcuffed her in front of her students. I heard the principal introducing the substitute as we were escorting Mrs. Tobias out of her classroom.

W e decided to extend our stay at the Willard for another day or so. We had stopped at our home and picked up a few more changes of clothing and toiletries before heading back to the hotel. The Oval Suite had an extra bedroom so we took Savannah back to the Willard with us and ordered room service for her. After what she had been through, I let her have a cheeseburger and fries. After she ate, she and I talked and talked for hours, it seemed. We talked about what Mrs. Tobias did to Luther. We talked about her feelings for Luther, which she denied, but that was okay. We talked about sex and the importance of purity. We talked about my job and all the time I spent away from her. We talked about all the concerts and other firsts that I missed. When I got finished talking, I listened, and listened, and listened some more. I felt so bad for not being the mother I needed to be, but I was also assigning blame to teachers like Mrs. Tobias.

I don't think I slept at all the night we picked my daughter up from the police station. I think I couldn't sleep because I couldn't wait to go into that school and see Mrs. Tobias' face when the cops arrested her. I thought it was going to feel good to see her get what was coming to her. But when I saw the anguish, the guilt, and the embarrassment Mrs. Tobias felt, I was deeply moved. My heart felt for her, not because she was a woman too, but rather, because she too had been a victim. I think it was then that I realized that when she had been molested as a little girl, nobody noticed. And if they did notice, they either didn't care or didn't know how to help her. On the way home, I wept for her, her husband, and especially for her three daughters. It was truly a tragic situation for the entire community.

Of all the people hurt by this tragedy, I felt the sorriest for Luther Pleasant. He was a young black male who had sampled the pleasures of the flesh from a good-looking grown woman. His peers, and probably some of his male teachers, and men in general were going to envy him for being with a teacher that they all wanted to get up in. That, more than anything, could twist his mind and turn him into a monster when he got older. My husband and I promised his parents we would do whatever we could to help him. What bothered me more than anything else was the fact that Bobby Tarantino had gotten clean away—at least for now.

Coming Soon!

FLESH II: The Hunt for Bobby Tarantino.

Excerpt:

The Barrington case was over. We had captured just about everybody involved except Bobby Tarantino who was probably far away from my arms of justice in Fortaleza by now with his two daughters. It was up to the Bureau's Legal Attaché Office in Brazil to get him now. I didn't think they would get him either. A smart operator like him probably knew the FBI had legal attachés in other countries. For all we know, the woman caller could have been Francesca Ferrari. She could have said the South Atlantic because Bobby knows the hotel staff knew where Raquel was from. He could be back in San Francisco chilling out.

The good news, however, was that justice had caught up with two criminals that weren't even on our radar—Dr. Molly Lester and Mason Spivey. Lester and Spivey reminded me of the two thieves hanging on crosses next to Jesus. The first turned out to be a repentant child molester and the other turned out to be an unrepentant accessory to first degree murder. I wondered if Lester had made it through the pearly gates. Would Spivey? Assuming Lester had made it into heaven, were the streets up there really made of gold? And if they are, I also wondered if there was a tree of life that yielded twelve different fruits every month on either side of the river of life as Revelation 22:2 says. If so, that must really be a sight.

I was still troubled by the fact that we still hadn't found the bodies of Jack Ryan and Raquel Mendes. Neither was officially listed as dead, but there was no reason to believe they were alive at this point. There was nothing we could do until we caught up with Tarantino. We might have a chance of catching him if he was stupid, but he wasn't. He was a clever criminal who, with the exception of what may have happened in his penthouse the day Jack Ryan showed up, planned his moves carefully; every cop's worse nightmare. I didn't think he'd ever come back to the States.

It bothered me that I ignored the alarm bells about Mrs. Tobias because I didn't want to believe that she could have been sexually involved with my daughter like Kelly had suggested. Even though it wasn't Savannah, it could have been. I apologized to Kelly and Keyth for getting angry with them when they had followed their instincts. They were quick to forgive me and we all moved on. I realized that I had a wonderful husband who loved me and our daughter enough to make the hard choices I couldn't or wouldn't make. It was also good to be reminded that my best female friend wasn't intimidated by my martial art skill and cared enough to call my husband and inform him of her suspicions.

With the Barrington case being officially over, I wanted to spend as much time with my daughter as I could. Even though Savannah could return to school immediately for the summer session, I held her out a few more days so we could do what we've never done together which was take a tour or two of Washington. We decided that since we had both been on separate tours, me with my father and she with Keyth, we should do a tour that neither of us had been on. I had the concierge book the Washington DC *After Dark Tour*. After seeing all the Memorials, the Capitol building, and the Washington Monument lit up at night, we both wondered why we had never taken the tour together before. We had lots of fun. And on the way back to the hotel, Savannah told me that she understood now why my job as an FBI agent was so important. She said that somebody had to stop the bad people in this world and put them in jail so they wouldn't hurt people like Luther Pleasant again. I tried not to cry, but the tears fell anyway.

By the time the bus dropped us off at the hotel, Kelly, Keyth, and Sterling were waiting in the lobby for us. Whatever they had to say, I knew it couldn't be good judging by the looks on their faces. I figured the bodies of Jack Ryan and Raquel Mendes had been found and that we had a line on how we could get our hands Bobby Tarantino. But when we walked over to them, neither was true. Keyth gave Savannah the key to the Oval Suite and sent her up there. Kelly waited until she was out of earshot before she told me what had happened. It turned out that Blaze, Kelly's sixteen year old daughter was missing.

Also by Keith Lee Johnson

Fate's Redemption
Little Black Girl Lost
PRETENSES
Sugar & Spice
Little Black Girl Lost 2
The Honeymoon is over
Little Black Girl Lost 3
Hell Has No Fury
Little Black Girl Lost 4
Little Black Girl Lost 5
Little Girl Lost: The Return of Johnnie Wise
Little Girl Lost: Johnnie Wise In the Line of Fire

CPSIA information can be obtained at www.ICGtesting.com
Printed in the USA
LVOW090806210212

269688LV00001B/36/P

9 781935 825029